THE WALK AWAY

A MEMOIR OF SURVIVAL, FAITH, AND THE ROAD TO
REDEMPTION

Federico Botero

Published by Walk Away Media

United States of America

ISBNs — English Edition (*The Walk Away*)

Paperback: 979-8-9936793-2-7

Hardcover: 979-8-9936793-4-1

Ebook: 979-8-9936793-0-3

ISBNs — Spanish Edition (The Walk Away/*La Renuncia*)

Paperback: 979-8-9936793-3-4

Hardcover: 979-8-9936793-5-8

Ebook: 979-8-9936793-1-0

First edition

Printed in the United States of America

For additional resources and updates, visit:

www.thewalkaway.com

Dedication

To every soul brave enough to let go.
To every heart still seeking the strength to begin again.
This book is for you.

— Federico Botero

Acknowledgment

This book was not written in solitude, though much of it was born out of silence. Every page carries the weight of people, moments, and unseen hands that shaped me through both light and shadow.

I give my deepest thanks to Jesus Christ, who has been my compass in every season of my life. Through hardship, He transformed me. Through pain, He refined me. And through His mercy, He showed me that even when everything falls apart, His presence remains. Every miracle He has worked in my life, seen or unseen, reminds me that grace is not earned; it is received.

To my children — Amalia, Elizabeth, and Matthew —, I wrote this book with the hope that it might serve as a bridge, a way for us to draw closer again through truth, faith, and understanding. Beyond distance or silence, my love for you runs through every chapter of this story.

To my father, for the difficult lessons, for shaping my path through contrast, and for reminding me of the life I truly wanted to build.

To Estelita, for her tenderness, her simple faith, and the quiet prayers that carried me more times than she ever knew. Her presence was a reminder that genuine kindness leaves eternal marks.

To my mother and my brother Eduardo, whose love continues to live beyond time and life itself. I thank Christ for revealing to me that they rest in peace, in joy, and in His perfect glory. Knowing this has brought comfort where once there was only pain and emptiness.

To my brother Enrique, for being a steady voice of wisdom and strength whenever I needed to remember who I am. Your guidance and faith in me have carried me through some of the hardest moments. And to all the people who walked beside me at different times, thank you for serving a purpose in each season. Through joy or through pain, every shared step helped me grow and understand myself more deeply.

I am also thankful for the hard moments I had to endure, for the nights when faith was all I had left, for the losses that taught me to let go, and for the storms that forced me to start over. Each one was a lesson disguised as a trial.

Finally, I thank you, the reader, for holding this book in your hands and stepping into my story. May you find in these pages the strength to forgive, the faith to begin again, and the courage to walk away when life calls you forward.

This book is not about endings. It is about redemption, grace, and the quiet power of transformation. It is about walking away, not in defeat, but in faith.

Contents

Preface – The Courage to Walk Away

When people hear *walk away*, they often think it means to quit. But walking away is not giving up. It's an act of faith, a quiet rebellion against the things that no longer serve your soul. It's the moment you realize that staying still can be more dangerous than letting go.

This book isn't a manual, nor a list of steps to success or survival. It doesn't promise formulas or rules. It's a journey through lived experience, moments of clarity carved out of chaos, lessons learned not from theory but from scars. These pages don't aim to teach; they aim to tell the truth.

Walking away doesn't always mean leaving something broken. Sometimes, it means releasing something beautiful — a dream that no longer fits, a place that once felt like home, a version of yourself that the world still expects you to be, even the memories and habits that once defined you but now quietly drain the life out of you.

To walk away is to heal. It's medicine that time alone cannot give, the brave decision to stop clinging to what once was and open your hands to what could be. It's not about rejection; it's about redirection. It's not about forgetting; it's about forgiving — yourself, others, and the past that shaped you.

Sometimes life demands that you leave not just people but patterns — ways of thinking, reacting, and surviving that once kept you safe but now keep you small. You learn to walk away from the noise, the expectations, the endless need to prove that you are enough. And in that silence, you finally begin to heal.

This is not a story about running away. It's a story about returning to yourself, to truth, to peace. Because when you walk away from everything you thought you needed, what remains is the purest form of strength: faith. Faith that the unknown will not destroy you, but transform you. Faith that even in loss, you are being led.

When everything is gone — the noise, the names, the masks — all that's left is you and God. And that is where the real journey begins.

The Walk Away is not about endings. It's about beginnings that disguise themselves as endings — the kind of endings that heal instead of hurt, rebuild instead of erase.

If you're holding this book, perhaps you, too, have reached a crossroads. Maybe you feel that pull to release what no longer belongs to you, even if it once meant everything. If so, this story is for you.

Because walking away is not quitting. It's choosing to live again — lighter, freer, and unafraid to begin anew.

Federico Botero
The Walk Away: A Memoir of Survival, Faith, and the Road to Redemption.

Chapter 1

The Road Ahead

The bike surged forward, steady and alive beneath me. Wind pressed against my chest and tugged at my jacket as the throttle responded to the smallest twist of my wrist. The engine's vibration crawled up my arms and settled deep in my body, pulsing through every pore. The road blurred ahead, each shift and lean syncing with my heartbeat. My eyes tracked the movement of cars, the play of light on the asphalt, every sound sharp and clear. I could feel the weight of the machine, the pull of gravity in every curve, the hum of the tires gripping the ground. Every sense was awake, locked into the rhythm of speed and balance. The rest of the world fell quiet behind me.

As I entered Pereira, the streets began to change, the turns growing more familiar with every block. My eyes caught flashes of places I half remembered: the San Mateo Army Base, the Fátima Church, the neighborhood where I grew up. The wind carried the scent of the Otún River and the faint echo of home. I eased off the throttle, feeling the bike settle beneath me, steady and responsive. Every vibration through the frame and every breath of air past my helmet drew me deeper into the rhythm. The town moved around me, traffic lights flickering, people crossing, the low hum of evening rising and fading. It all felt distant, slowed by motion. The road led me forward, straight through the heart of the place where it had all begun.

I weaved through the streets, my eyes tracing the outlines of buildings that felt both familiar and foreign. It was like riding through a memory that no longer belonged to me. The playgrounds were gone, replaced by neat rows of shops with bright signs and mirrored windows. The schools stood larger now, their walls cleaner, newer, hiding the cracks I used to know by heart. The town looked busier, more defined, although something about it felt hollow, as if the innocence of the place had been paved over with progress.

But then, there it was.

My eyes landed on it, the way they always did, as if it had been waiting for me. The damned building. It stood there like a ghost, untouched by time.

The awning sagged as if it were struggling to stay in place, while the concrete walls still stood firm, holding up the roof with quiet resilience. But it was still there. Still standing. Still defiant, even though everything around it had changed. I slowed down as I approached, my hands tightened on the handlebars. My mind raced, memories flooding back faster than I could process them.

That place wasn't just a building. It was a time capsule. It was a hard, disgraceful memory of my younger years, a reminder of the abuse I suffered as a child, especially knowing the abuser had lived there.

I could feel my chest tighten, my breath coming a little faster. I tried to focus on the road ahead, tried to ignore the tug of the past, but it was like a magnet. I tried to push it away, tried to block out the flood of emotions, but it was impossible. I had spent so much of my life trying to bury those memories, trying to move on. But this building, this stubborn, weathered structure, had a way of pulling them back to the surface.

I gripped the handlebars tighter, the leather beneath my palms suddenly feeling slick. Then the past broke through—her face, her wide, almost playful eyes, the way she had smiled at me, as if there was something between us that shouldn't have been there, something far too heavy for a five-year-old to understand. I didn't want to remember, didn't want to let the memories creep back in. But they came anyway, relentless and suffocating.

She was around twenty-one when she lived in that prison, serving time for what she had done. I was five. Too young to understand, too naive to know the difference between what was right and wrong. My parents had never talked about it. They'd never even tried to explain it. Eventually, I stopped asking, stopped begging for answers. It was as if they couldn't see it, couldn't feel the weight of that building, that memory, the way it clung to me like a shadow. They didn't know how much it haunted me, how much I carried it with me, even when I wasn't thinking about it.

I could still see it all clearly, the shame I wore in middle school like a heavy coat, trying to laugh off the darkness. I had learned to turn those memories into jokes, something to brag about to my friends like it made me something special, something older, cooler. "I started early," I would say with a forced smile, as if that somehow changed the truth. They laughed, unaware that what sounded like pride was really pain they could never comprehend.

Still, her voice lingered in my head. I could feel her hands on my small frame, the confusion twisting in my gut. That wasn't what a kid was supposed to feel. I wasn't supposed to feel the weight of that kind of power. I wasn't supposed to be made to feel like I was something to be used, molded into something that didn't belong in the innocence of childhood.

I told myself a story. I told myself it wasn't so bad. Maybe I didn't cry because I was strong. Maybe I even liked it, I convinced myself, as if that would make it okay. Anything, anything was better than facing the truth. The truth that I was just a child. That I didn't ask for any of it. That it wasn't my fault.

The building was still there, maybe wearing new layers of paint, a few repairs here and there, but it remained. Just like the memories. No matter how many coats I'd tried to paint over them, no matter how many fixes I'd attempted through the years, they always bled through. That building had become a metaphor for it all—persistence and pain, endurance and imprisonment. It stood there like a cell with the door wide open, daring me to step inside again.

The bike slowed as I approached another red light, the engine purring softly beneath me. The world seemed to hold its breath, balanced between the past and the present. A car idled beside me, headlights flickering on the pavement.

The light turned green. I twisted the throttle, and the pull of acceleration snapped me back—the wind against my face, a cold reminder that the world was still moving, even if I wasn't ready to move with it.

I let the wind rush past me, pulling me forward, away from the darkness of the past, even if just for an instant. The road stretched ahead, smooth and open, offering a freedom that felt almost unreal—fragile, fleeting, but enough to breathe again. For a moment, I almost believed the weight had lifted.

Then, as if the universe had a sense of humor, a bird swept across the sky and left its mark on my helmet. I slowed, blinking in disbelief. For a second, I didn't know whether to smile or curse. Maybe both. The timing was cruelly perfect—either life reminding me that it doesn't stop throwing things at you, or maybe just a blunt message to stop dwelling on the crap, because that's exactly what I'd get.

I shook my head, a reluctant laugh slipping through. The tension inside me loosened, and in that fleeting instant, I understood something.

Healing isn't linear.

It wasn't a neat little package I could wrap up with a bow and move on. Healing came in the most unexpected forms. That day, it came from a bird with terrible aim, an absurd moment that reminded me that life doesn't stop. It doesn't care about pain, history, or scars. It just keeps moving.

And whether I was ready or not, I had to move with it. I had to let myself smile at the mess, to find something, anything, to break the tension. The road was still there, stretching ahead, waiting.

As I rode on, I understood that healing wasn't about forgetting what happened. It wasn't about formulas or easy answers either. No one could promise a way to erase the pain, and what works for many has rarely worked for me. I'm human, and my path has never fit into a pattern someone else could outline. But I've learned that acceptance and the choice to forgive, even her, can soften the weight of memory.

It still hurts to remember, but the pain feels lighter now. I don't feel trapped in that building anymore or in what it represents. I'm no longer the child who couldn't understand what had been taken from him. I'm a man on a bike, learning that freedom isn't the absence of pain, but the grace to keep moving despite it.

Chapter 2

Brushes with Death

The door creaked open. The air reeked of gasoline—sharp, acrid, invasive. Under the dim light, a small pool of liquid shimmered, its edges crawling toward the table where the phone sat. On the floor, a limp figure lay motionless.

Footsteps slapped against the wooden floor, quick and uneven, driven by panic. My father stepped through the doorway, his breath catching as his eyes locked on the figure. The briefcase slipped from his hand and hit the floor with a dull thud that shattered the silence. He dropped to his knees, his hands trembling as they hovered over my body.

"Jesus Christ," he whispered, his voice barely audible before it broke. "What happened?" His words were raw and desperate, the panic in his voice thickening the air until every breath felt heavy.

The house, still as it had been moments before, suddenly filled with noise. Piercing cries and rising voices collided. A chair toppled, crashing to the floor. Someone ran a hand through their hair, pacing in wild circles. Others stood frozen, eyes wide with terror, their hands shaking as they tried to grasp the horror unfolding before them.

"It smells like gasoline!" Estelita shouted, her voice slicing through the chaos. "Oh God... he must have swallowed it!"

The room fell into stunned disbelief. Gasps broke the air as the truth settled in. My face, pale and purple under the cold light, became a brutal reminder of what was happening. Someone sobbed uncontrollably, their cries muffled behind trembling fingers. Others stood rooted to the spot, their eyes darting between one another, searching for what to do next. And I, small and still, lay there, a lifeless weight on the floor, the gasoline still clinging to the inside of my throat.

From outside the metal gate, a neighbor caught sight of the scene through the open doorway. She screamed, the sound rising with alarm, and the small garage door clanged as she forced it open. "Pick him up! Take him to the hospital!"

My father didn't waste a second. He moved with the kind of determination only a parent can possess in the face of unimaginable terror. His arms slid under my lifeless form, lifting me as if I weighed nothing, his face ghostly pale, his hands trembling as they clutched me tighter. He muttered to himself, like a mantra, his voice low and strained. "Please, please don't leave me, son."

"Stella, call the hospital! Tell them we're coming!" my father shouted, his voice cutting through the frenzy. He moved with urgency, every motion deliberate, as if each passing second could decide my fate.

A flurry of movement followed, neighbors scrambling, fumbling with the rotary phone. The sound of the dial turning was like a twisted, hollow echo in the thick, tense air. My father was already out the door; my limp body pressed tightly to his chest.

The car door slammed, its metallic sound echoing through the night. The engine roared to life, and tires screeched as we sped down the street with reckless abandon. My father's hands were firm on the wheel, but his other arm, the one that wasn't steering, was wrapped around me, pulling me close, keeping me safe even though there was nothing he could do to fix what had happened.

"Stay with me, son!" he shouted, his voice trembling, cracking under the weight of his fear. He shook me gently, his words a frantic plea. "Don't go! Breathe! Please, breathe!"

His face, usually composed and strong, was now drenched in sweat, his knuckles white against the steering wheel. His focus was absolute—every breath, every glance fixed on me. Streetlights blurred past, red lights and honking horns fading into nothing. All that existed for him in that moment was the fight to keep me alive, as if sheer will could keep my heart beating.

His hand shot to my mouth, desperate, as if he could somehow force my small, lifeless body to respond. He jammed a finger between my lips, probing with desperate urgency, hoping to clear any gasoline still in my mouth before it went farther. My jaw hung slack, unresponsive, the gasoline still a bitter, burning taste in my mouth that I couldn't swallow away. He pressed harder, more desperately, trying to stir me, to bring me back to him.

But nothing happened. There was no movement.

He cursed under his breath, his body shaking with helplessness. He kept his other hand on the wheel, eyes darting between me and the road. The car seemed to fly, as though the world around him had dissolved into nothing.

The speedometer climbed as he tightened his grip, his focus locked forward. Panic surged inside him, but he drove through it, every thought narrowed to one purpose—getting me to someone who could help before it was too late. The tires screeched around corners, the night blurring past as if he could outrun what was happening. He glanced at me once, terror flickering across his face, then back to the road. When the hospital lights finally appeared ahead, he accelerated, chasing that single glimmer of hope.

Before the car came to a full stop, nurses rushed toward us, their footsteps echoing against the pavement in perfect unison. The door flew open, and strong hands reached in, pulling me from my father's grip and onto a stretcher. The motion was swift.

He stumbled out of the car, his legs weak beneath him, but his eyes never left me. He was already moving, following the nurses' rapid steps as they whisked me toward the emergency room, his face drained of color. He didn't speak. His silence said everything.

"Wait here, sir," a nurse ordered, holding a firm hand against his chest as they reached the door to one of the trauma rooms. "We need to take him in now."

"Please," my father pleaded, his voice trembling with desperation. He reached for the stretcher as they pushed it through the doors. "Let me go with him—he's my son."

The nurse's grip on him tightened, but the swinging doors to the trauma room clanged shut in his face, sealing him out.

He stood there, frozen in place, the weight of everything crashing down. The cold, sterile air of the hospital's waiting room felt suffocating, and the silence closed around him like a vice. His heart pounded so hard it hurt, each beat echoing in his ears.

The minutes dragged on like hours. The ticking of a clock on the wall became the only sound, each second stretching painfully as if the world had slowed down for him alone. He began pacing, his shoes scuffing rhythmically against the polished tile floor. His lips moved silently, a string of prayers spilling out in desperate whispers.

The seconds, the minutes, the hours—they all blurred together, time becoming a cruel illusion. All that mattered was me, and all he could do was wait.

Finally, the doors swung open again, and a doctor stepped out. His expression was unreadable, but there was something heavy, something unspoken, pressing down on his features. He stopped in front of my father, his eyes flicking toward the before meeting my father's gaze.

"Sir, your son is in critical condition," the doctor said, his voice steady but heavy with concern. "The gasoline has affected both his breathing and his nervous system. We're giving him oxygen and working to clear the toxins from his body, but he's still unresponsive. We're doing everything we can to stabilize him."

The floor seemed to tilt beneath my father, and he grabbed hold of the back of a chair to steady himself. His knees buckled, the strain of the news taking its toll on him all at once. The raw, choking weight of the words hit him like a physical blow, and for a moment, he couldn't breathe.

"Critical?" he repeated, barely above a whisper. The word seemed to hang in the air, impossible to accept. His eyes fixed on the doctor, searching for a different meaning. "You mean he might not make it?"

The doctor's shoulders sagged, the burden of the moment too heavy to bear. He placed a hand on my father's shoulder, a silent acknowledgment of the pain that swirled around them both.

"He's in the best hands we have," he said gently. "Right now, we're keeping his breathing stable and watching how his body responds to treatment. The next few hours are critical, but he's holding on, and we're doing everything possible to help him recover."

My father nodded, but there was no strength in it, no belief. His chest felt hollow, as if life had drained out of him, leaving only a shell. He couldn't imagine a world that went on without me in it.

Suddenly, the doors to the waiting room burst open, and my mother rushed in. Her face was pale, her eyes wide with terror, and tears streaked down her cheeks, leaving trails of salt on her skin. Her elegant dress, so crisp and clean just hours before, now seemed crumpled, forgotten. She stumbled forward, breath coming in shallow gasps as she scanned the room, her eyes desperate, searching for the one thing she feared most—me, lifeless or slipping away.

"Where is he?" she cried, her voice cracking with panic. A nurse stepped forward, trying to calm her, but my mother wasn't listening. Her movements were hectic, her mind a whirl of confusion and anguish. She brushed past the nurse, her gaze locking on my father, who sat hunched in the corner, his face buried in his hands. His shoulders collapsed slightly, and the moment she saw him, the world seemed to tilt beneath her too.

She ran to him, her steps unsteady on the cold tile as she reached out, grabbing his arm with a force that seemed to rise from the deepest pit of her fear. "Where's Fede? How is he?" she cried, her voice quivering, a mixture of terror and disbelief clawing at the edges of her words.

My father looked up at her then, his eyes red and swollen, a silent proof of his own torment. He shook his head slowly, his lips parting but finding no words. He struggled to speak, to offer her something, anything, but his voice cracked with the weight of it all. "They're treating him," he whispered, his voice hoarse. "But it doesn't look good."

Her knees buckled under the weight of his words, and she sank into the chair beside him, clutching his arm with desperate strength. A sob caught in her throat as she pressed her hands to her face, shaking her head as if she could push the moment away.

"Not my baby," she whispered, her voice barely audible, lost in the storm of her grief. "Please, God, not my baby."

My father reached over and gently pulled her into his arms. "Shh, he is going to be ok. We can't give up hope. Not yet."

But her sobs only deepened, and she pulled away from him, her face tight with grief and desperation. "How can you say that? How can you be so calm?" Her voice rose, a sharp edge of anger cutting through the pain. "I need to know what's happening to him, I need to be with him."

A nurse stepped closer, her tone gentle but firm. "Ma'am, I know how hard this is. The doctors are with him right now — he's not alone, I promise you. Please, let them work."

But my mother shook her head, stepping back as tears blurred her vision. "You don't understand," she cried. "I need to see him. He's my son — please, let me see him!"

"Please..." my father said softly, reaching for her hand, but she pulled away.

"He's my baby," she sobbed, her voice breaking. "If he hears me... maybe he'll fight harder. I just need to be with him."

"I know, Lucre," my father whispered, his voice trembling but controlled. "Please, try to breathe. They're doing everything they can. If we lose ourselves now, we won't be any help to him."

But my mother barely seemed to hear him. She was lost in her own world, as if the room had closed in around her. She was suffocating, drowning in uncertainty.

My father's shoulders slumped, his body drained by the weight of worry. He reached for her hand and held it tightly, as if that small connection were the only thing keeping him from falling apart. "I can't lose him either," he said softly. "But we have to hold on—for him."

"I'm trying," my mother gasped, her body shaking with sobs. Her voice faltered, barely a whisper, as she stared at the door where the doctors had taken me. "What if it's already too late?"

The words struck him hard. The tears he had fought to contain broke free, his breath catching as his composure gave way. "I don't know," he whispered. "I just don't know."

They sat there in silence, both of them hollowed, clinging to each other as if the smallest thread of hope might still hold.

After a few hours, my parents were finally allowed to see me, and they rushed into the trauma room. My mother stopped a few steps inside, frozen by the sight before her. Her body trembled, her breath shallow and uneven, as her eyes locked on the small, fragile figure lying in the hospital bed—me, her child.

My father sat close by, elbows on his knees, eyes fixed on my tiny chest. His face was drawn and pale, a reflection of the exhaustion that had slowly consumed him over the past two nights. Each rise and fall of my breathing seemed like a fragile promise—a promise he feared would break if he looked away.

Every breath I took was a gift. Every exhale, a moment longer. And through that stay in the hospital, my father remained steadfast, his vigilance a reflection of his deep, unyielding love. But in the quiet moments between each breath, his exhaustion was impossible to hide. Dark circles had formed beneath his eyes, his shoulders slumped under the weight of sleepless hours and the terror of not knowing. He hadn't left my side. Not once.

My mother, too, had not left. But her presence was different. It wasn't the quiet strength my father carried—it was a gentle, watchful presence. She stayed close but often sat a few steps back, her arms crossed tightly over her chest as if holding herself together. Her eyes shifted between me and the floor, and tears would gather but not fall. Her lips wavered, her expression tense with longing, as though she could will me to open my eyes, to breathe, to speak.

Every few minutes, she would rise from her chair, her movements slow and deliberate, and walk to my bedside. She would smooth a hand over my forehead, her touch gentle but uncertain, as if she thought I might break beneath it. Then, after a moment, she would step away, returning to her chair, her nails pressed against her lips, biting softly in a futile attempt to calm herself. Her every motion carried an anxiety I couldn't fully understand.

While my father's steady presence anchored the room, my mother's closeness kept it from falling apart. Where my father stayed strong, my mother stayed near—frayed, yes, but unyielding. Two different forms of love, both equally powerful.

Through the fear and the waiting, they stayed close, bound by something deeper than hope. Whatever distance had grown between them before that night seemed to fade, swallowed by the urgency of keeping me alive. Love, stripped of its arguments and silences, had no conditions, no questions, no thought of leaving. It simply remained—quiet, steady, and unbroken.

I was aware, in some distant part of my mind, of their presence. The weight of their worry, the constant, unspoken tension that filled the room. My heart wanted to reach out to them, to offer comfort, to show them that I was still here, still fighting. But I couldn't.

In the stillness, my mind replayed everything—the chaos of that night, the frantic drive to the hospital, the anxious looks of the doctors, and the sheer panic in my father's voice. The neighbor's voice echoed in my mind, sharp and urgent, calling for someone to act, to do something.

Estelita's face flashed in my thoughts next. Her calm demeanor, the way she simply stood by, like an anchor in the storm. She had done nothing more than be present, offering what little help she could in the face of so much unknown. But somehow, her quiet strength had been a balm to my father's frantic mind, a calm presence in the storm.

I could sense the faces around me, the ones who had fought to keep me here—their voices low, their movements careful, as if the air itself could break me. Each breath I took felt like a promise to them, to the love that refused to let go.

As the sounds of the room faded, something inside me began to drift—not away, but inward. In that soft space between sleep and waking, a memory rose to the surface. It wasn't a dream or a thought; it was something deeper. I was back in my room, small and afraid of the dark. My door stood open, the way it always had, and in the doorway there was a figure made of stars. Arms stretched wide, filling the frame. I remember rubbing my eyes, thinking it couldn't be real. But when I tried to walk closer, I felt it there—solid, unseen, stopping me.

At the time, I didn't understand. But lying in that hospital bed, suspended between life and whatever waits beyond, I felt the same stillness, the same presence. As if that figure had been there all along, waiting in the doorway between worlds, guarding me then, and now again.

The faint hum of machines filled the room—the breathing, the pulse, the sound of life returning. And somehow, I knew I hadn't come back on my own. I had been carried.

Chapter 3

The Man in the Stars

My shoes were the first thing you'd notice. Big, clunky things, like heavy bricks strapped to my feet, impossible to ignore. Every step I took, the soles slapped against the pavement as if announcing my difference to the world. That I didn't fit in. That I wasn't like the other kids who could run and play without thinking twice about their feet. I hated those shoes.

They were corrective shoes, meant to straighten my gait. But instead of helping, they made every step feel like work. The thick soles were awkward and heavy, and each footfall reminded me of my legs, which weren't quite right. Slightly turned inward, they made me feel like I was walking in the wrong direction, out of rhythm with the world around me.

Each step sounded louder than it should have, as if the pavement itself wanted everyone to look. I could feel their eyes before I even looked up. And in my mind, I could almost hear their silent judgment: *You don't belong here. You don't look like us.*

At that age, every feeling I had was exaggerated, magnified by the belief that everyone noticed me the way I noticed myself. It wasn't just that I felt different; it was that I believed everyone could see it too. Every awkward step, every stumble, every reminder that something about me was just a little off.

The shoes weren't the only thing I hated. My hair was almost as bad, maybe worse. I never understood why my mother insisted on keeping it the same way every time, a perfect bowl cut. It made my head look even bigger, especially next to my brother's. His hair always seemed to fall naturally into place, while mine sat stiff and round, like someone had placed a helmet on me and called it a style.

My mother thought it was adorable. She loved to tell everyone how cute it looked, how well it suited me, how it was the perfect haircut for a boy. But I never saw it that way. Every time I looked in the mirror, I saw a boy whose hair didn't move, didn't breathe. It sat there, stiff and lifeless, another part of me that felt wrong.

In my mind, I imagined it different, longer, a little messy, with some life in it. I could almost feel the softness between my fingers, the way it would move if I ran or played. But it was only a thought I never dared to say aloud.

She wouldn't have understood. She would have laughed, thinking I was being vain. She wasn't unkind; she was simply proud of her little boy. She loved my hair the way it was, neat and proper, like a small soldier ready for inspection.

My mother loved to tell stories about when I was born. She would laugh and say, "You were the ugliest baby I'd ever seen," as if it were a joke meant to make people smile. Everyone laughed when she said it, but I never did. I knew she meant it playfully, but to me it never felt funny. I didn't understand why she kept repeating it, or why it mattered so much to her that I wasn't the kind of baby people called cute.

Unlike other mothers, she never showed me pictures of myself as a newborn. To this day, I can't recall ever seeing one. When other parents filled albums and burned through rolls of film capturing every new expression, I had none. There were no pictures of me sleeping, crying, or being held for the first time. It was as if my beginning had been left undocumented, erased before I could remember it.

She used to say I had terrible hair, a round face, and eyes too big for my head. I suppose she thought those details made the story funnier. But I always wondered what it meant that the story she chose to tell about my birth was that I was ugly. Maybe it was her way of softening something she didn't understand, or of laughing away discomfort. Still, each time she told it, it landed somewhere deep inside me, a quiet reminder that even from the start, something about me seemed to stand out for the wrong reasons.

I couldn't stand being away from her. I used to make my mother wait outside the bathroom door while I went inside, just so I could hear her voice when I called. I was terrified of silence. Silence meant she might be gone. That fear never really left me; it only changed shape.

Maybe that's why I never wanted to let her out of my sight. When my mother was near, I felt visible. When she left, I disappeared.

Every New Year we traveled to Cali to visit my grandparents and the rest of the family. The house was always full of noise—laughter, music, cousins running through the rooms. Everyone loved those gatherings. But for me, they always carried a quiet dread.

When it was time for my mother to leave and return home, I cried until I had no breath left. I clung to her skirt, begging her not to go, promising I'd behave, that I wouldn't make trouble if only she'd take me with her. She would hug me tight, tell me she'd be back soon, and smile to soften the moment. But I didn't want *soon.* I wanted *now.* I wanted the warmth of her perfume, the sound of her voice, the proof that I still existed when she looked at me.

When the car pulled away and her figure faded behind the gate, the air itself seemed to lose color. The house was still alive with laughter, but none of it reached me. My cousins kept playing, my grandparents kept talking, and I just stood there, feeling the silence grow inside me.

That night, I couldn't sleep. I pressed my face against the cool window and stared at the sky. The stars looked like tiny holes poked through heaven. I didn't know who lived beyond them, but I imagined there was a man up there who could see me. I called him *the man in the stars.*

I whispered to him the things I couldn't say to anyone else—how much I missed my mother, how afraid I was that she might never come back, how the world suddenly felt too big without her in it. I didn't know what prayer was then, but something in me reached out all the same.

Some nights, when the loneliness felt too heavy, I would look up again, searching for that same light. Maybe I thought if he could see me, I wasn't truly alone.

The man in the stars gave me a sense of peace, but he wasn't always in my thoughts. Most days I was still the imperfect child who carried more feeling than he knew what to do with.

By the time I was five, I had perfected the art of throwing tantrums. I had learned how to make my anger loud and unstoppable, a storm that no one could ignore. I could scream for hours, my voice rising in pitch, becoming hoarse and desperate until it felt like I was coming apart at the seams. The tears were always there, always flowing, like a constant stream I couldn't turn off.

I wasn't a quiet child. I wasn't the one who sat still in the corner or followed every rule without question. I was restless, demanding, and full of energy that had nowhere to go. Whenever something didn't happen the way I wanted, or when I felt unheard, I erupted. I would cry, yell, stomp my feet, and fight the air until I ran out of strength.

Looking back now, I can see that those outbursts weren't just about getting my way. They were the only language I had to show the world how deeply I felt everything.

My parents didn't know what to do with me. They tried everything. Timeouts. Redirection. Calm talks. But nothing worked. No matter what they did, my tantrums kept coming. It didn't matter how much they tried to reason with me. It didn't matter how many times they took me aside and asked me to calm down. My emotions didn't make sense to them, and neither did my outbursts.

One day, during one of my worst tantrums, my dad lost his patience. We were on a road trip, heading from Orlando, Florida, to Ohio, on our way to explore more of the world. The heat in the car was unbearable, the long hours of driving making everyone irritable and tired. The trip had been fun in some ways—theme parks, roller coasters, and sights I had never seen before.

I can't tell you what set me off that day. Maybe it was the hours trapped in the car, or maybe something small—a simple frustration, a tiny spark that caught fire. Whatever it was, it ignited something inside me. My throat tightened as I began to scream, and in an instant, I was lost in the storm of my own emotions. I kicked and cried, tears streaming down my face, my body shaking with the force of it. I didn't know why I couldn't stop. I just couldn't.

My dad, already worn thin from the endless drive, snapped. His patience, already stretched beyond its limit, finally gave way. "If you don't stop crying," he yelled, gripping the steering wheel so hard it creaked, "I'll leave you here."

At five years old, I didn't believe him. I didn't think my parents could ever do something like that. Parents didn't leave their kids. They were supposed to protect them, take care of them. They couldn't just leave me behind.

So, I kept going. I screamed louder, threw my body around harder, testing every limit my parents had left. I didn't care. I had to get it out, and nothing was going to stop me.

The next thing I knew, we had pulled into a gas station. I was still lost in the storm inside me, sobbing and gasping for air. When the car stopped, I bolted for the bathroom, my cries echoing off the walls as I tried to calm myself down.

I don't know how long I stayed there, but when I finally stepped outside, something felt wrong. The air was too still. The parking lot was empty.

The car was gone.

I stood there, stunned. I thought maybe they had parked around the corner, or maybe they had gone to the store next door. But as the minutes ticked by, I realized something much worse—my family was gone. They had left me behind.

My heart began to race. The blood in my ears pounded louder with every passing second, and I began to feel dizzy. Panic crept up my spine like cold fingers. I turned in circles, my eyes darting anxiously over the parking lot, looking for something, anything that would tell me they were coming back. But there was nothing. No sign of my parents. No sign of the car.

They had really left me behind.

I couldn't breathe. The world around me felt suddenly too big, too unfamiliar, and I couldn't stop the panic that threatened to swallow me whole. My small legs, still trapped in those clunky corrective shoes, didn't know what to do. They felt heavy, clumsy, and I could feel the weight of the entire situation pressing down on me. I wanted to cry out, but I didn't. I couldn't.

My legs started to move before my mind caught up. I didn't know where I was going; I just knew I couldn't stay there. The stillness scared me more than the road ahead. So I walked—because walking felt like doing something, like maybe if I kept moving, they would see me again and come back.

I walked down the highway, my feet slapping against the pavement with each step. The sound was louder than it should have been, echoing through the emptiness around me. I didn't know how far I was going or what I would do when I got there. I just kept moving, my legs aching, my breath shallow, my heart racing with something I didn't yet understand—part fear, part hope, and something that felt like both.

Meanwhile, my parents realized their mistake. My dad had miscalculated and ended up on the interstate. They had to drive six miles before they could turn around and get back to the gas station where they had left me. However, by the time they returned, I was long gone. Now, it was their turn to panic. They asked everyone they could find at the gas station, but no one knew where I had gone. Desperate to find me, they began driving down the road again, searching for any sign of their lost child.

It wasn't until they saw me, a tiny figure trudging down the side of the highway, that the full weight of their mistake hit them. My dad slammed on the brakes, the tires squealed as he jerked the car to a stop. He didn't even wait for the car to come to a full stop before he leaped out, his face gone ashen. His voice cracked as he shouted, "Get back in the car!"

I froze. The anger and hurt from the tantrum still burned inside me, making my body stiff and unyielding. Part of me didn't want to move. I didn't know whether to run to them or stay where I was. But something in my dad's voice cracked through the noise inside me. I saw the fear in his eyes—the same fear I had felt moments earlier when I realized I was alone—and slowly, reluctantly, I climbed back into the car.

There was no shouting on the way back. No angry words. Just silence. My parents were lost in their thoughts, and I was lost in mine. I stared out the window, watching the highway fade behind us, my small reflection shifting in the glass.

It struck me how close I had come to disappearing, how a single moment of anger could separate a family from everything it loves. The road stretched endlessly ahead of us, but something in me had changed. I didn't have words for it then, only the sense that life could vanish in an instant, that love itself could be fragile. I pressed my hand against the glass, watching my reflection tremble with the hum of the car, and wondered if the man in the stars had seen it all. Maybe He had been there, quietly reminding me that even when we lose our way, we are never completely lost.

Chapter 4

The Day I Stopped Running

The Catholic school I attended felt more like an institution built for obedience than a place meant to shape hearts. The exposed brick walls, open-air walkways, and bare bulletin boards gave the campus a stark, almost ascetic atmosphere. Nothing colorful. Nothing soft. Just structure and rules. You couldn't get away with much. Step out of line and a teacher's reprimand landed instantly. But discipline is not the same as compassion. No one taught us how to treat each other with dignity. No one explained how to defend someone being mocked. Respect was something teachers assumed you brought from home, even if home wasn't a place where respect was taught or lived.

That lack of compassion showed up early in my life. Back in third grade, every trimester, one of the priests would walk into our classroom with a list in his hand. He'd clear his throat and call out the names of the ten "worst students," the "last ten of the class," as he liked to say. Then he ordered us to stand outside along the hallway wall for everyone to see. I was on that list more than once.

Standing there, small and silent, I didn't understand what lesson I was supposed to learn. I only knew how it felt: humiliating. Like I was being held up as an example of failure. That moment didn't teach me to work harder; it taught me how to shrink. How to accept the idea that I was inferior and less smart, because that's exactly how he made me feel. Looking back now, I realize it was its own form of bullying, just delivered by someone wearing a priest's habit. The school preached about shaping souls but forgot the responsibility of protecting the hearts standing right in front of them.

Cruelty didn't roar there; it whispered. It showed up in snide jokes, in exclusion, in the casual brutality kids use when no one teaches them better. Teachers corrected misbehavior, but they didn't prevent the roots of unkindness from forming. You could get an A in religion and still fail miserably at empathy.

Later in high school, we had spiritual retreats meant to guide us, but they often felt heavy, as if I was being asked to carry emotional weight I didn't know how to process. I left those retreats feeling more confused about myself than enlightened. And beneath it all was bullying. It wasn't always aimed directly at me, but it hovered everywhere like background noise. Sometimes I stood silently by, wishing I had the courage to defend someone—or myself—but afraid of becoming the next target.

There was, however, one place where things felt different. The school garden sat tucked behind the buildings, a quiet sanctuary where I often went to breathe. It was a small patch of green in a world of brick and concrete, a rare moment of peace in a place where peace felt optional. One afternoon, I wandered there as I often did, lost in my thoughts. The light was warm. The air calm.

Then the world shattered.

A sudden whoosh cut through the air—and then: CRACK. A blinding impact slammed into my left eye. Pain exploded across my face. My knees buckled. I grabbed my eye, gasping as the world spun wildly around me, and then everything in that eye went dark. Not blurry—dark. As if someone had shut a door inside my vision.

"I can't see!" The words tore out of me before I could think. Shock took over. My mind scrambled for answers. What hit me? Who threw that? Why? Voices rushed toward me, distorted and far away. It turned out to be a green almond, taken straight from the tree and thrown by another student. In that moment, though, none of that mattered. All I felt was the pain, the confusion, and the terrifying darkness in my left eye. Hands grabbed my shoulders, guiding me, while everything around me blurred into noise. The only thought pounding inside me was: Will I ever see out of this eye again?

My dad's voice on the phone was tighter than I had ever heard it. My mother was miles away, frozen by the news, unable to reach me. At the hospital, everything moved fast. Shapes and shadows passed in front of me, voices overlapping in tense bursts. I could feel the cold of the instruments more than I could see them, and every sound seemed sharper than it should have been.

After the examination, the doctor looked at me with a seriousness that made the room feel smaller. "Your retina is at risk of detaching. No movement. No strain. I'm patching the eye for a week." I wasn't going blind, but I could lose the sight in that eye permanently. The thought alone made my chest tighten. He covered the eye immediately. My world tilted—light on one side, darkness on the other.

I spent the next week immobilized at home, head tilted upward, body still. I stared at the ceiling for days. Silence became loud. Time stretched thin. Dread whispered constantly: What if I open the patch and it's still dark? Somewhere in that stillness, another thought surfaced, faint but steady—a sense that I was being protected, spared again. That realization didn't erase the dread, but it gave me a small sense of hope to hold onto. After a week, the doctor removed the patch. Slowly, light returned. Shadows became shapes again. Relief washed over me like a prayer.

The bullying didn't stay behind at school. One boy, my classmate who also lived in my neighborhood, made sure of that. He seemed to exist everywhere—mornings in the hallways, afternoons on the walk home, outside his house when I tried to pass. He knew exactly what words would sting, how to shove without getting caught, how to make me feel small without ever raising a hand where a teacher could see. Avoiding him became its own routine. I took longer routes, delayed going home, found ways to disappear. But avoidance can only protect you for so long.

One afternoon, I turned a corner near the store and there he was, surrounded by his friends. His grin widened when he spotted me. "Hey, freak!" The laughter behind him hit like a slap. My chest tightened. Normally, I would have taken a different route, even if it meant walking several extra blocks just to avoid him. But after the injury, something in me had shifted. Hiding hadn't protected me—not even the quiet garden had kept me safe before. They had found me there, in the one place I thought I was untouchable, and they attacked when I was most vulnerable. So when I saw him, the urge to flee wasn't there. Instead, a new resolve formed: if I kept showing fear, they would keep hunting it. If I didn't defend myself, the next injury could be worse. I walked toward him, not away, carrying the quiet determination to protect what I had nearly lost.

"Leave me alone," I said.

Even I was surprised by the firmness in my voice. He shoved me hard onto the dirt. The old fear tried to rise, but it didn't take hold like before. A strength I didn't know I had erupted, pushing me forward. Before I could think, I got up fast and tackled him. My knees pinned his arms. My hands grabbed his collar. His eyes widened in shock.

"Say you're sorry."

My voice shook with a fierceness I had never felt before.

"Say it."

He finally whispered it: "I'm sorry..."

I let him go. My chest heaved. My hands trembled. For the first time, the tremble wasn't fear.

The days that followed were quiet. Slowly, almost awkwardly, we began to talk. Against all odds, we became friends. Not immediately, and not easily, but honestly. He wasn't the monster I had imagined; he was just another kid trying to survive himself. And I realized that holding onto anger would only keep me tied to the past.

That day didn't make me strong—it revealed the strength that had always been there, the quiet courage to stop letting fear define me. It was the day I chose to stand, to claim my space, to protect my peace. And that strength has stayed with me ever since, steady and unshakeable.

Chapter 5

The Farm

The morning air was cool, clinging to my skin like a soft, invisible blanket. It smelled fresh and earthy, a sharp contrast to the usual thick, warm air of midday. The sun hadn't quite made its entrance yet, but the world was beginning to stir, with the faint sound of cows lowing in the distance. That was my alarm, much more reliable than any clock or buzzer—hooves shuffling and the cowboy's steady calls as he guided the herd toward the corrals.

The farm was still shrouded in darkness, the only light coming from the flickering glow of a candle on the kitchen table and the soft amber of an oil lamp in the corner. Electricity was something we didn't often rely on. The generator, stubborn and unwilling, sat silently in the corner of the warehouse. My uncle had spent more than his fair share of hours tinkering with it, but it had long since given up the fight. So, we adjusted, learning to navigate the shadows with the quiet company of our lamps. The candlelight's gentle sway had become as familiar as the rising sun, something that didn't need to be questioned.

That morning felt different. It was my ninth birthday, and a quiet excitement bubbled inside me—not the kind that comes from expecting a big surprise, but the steady happiness of knowing something special was about to happen. My dad was already up, moving around the kitchen, his movements deliberate as he poured a splash of rum into two small tin cups. The scent of it mixed with the lingering smell of early coffee.

I padded in barefoot across the red tile floor. He looked up and gave me a quick hug and a kiss on the cheek—simple, familiar, the way birthdays always began in our family.

"Happy birthday," he said quietly.

"Thank you," I murmured.

He added a small spoonful of sugar to each cup, swirled them once, and handed me mine.

"Come on," he said, tipping his head toward the yard. "Let's go to the cows."

We walked out into the yard, where the morning air was still crisp, and I could almost feel the earth waking up with every step we took.

The cowboy was already there, his silhouette outlined against the dim morning sky. When he noticed us approaching, he straightened respectfully.

"Good morning, sir. Good morning, Federico," he said.

"Good morning," my dad replied. "It's his birthday today."

The cowboy's expression warmed.

"Is it? Well, happy birthday, young man. Here, give me your cup. Today you get milk from our best cow, Anita."

I handed him my cup, and he went back to work, his hands moving with the practiced ease of someone who had done this every morning of his life. The warm milk streamed into the tin cups, still steaming in the cool air, and there was something about the way the cow's milk mingled with the rum and sugar, a simple concoction that felt like magic in a cup. It was not like any drink I had tasted before. It filled me with warmth and energy, the kind that does not come from running around or playing but from something almost enchanted, something very comforting.

We sipped the drink slowly, the chill of the early morning fading with each swallow. The light began to grow just a little, enough to make the world around us look softer, quieter. The cows had settled into their pens, and the cowboy was now moving to check on the horses, his boots making soft thuds on the earth. It was a peaceful sort of busy. Nothing rushed. Everything had its time.

Inside, the smell of breakfast was beginning to fill the house. My grandmother sat at her usual spot at the table, still in her pajamas, her eyes bright with joy. Our cook was in the back, working over the wood stove and skillfully preparing the arepas, then bringing them out one by one. My grandmother took each one, cutting it in half and spreading the perfect amount of butter and *queso campesino* made from our own cows. She had perfected the rhythm of it, making sure each arepa was just right. We all waited for her to begin, knowing that no one could prepare them quite like she could.

We spent our vacations on the farm with some of our cousins on my father's side, and that morning we were all gathered around the table waiting for breakfast when my mom arrived. She and my dad had been divorced for about three years, and she didn't usually join us on the farm. So when I saw her car pull up in front of the house, a burst of happiness shot through me, sudden and bright. I jumped out of my chair and ran outside as fast as I could. The moment she opened her car door, I threw my arms around her. She had come to be part of the moment, and that meant everything to me.

The table was already set. Cups of milk, fresh from the cow, sat waiting to be poured, and the butter was ready, soft and creamy. My mom slid into her seat, her eyes lighting up when she saw the food. Although my parents were long divorced and often disagreed, they still managed to share moments like this when it mattered.

After breakfast, my family began singing "Happy Birthday," their off-key voices drifting through the house with a warmth that felt simple and genuine. I listened quietly, letting the sound mix with the morning air that slipped in through the louvered windows. The scent of wet grass and flowers carried in on the mist, filling the room with the freshness of the valley. From where I sat, I could see all the way down to the Cauca River, glinting faintly in the early light. The voices, the view, and the soft morning breeze made the moment feel peaceful in a way I still remember.

Earlier that morning, my dad had handed me my birthday gift: two cans of peaches. He had discovered once that I liked them, and from then on it became the only thing he ever gave me. I thanked him the way I always did, even though I had hoped for something different that year.

Then, they started to lead me outside, hands gently covering my eyes, their laughter ringing in my ears. My heart raced as they moved me across the yard, teasing me with their giggles and playful nudges. The anticipation built like a pressure cooker, and I couldn't stand it. When they finally let go of my eyes, I opened them to the bright morning sun—and saw it.

The bike.

It was white, clean and simple, with long handlebars draped in shiny pink tassels. A small pink rose sticker adorned the frame, making it look like something out of a fairy tale. And then I saw the training wheels. Big, clunky, and undeniably childish. My heart sank. This wasn't the sleek, cool bike I had imagined, the kind that would make me feel free and adventurous. No, this was a toy, the girly kind, a beginner's bike that screamed "not cool" to a nine-year-old.

My excitement evaporated faster than it had built, leaving behind a sinking feeling in my heart. This wasn't what I had hoped for at all. It wasn't the bike that would take me on wild adventures. But I forced a smile, my mind racing for something positive to say. It was still a gift, still mine. Even if it wasn't what I had envisioned.

I swallowed my disappointment, smiled, and thanked my mother with as much enthusiasm as I could muster, and then they encouraged me to give it a try. Despite my reluctance, I climbed onto the bike. The metal frame felt strange under my legs, but I pushed forward. Wobbling at first, I made my way over the dirt paths of the farm. I learned quickly, though, gaining confidence as I balanced myself and pedaled harder. My legs were weak, but the thrill of moving forward, however ungracefully, kept me going.

When vacation ended, I had to take the bike back with me to the city. The thought of leaving it behind tugged at my heart. The familiar streets and noise of the city felt like a world apart from the wide-open spaces of the farm. I decided to ride it to basketball practice one afternoon, figuring it would be faster than walking. The school was only a few blocks away, but the streets had a lot of traffic, making it harder to navigate. Still, the bike made the trip easier, and I liked having that small bit of freedom.

Practice ended later than usual, and I swapped my sweaty basketball shorts for a pair of new jeans that made me feel like I fit in. I didn't want to draw attention to my skinny legs, so I pulled the denim tighter around my calves, trying to look more grown-up. I mounted the bike again, self-conscious but determined to get home.

Two blocks from my house, I was riding up the hill, pushing hard on the pedals and trying to keep my balance in the late afternoon sun. I was focused on the climb when a car came up behind me and hit the back of my bike with a force I never saw coming. The impact lifted me high into the air, throwing me forward before I could even understand what was happening. One second I was pedaling uphill, and the next I was crashing down onto the hot asphalt, the world snapping back into place as the ground rushed up to meet me.

When I hit the ground, everything went strangely quiet. I could hear my own breathing and the hard thump of my heartbeat, but the rest of the world felt distant, as if the sound had been pulled away from me. I stared at the pavement, trying to understand what had just happened. I felt disoriented, unsure if I could move or even stand. There was no pain yet, just a heavy confusion and the unsettling sense that my body hadn't caught up with what my mind was trying to process.

After a few seconds, I tried to move, unsure if my legs would respond. Somehow, they did. They felt shaky, but they held, and I pushed myself up to my feet. I brushed the gravel from my jeans, my mind suddenly locking onto something I hadn't noticed at first. My jeans. There was a hole in the knee — a big one. I froze, a wave of panic rising in my chest. They were new, a Christmas gift, and I could already hear my mom's sigh of frustration in my head. She was going to be so mad.

"Are you okay? Sit down! You need to sit down!" a stressed voice called out from behind me.

I turned to see a woman rushing over, her eyes wide with concern. But I waved her off, brushing more gravel off my jeans. In my confusion, I didn't want anyone to help me; I just wanted to stay on my feet. All I could think about was the hole in the knee of my brand-new jeans.

"Look at your leg!" the woman said, her voice rising in panic as she pointed to my leg.

I glanced down, my eyes finally focusing on the sting in my skin. Blood was starting to seep through the fabric of my jeans, a red line tracing down my calf. The wound was large, and I could clearly see bone through the exposed tissue.

The realization hit me hard. I wasn't fine. The bike ride, the accident — it all suddenly felt too real. But the worst part wasn't the pain. It was the thought of my mom's disappointment over my ruined pants. She was always telling us to take better care of our things, and all I could think about was how this would look to her.

The bike sat a few feet away, bent and bruised from the impact. The handlebars were twisted, the wheels warped and no longer straight, and the pink tassels dragged along the ground. Even the rose sticker was scratched, its bright pink now just a dull smear.

The woman who had hit me picked it up carefully, trying to gather the broken pieces. She placed it in the back seat of her car and then helped me into the front. She drove me to my house first, but when she saw that my mom was still at work, she took me to the hospital herself. By then the pain in my leg had begun to catch up to me, and all I could think about was how my mom would react when she saw the bleeding, the torn jeans, and the broken bike.

At the hospital, my mom arrived a few minutes later, still dressed in her usual elegant, casual way, but her face was tight with worry. I waited for her to look at the torn jeans or ask what had happened to the bike, but she didn't mention any of it. She came straight to me instead, touching my arms and my face, checking if I was hurt anywhere else. She kept asking where it hurt and saying how thankful she was that I was alive, that nothing else mattered. I had spent the whole ride worrying about the jeans and the bike, and suddenly none of that seemed important anymore.

Back at home, the bike was waiting by the door. Seeing it stopped me in my tracks. The metal frame was bent and twisted, the wheels crushed, the whole thing looking as if it had been folded in half. It was hard to believe something that strong could end up like that. And then there was me—skinny, tender, mostly skin and bones—still standing. Looking at the bike made it impossible to ignore how lucky I had been.

The bike was never replaced, and for a long time I felt its absence. But even then, I knew the real story wasn't about the bike. It was about how close I had come to losing my life and the strange feeling that followed me home.

That night, and in the days after, I kept thinking about the moment I opened my eyes on the pavement. The sky felt close, almost watching me. I didn't understand why I was still there, standing in front of a bike that looked folded in half while I had walked away with only stitches and a scar. It felt as if something had kept me from falling harder than I did, as if something had caught me before the ground did.

Trying to make sense of it didn't lead anywhere. My mind went instead to Jesus, and I wondered if He had been there with me somehow, in a way I couldn't see. It wasn't a question or a prayer. It was just the quiet thought that came naturally to me then.

There was nothing I could explain about what happened on that street. I only knew that something had taken place, something I wasn't ready to understand yet. And even though I didn't have the words for it, I felt grateful every time I thought about it.

Chapter 6

Witness to Violence

The street was ours. It was where we grew up, where the world felt small enough to make sense. Beneath the glow of the setting sun, our laughter echoed like the music of our youth. That amber light painted everything in a warm glow, even the cracks in the pavement, the worn-out bikes leaning against walls, and the faded goalposts made of rocks. It was as if the street had been waiting for us—waiting to be filled with the sound of children running, playing, and pretending the world was always this simple.

Our games had no rules, only the rhythm of our feet and the joy in our voices. The streetlights, which flickered on as the sun dipped lower, became our guides when it was time for hide-and-seek. We would dive behind bushes, slip into shadows, and sometimes, if we were brave enough, run straight into the open just to test our luck. When a car approached, everything stopped. We scattered like birds taking flight, only to return the moment it passed.

We owned the road.

That evening started like any other. It was one of those perfect nights— cool enough for sweatshirts but warm enough for the kind of freedom you only get when you're young. The air was thick with the smell of dinner from open windows, and the sounds of chatter mixed with the distant hum of television sets. "Ready or not, here I come!" someone yelled, followed by the pounding of feet against the asphalt as kids scattered in every direction.

I crouched low behind a palm tree, one of the few in our neighborhood, pretending to be a shadow in the dimming light. My heart was steady, the kind of calm that comes from knowing the game inside and out. No one had found me yet, but I knew I couldn't stay here too long. Sooner or later, footsteps would come my way, and I'd have to break cover.

But then—then it happened.

The first sudden crack split the air like a slap. I didn't understand it at first—my mind refused to register the sound. The second came quickly after, louder, more violent—like an explosion reverberating through my entire body. It was gunfire, the kind that leaves no room for confusion. My body went rigid, my breath trapped in my throat. It didn't feel real.

Then came the engine's roar, deafening and furious. A jeep sped down the street, swerving and kicking up dust, its tires screeching against the cracked road. Behind it, motorcycles raced—men in helmets, faces hidden, their hands gripping guns. Bullets tore through the air, striking the jeep's frame and throwing sparks. I could feel them ripple through me, each shot like a hammer pounding against my bones.

My pulse quickened. My thoughts scrambled. I pressed myself harder against the tree, the rough bark digging into my skin as I squeezed my eyes shut, wishing I could disappear. The laughter, the games, the carefree moments—everything vanished in an instant. The world felt like it was falling apart, and all I could do was hold my breath, praying to stay hidden, praying for the danger to pass, praying that we would all be okay.

It was a police chase. The two motorcycles, each carrying two policemen in full gear, pursued the jeep with unyielding focus. Their engines surged like a storm on the horizon, slicing through the heavy air thick with exhaust and the faint metallic edge of fear. I could feel the tremor of it in my guts, the kind of fear that makes your skin prickle and your breath hitch. Every sound was amplified—the screech of tires, the thunder of the pursuit, the dull whine of the engines carving through the quiet evening.

Then, with horrifying suddenness, the scene became even more nightmarish. One of the men in the jeep, a figure I had barely noticed, was hit. The shot came so fast it felt as though time had stretched, and in that same moment, his body jerked violently. He was thrown from the jeep with unnatural force, spinning mid-air before crashing onto the road just feet from where I was hiding. His clothes—white pants, a white jacket, even white shoes—stood out starkly against the darkening street, an eerie contrast to the chaos unfolding around him. In that instant, it felt like the world had slowed down, every detail freezing in place, suspended in horror.

The jeep, without a moment's hesitation, sped away, skidding, the motor erupting with the same relentless fury. The motorcycles followed close behind, their noise fading quickly into the distance. The street, once alive with the voices of children and the hum of summer evenings, was now swallowed by an unsettling silence. I could hear only the quick, uneven rhythm of my own shallow breaths, my heart thudding hard inside me. Slowly, almost without realizing it, I stepped out from behind my hiding place and inched forward until I was close enough to reach the fallen man. My eyes locked onto the motionless figure on the ground. He looked almost unreal, like a mannequin dropped carelessly onto the road, but then his hand twitched.

A strange heaviness settled over me as I stood beside him, close enough to see his face clearly. His eyes were open, staring up at me with a mix of shock and fading awareness. It felt as if the whole world narrowed to just the two of us. He never imagined that the last image he would see in his life would be a child—me—standing there with my eyes wide, frozen somewhere between terror and disbelief. I didn't run. I didn't scream. I simply stood there, unable to move, held in place as his gaze clung to mine for what felt like an eternity.

That's when the policeman appeared. I could barely make out the blur of his uniform as he sprinted toward the fallen man. "What the hell are you doing?" he barked, his voice urgent and laced with authority. "Get back! Now!"

I stumbled backward, too stunned to react, feeling the officer's hand on my shoulder as he pushed me aside with quick, practiced force. My mind was in a fog, my senses numbed by the chaos, and for a moment it felt as though I were watching everything unfold from a distance, trapped in a dream where I could only observe. The officer dropped to his knees beside the man, moving with sharp efficiency as he checked for a pulse, his fingers pressing firmly against the side of the man's neck. His face hardened with grim certainty. As I stepped away, the man's eyes lost their focus, the faint rise of his chest stilled, and in that quiet, he was gone. The chase wasn't over yet.

At the far end of the neighborhood, the jeep came to a sudden stop where the street simply ended, just a few houses from my own. Beyond that point stood the back perimeter of the San Mateo Army Base and the coffee plantations of my elementary school. The fugitives didn't hesitate; they abandoned the vehicle in an instant and slipped into the thick shadows of the woods behind the neighborhood. Within seconds, they were gone, swallowed by the trees and the darkness beyond.

More police squads arrived in a flurry, sirens wailing as their cars swerved onto the street, filling the air with their flashing lights and sharp, serious commands. The peaceful neighborhood had become a war zone in the blink of an eye. I could feel the tension creeping through the air as army personnel, their uniforms stark against the night, arrived and joined the search. Their presence only amplified the weight of the moment, as if the danger was far from over.

The street had never felt so small, so vulnerable. All the years of games, laughter, and innocent mischief felt a world away.

Terrified, my friends and I darted into our houses, slamming the doors behind us, the force of our panic pushing us faster than our feet could carry us. Our hearts were pounding, and I could feel the adrenaline surge through my veins, making everything feel surreal. The world outside had turned into something unrecognizable, a twisted version of our street where children no longer played but ran for their lives. I had never imagined something like this could happen, not here, not in the place I'd grown up, where every corner felt familiar, every face comforting.

Inside, my house felt like a small fortress, but one held together more by panic than protection. My mother was already there, pulling the curtains tight with unsteady hands, her face nothing like the calm I had always known. She locked every window and door, her movements quick and anxious, as if she could somehow build a barrier against whatever danger might still be out there. But even she was trembling, and I could see something in her eyes I had never seen before. I had always believed she could handle anything, that she was the one who kept us safe. Seeing her shaken unsettled me in a way nothing else had.

I stood frozen by the door, watching her. My breath caught in my throat as I tried to steady myself, the reality of what I had witnessed still echoing inside me.

"Mom… are we going to be okay?" I finally asked, my voice barely audible.

She didn't answer immediately, but her eyes flicked to me, and then she quickly pulled me into her arms. "We're safe, we're safe," she muttered under her breath, as if repeating the words to herself, trying to convince us both. "Stay with me."

We huddled together in her room, a small island of warmth and comfort in a world that had suddenly turned cold. My brothers' anxious chatter filled the space, but it did nothing to ease the nervousness hanging in the air. Outside, the chaos continued, though it felt farther away now. The sounds of sirens, shouted commands, and the occasional burst of gunfire cut through the night, each one hitting us like a jolt. We flinched at every creak of the house, at every shadow passing by the window. The night felt heavier than it ever had before.

Then came the knock. A loud, insistent tap at the door that made all of us jump. My heart raced. Who could that be? I didn't want to know.

My mother slowly stood up, her movements stiff and hesitant. She glanced at me, her eyes wide with uncertainty. "Stay here," she whispered, though I could see the worry in her gaze. She didn't want to leave me and my brothers alone, but there was no choice.

She opened the door and the cool air outside rushed in, carrying the lingering smoke from the police patrol cars. Two officers stood there, their faces obscured by the darkness but their uniforms unmistakable. "We need to search your backyard," one of them said, his voice sharp and clipped. "We believe they may be hiding behind your yard's wall. Stay inside and keep the doors locked."

I heard the pounding of heavy boots as a group of agents rushed into our house, almost ten of them storming down the stairs and moving quickly through the living room and dining room toward the backyard. My mother nodded silently, too stunned to speak. I stood behind her bedroom curtain, peeking through a narrow gap, afraid that someone outside might see me. From there I watched the policemen reach the yard and climb our wall one after another, trying to surprise the criminals they believed were hiding on the other side, their movements tense and deliberate as the whole scene tightened with uncertainty.

I waited in silence, unable to tear my eyes away. After what seemed like an eternity, the agents finished their search. I heard them muttering, frustrated, and then the sound of their boots fading into the distance. They had found nothing. But still, the unease lingered, thick and suffocating.

The night dragged on in a blur of whispered conversations and anxious waiting. We tried to calm each other, but the fear sat heavy inside us, a weight none of us could escape. Every noise outside felt too loud and every minute seemed slower, as if the whole neighborhood had gone still. Then a final crack of gunfire cut through the quiet. I counted the shots one by one, matching them to the men who had fled into the dark. When that last one echoed, I did not need anyone to tell me what it meant. I knew the final man had fallen.

More than anything else, what stayed with me was the image of the man in white, lying in the street with his gun still in his hand, close enough for me to touch. His bright clothes looked almost unreal against the dark pavement, and I couldn't stop seeing them in my mind. Moments earlier he had been alive, running for his life, and then he wasn't. Just like that. In the same street where we had been playing.

I was lucky in a way. After that night, I went back to my games, my school, my summer. Life around me slowly returned to what it had been. But the image of the man in white never left me. He didn't die with someone he loved holding his hand. He didn't get to say goodbye to anyone who knew his name. His last moment was spent looking at a stranger — a boy he had never seen before. Sometimes we don't leave this world the way we imagine. Sometimes we die in front of people who were never meant to know us. And somehow, that moment became part of my story.

Chapter 7

The Story Did Not Repeat

Evenings in our neighborhood softened everything. The sun dipped behind the brick roofs, dragging the last strips of light across the courtyard and stretching the shadows over the sidewalk. Kids tore up and down the block, yelling out soccer plays, arguing over fouls, breaking off into games of tag. Somewhere, a broom scratched over wet cement. The mix of soap, dust, and warm air smelled like home. On the corner, a neighbor knelt in his yard, shaving the grass with a machete, each slow chop keeping time with the sounds of the street.

A few weeks earlier, the whole place had felt different—sirens, shouting, the blur of police running past. Now the neighborhood seemed like it was trying to breathe again. Not untouched, not innocent, but quieter. Routine. Adults stepped into their doorways or stood by the sidewalk, talking in low voices while keeping an eye on the kids as the afternoon light faded. Life was settling back into its old rhythm, or at least trying to.

I wanted to believe things were normal again.

That's when the guy started showing up. Nobody knew his name or where he lived. He didn't look like anyone from the block, but he drifted in like he belonged—standing near the sidewalks, watching us play soccer and yelling things like, "*Pásela!*" before any of us even knew who he was.

He was older, too old to be running around with us, but kids don't think much about that. If someone wanted to play, we just let them. So a few times, he jumped in. He chased the ball, laughed too hard at our jokes, and tried to tag us like he was already part of the group.

But something about him didn't sit right. His smile looked like it didn't fit his face. And even when he laughed, his eyes stayed empty.

The adults noticed him too. They didn't say anything to us, but you could feel the way they watched him quietly, like something about him made them uneasy.

Still, he kept coming back. A little closer each day. Watching more than playing.

That afternoon, I was upstairs in my room, leaning on the windowsill like I always did, letting the sounds of the street drift in. Kids arguing over a goal. A ball bouncing. And somewhere in the distance: "Mangos! Mangos maduros!"

It was one of those ordinary afternoons, so normal it made what happened next feel even stranger.

Because that's when I saw him walk into our open garage, slipping through the front metallic gate we never remembered to lock.

He stepped inside like he had done it a hundred times before. He didn't look around or hesitate, just walked in slowly, almost casually, until he stopped right under my window.

I leaned forward a little, trying to understand what he was doing. I hadn't invited him in, and all my perceptions about him—everything that had felt "off" before—started to kick in at once.

Then he lifted his head. And looked straight at me.

Everything in me went quiet. The sounds outside, kids shouting and the mango vendor calling from the distance, all faded into the background. It was just him and me, locked in a stare that felt too direct, too intentional.

"Hi," I said automatically, the word slipping out before I could think. My voice sounded thin, unsure, like it didn't belong to me.

He didn't smile. Not the too-big smile he used when he played soccer with us. His face was blank, like he was trying to decide something. Then he spoke.

"You wanna play?"

His voice didn't match the question. It wasn't light or friendly. It was slow, heavy, like he wanted the words to stay inside the room with me. Something about it made my stomach twist.

"I'm okay," I said, trying to sound normal even though my throat felt tight.

His eyes narrowed just a little. "Come on," he said, the tone shifting— soft on the surface, but wrong underneath. "Don't you wanna have some fun?"

I didn't answer. Something felt off, something I didn't know how to name at that age, but every part of me felt it.

The air felt different then, thicker somehow, like the room had shrunk around me. He didn't look away. He didn't step back. He just stayed there, staring up at me with a look I couldn't read but instantly feared.

My fingers dug into the windowsill. I wanted to call for my mom, or my dad, or anyone—but my voice wouldn't come. My body wouldn't move. I felt like I was glued to the spot, watching something unfold that I didn't know how to stop.

He took a small step closer to the wall. Not a big step. Not enough to be obvious. Just enough to close the space between us in a way that made every hair on my arms stand up.

"Come on," he said again, softer now, almost coaxing. "Just you and me."

I didn't know what he meant. But I knew it wasn't good. The way he said it made my stomach clench.

Then he placed his foot on the narrow cement ledge halfway up the wall—the one kids sometimes used to reach the roof when we chased our soccer ball. His hand found the edge of the window frame, testing it, gripping it like he was checking how solid it was.

My breath caught.

Then his other hand reached for the stone veneer patch on the wall, the decorative stones that created perfect little footholds for climbing.

He wasn't talking anymore. He was climbing.

His movements were slow, steady, like he'd practiced this somewhere else. His foot pressed onto the cement ledge, then onto the stones, and he pulled himself upward, inch by inch. I couldn't look away. My whole body went cold, like my blood had stopped moving.

By the time I realized what was happening, his face was almost level with my window. His breathing was louder now, shallow and quick, and I could see the sweat on his forehead. One hand clamped onto the window frame. The other reached higher, fingers curling around the ledge like he was testing how much weight it could hold.

I stepped back on instinct—just one small step—but even that felt like too much. His hand slid farther inside, and his face crossed the line between outside and inside as if my room belonged to him.

I froze. Completely.

My legs wouldn't move. My arms wouldn't lift. My throat wouldn't open no matter how hard I tried. I felt trapped inside my own body, watching him climb closer and closer, unable to scream or run or do anything at all.

All I could hear was his breathing and my heartbeat crashing in my ears. He pulled himself one inch closer, then another, his eyes fixed on me like I wasn't a kid anymore—like I was something he already owned.

His fingers reached across the inside of the window, stretching toward me.

Something inside me broke loose, not a thought, not a plan, just a jolt that shot through my whole body. One second I was frozen, and the next something pushed me forward from the inside, like a sudden spark waking up my arms and legs.

I don't remember deciding to move. I just moved.

As his fingers reached farther into the room, I threw myself toward the window with everything I had. My palms drove into him harder than I thought I could. I felt his balance break before I saw it in his face. His grip slipped. His foot lost the stone. For a split second he hung there, eyes wide, searching for a hold.

Then he fell.

He hit the tile below, and the echo climbed the wall until it met my breath again.

And that's when my scream finally came. Raw and shaking, louder than anything I had ever heard come out of me. I shouted again and again, the sound tearing through the quiet of the house.

He scrambled to his feet, panicked, not in control. His eyes darted around before he bolted through the garage and out the open gate.

When he disappeared, everything went still, so still it felt wrong. My scream faded in pieces, and the only sound left was the pounding in my ears. I stayed by the window, gripping the frame so tight my fingers hurt, but I couldn't let go.

The garage below looked unchanged—open, quiet, nothing out of place. But to me, it didn't feel the same anymore. The spot where he had stood and climbed now felt tense, like the moment was still stuck there even though he was gone. My breath came in short, uneven pulls, as if my body was trying to catch up to everything at once.

I waited for him to come back.

I don't know how long I stood there—seconds, minutes—but every rustle of leaves, every distant shout, every ball bouncing on the street made my stomach jump. I kept watching the sidewalk, the gate, the wall beneath my window, convinced he would appear again.

But he didn't.

Slowly, the world outside drifted back into its usual rhythm. Kids arguing about a goal. Someone laughing. The mango vendor calling out a few blocks away. All the familiar sounds returned one by one, like the neighborhood had no idea what had just happened.

I stayed there a little longer, hands trembling, staring at the empty wall where he had been climbing.

That night, I lay in bed with the lights off, staring at the ceiling. My room felt different too—like the darkness had too many corners. Every little sound made me jump. A car passing outside. A dog barking two houses down. Even the wind moving the window made my stomach flip.

I kept replaying everything in my head. The way he looked at me. His hands on the stones. His face coming closer. The moment I pushed him. It played over and over like a movie I couldn't turn off.

And every time, the same question came back: What if I hadn't moved? What if I had stayed frozen the whole time? What if he had made it all the way inside? I tried to stop thinking about it, but my mind kept going back to that window, to his hand reaching in like it belonged there.

Lying there in the dark, another kind of fear stirred, one I hadn't felt in years. This time it wasn't only a feeling. Images came too, fast and unwanted. The way he had looked at me, the way he came closer, pulled at something I had carried since I was five. I had learned that a memory like that does not disappear. It only goes quiet. It sleeps. And then a moment like this wakes it up. It wasn't the same place, not the same person, but the fear had the same shape.

I curled tighter under the blankets, wishing I could push that feeling away the same way I had pushed him off the wall.

As I lay there, trying not to look at the window, one thought kept circling in my mind—how I had been frozen one second, and then suddenly moving the next. I didn't know where that push came from. It didn't feel like something I decided, or even something I planned. It felt like a part of me woke up right when I needed it.

And I knew what it was.

It wasn't bravery, not the kind kids talk about. It wasn't anger either. It felt different. Steadier. Like someone bigger than me had grabbed hold of my fear and shoved it out of the way.

I didn't say it out loud, but I knew God helped me push him.

That was the only thing that made sense to me then—the only way I could explain how my body moved when the rest of me felt like it couldn't. I held onto that thought like a lifeline in the dark, because it made me feel less alone. Less trapped in the replay of the moment. God had shown up right when I needed Him most.

I closed my eyes and tried not to think about the window anymore. Morning felt far away, but I kept telling myself the sun would come eventually, and when it did, things would look different. Maybe the fear wouldn't leave right away. Maybe it would stay for a while.

But I was still here. And that mattered.

Chapter 8

The Christmas She Saved My Life

They say energy cannot be destroyed, it only changes form. If that is true, then my mother must have been made of the purest kind. She did not just enter a room, she filled it. Always moving, always creating, always giving life to whatever she touched. Even on the days when the world pressed hard against her, she carried herself with that same unstoppable spark. Her laughter was loud and contagious, the kind that spilled into hallways and lingered in the memories of anyone lucky enough to cross her path.

She did not have much formal education, only high school and a certification as a counselor for couples in crisis, but her real schooling came from surviving life with equal parts grit and grace. She never actually worked as a counselor. Instead, she poured that instinct to help into the toy store she built from scratch. It was not just a business. It was her creation, her refuge, her heartbeat. Kids and adults alike came for more than toys. They came for her. The colors on the walls, the warmth in the air, the sense that life could still be playful, all of it came from my mother.

The store was her independence made visible. She held onto it through financial storms and emotional battles, fighting until she had nothing left to give. When she finally lost it, after the divorce and the endless strain, something inside her cracked. She did not show that crack to the world, but I saw it. Yet even then, she did not disappear. She did not crumble. She let the store go and somehow rebuilt her life from what was left.

People loved her for that kind of strength, but they also loved her because she was truly beautiful. She had the kind of beauty that made people notice her the moment she stepped into a room, not loud or showy but naturally striking. There was an undeniable presence about her, a confidence that wrapped around her like a second skin. Her eyes were warm and expressive, her smile bright and disarming. Her hair was naturally brown, though she often wore it blonde, and her skin carried a sun-kissed glow that seemed permanent. She loved color, deep purples, bright reds, vivid yellows, and she wore bold earrings and bracelets that announced her before she spoke. She was not trying to impress anyone. She simply had impact, the kind that turned heads without her ever meaning to.

What set my mother apart more than anything was her strength. It was not only emotional, but also physical in ways that surprised people. I had seen her carry several heavy boxes up a full flight of stairs by herself, her breathing steady, her steps firm, never asking for help. Her resilience was something people talked about. She believed that no matter how hard life hit you, you got back up. You rose. When the toy store slipped from her hands, she did not mourn it forever. She pivoted. She stepped into a new world and became the manager of a well-known clothing store chain. In a short time, she was managing eight stores across three cities. Her work ethic was relentless, and each store she ran seemed to carry her touch. She had become a leader, someone people looked to for direction and inspiration.

Even with that strength, she had a softer side that showed in the way she cared for us. She was a naturally nervous person, always carrying a quiet tension beneath the surface, but she also believed in giving us independence. She let us explore and be kids. She never wanted to clip our wings. But when we came home later than she expected, the worry settled in her eyes before she said a single word. She did not panic or create scenes. She simply waited, trying to stay calm, and when we finally walked through the door, she let out a long breath she had been holding. She never yelled, but you could see the hurt in her face, the kind that came from imagining something bad had happened.

When she was nervous, her thoughts sped up so quickly that she sometimes forgot our names in the middle of a sentence.

"Where is your brother? Oh, where is the dog? Oh, where is... Eduardo?" she would say, shaking her head and laughing at herself. We teased her about it.

"Third time is the charm, right, Mom?"

She would roll her eyes at us, but always with a smile.

No matter how chaotic life became, she made sure we felt safe, loved, and genuinely happy. She lived surrounded by responsibilities and worries, yet she handled it with a grace that made it look almost natural. Still, nothing could have prepared her for what would happen that Christmas.

The holiday season was the busiest time of the year for the store. Streets were crowded, people rushed in and out searching for gifts, and my mother needed all the help she could get. I was thirteen, old enough to understand the pressure she carried but still young enough to find the chaos exciting. My job was simple: run errands between stores and pick up inventory. It made me feel useful. It made me feel important.

One afternoon, during the rush of the season, I was helping in the back of the store, sorting boxes and checking inventory. My mind was on the task, the usual noise drifting in from the front. Then a conversation floated through the room and caught my attention. A woman who worked there, someone I barely knew, was talking to another employee. She was laughing softly, sounding lighter than I had ever heard her.

"I took something to calm my nerves," she said. "It made me feel like I was floating. Everything felt easy, like I could finally breathe."

Her words slipped into me before I could stop them. The tone in her voice held a peace I did not understand yet, a quiet release that felt strange and inviting. I did not question it. I only felt a spark of curiosity that refused to leave.

I did not know it then, but something inside me responded to the idea of escape. Not from my family, not from my life, but from a restlessness I did not yet have the language to name. Her words kept returning in the following days, tapping at the edges of my mind.

What would it feel like to float? To turn the noise down? To feel nothing for a while?

At my age, those questions felt harmless. They were nothing more than curiosities. But they were enough to change everything.

Pharmacies in Colombia were loosely regulated at the time. No one asked questions, and curiosity mixed with a little cash could get you almost anything. One afternoon, that curiosity pushed me out of the store and toward a small pharmacy a few blocks away. I asked for the pills the woman had mentioned. I did not know their name, only the effect she described. The pharmacist reached behind the counter, grabbed two small cardboard boxes, and slid them toward me. I paid with sweaty hands and tucked the boxes into my pocket.

The store bathroom became my refuge, the only place where I could be alone. I closed the door, opened one of the foil strips inside the box, and pushed the pills through the aluminum. They fell into my hand with a small dry click. I swallowed them with tap water, the taste bitter but manageable. I waited, not knowing what I was waiting for.

Nothing happened at first. I walked out and kept helping in the store, feeling strangely calm. After a while, a lightness spread through me. Not the floating sensation I imagined, but a soft quieting. A fog that made everything feel distant and harmless. I liked it. I wanted more of it.

So I took a few more.

Time blurred. Hours folded into each other. I lost count of how many pills I took. Each one softened the world a little more, until everything felt muted, like I was watching life through a frosted window.

Then the quiet turned dark.

The world did not fade gently. It collapsed.

Everything went black.

When I opened my eyes again, I was on the floor of one of the stores. My body was stiff and heavy, my mouth foaming, sweat soaking through my clothes. Voices swirled around me, panicked and distorted. Then I heard the only voice I could recognize through the haze.

"Fede! Fede!"

My mother.

I tried to answer, but nothing came out. I was stuck inside a body that no longer listened to me. She pulled me up with her bare hands, desperate and terrified. There were no taxis on the street, no passing cars she could stop. She did the only thing she could. She dragged me across the pavement, inch by inch, crying for help as my body scraped the ground. I could barely see her face, only the blur of her silhouette against the sky.

She got me to the emergency room. After that, everything dissolved again into light, needles, voices, then nothing.

When I opened my eyes again, I was lying in my grandmother's apartment. Someone said I had been unconscious for three days. They said one more pill would have killed me. That sentence settled into me like a cold stone. I did not ask questions. No one asked me any either.

My father was sitting in a chair in the corner, quiet and still, his hands loosely clasped. He was not a man who showed anger, even when life pushed him to its limits. But when he looked at me, something in his face had shifted. His eyes were tired, as if sleep had not visited him since the day everything happened. There was no blame, only a sadness that filled the room.

"You have been out for three days," he said. His voice was steady, but the strain beneath it was unmistakable. He did not scold me. He simply watched, as if making sure I would not slip away again.

My grandmother stayed close. She was not someone who involved herself in my parents' affairs unless it had to do with our image, our reputation, or honoring the family name. She carried a quiet pride in who we were, and she expected us to uphold it. Yet her love for us ran deeper than any indignation she may have felt. That love overcame everything. She adjusted my blanket, touched my forehead, and straightened the pillow under my head. Her hands trembled slightly, but she said nothing.

Estelita came in and out of the room with her natural sense of responsibility, carrying water, bringing food, checking on my grandmother, keeping the house steady. She was the practical presence in our lives, the kind of person who kept things moving when others froze. Every time she walked into the room, she paused for a moment and looked at me with quiet concern. She did not need to speak. Her presence was enough.

My brothers were spared the details. They were too young to understand. All they were told was that I had been very sick. They stood at the door quietly, unsure if they were allowed to come closer. One of them slid a small toy onto the edge of the bed and slipped out again. Even without knowing the truth, they sensed the tension that had settled over all of us.

That was when the guilt began to take root. It did not hit me all at once. It arrived slowly, like a shadow that grew a little longer each day. I kept thinking about my mother dragging my body through the street, my father watching me with exhausted eyes, my grandmother's trembling hands, and the steady loyalty in Estelita's movements. I realized that what I had done had not simply happened to me. It had happened to them too.

There was no way to undo what they had felt, no way to erase the fear I had put in their hearts.

For a long time, I believed I had damaged something permanent in all of us. I was thirteen, and in my mind, I had already decided that some part of me was broken and that I had made everyone else carry the cost of it. In the quiet moments, I replayed everything, not the pills or the blackout, but their faces, the fear, the exhaustion, the love.

And that was what hurt the most: knowing that even after all of it, they still loved me enough to stay close.

With time, the guilt softened enough for me to see what I had missed in the moment. What happened that Christmas did not become a wound that followed us for life. My family never treated me like I was broken or shameful. They never used my mistake as a weapon. They simply kept loving me, quietly and without conditions.

I did not understand it then, but their silence was not avoidance. It was protection. It was their way of giving me room to grow out of what happened without burying me under it. They had been terrified, yet no one punished me, and no one demanded explanations I was too young to give.

Years later, when I look back at that moment, it no longer feels like the story of a kid who almost died. It feels like the story of a family who refused to let one terrible mistake define who I was. It taught me that love does not disappear when you fail. Real love stays. It bends. It absorbs. It carries you when you cannot carry yourself.

I did not earn their forgiveness. I did not even know to ask for it. But they gave it anyway, and that act shaped me more than the mistake ever did. It taught me that a person can fall hard and still be held, that a moment of darkness does not cancel the light around it.

What happened that Christmas became one of the first times I understood grace, not the kind you hear about in church, but the kind that sits beside you in the recovery of a small apartment, brings you water, adjusts your blanket, and watches over you while you sleep. It was the kind that does not announce itself. It just stays.

That Christmas will always be a scar on my memory, but it is also a reminder that even in our worst moments, we can be met with something stronger than our mistakes, something that lifts us back to our feet.

Something that does not let go.

Chapter 9

Negative Leader

The first photo arrived after weeks of waiting. My brother had been gone long enough for all of us to wonder how he was doing, and knowing him, we expected he'd delay writing just to build suspense. That was his style—quiet most days, but always saving the dramatic reveal for when he felt it mattered.

When the envelope finally came, we gathered around it as if opening a small mystery. Inside, he stood in the Oregon snow with mountains rising behind him, bundled in a thick jacket. His face looked fuller, his body noticeably stronger. In Colombia we used to joke that American water had vitamins because people there always seemed taller and healthier, and for a second that childhood theory crossed my mind. Whatever the reason, my brother looked like someone who had stepped into a bigger world and adapted to it.

He had always been disciplined and steady back home—the student who never needed reminders, who liked mountain biking and tennis more than crowds or noise, who stayed out of trouble without effort. Seeing him framed by that wide northern landscape, looking unmistakably stronger, filled me with pride.

I'd spent most of my life feeling too thin, painfully aware of it, wishing I looked the way I acted. That picture didn't spark envy; it sparked urgency. He had gone somewhere that had made him stronger, and suddenly I wanted my own chance at that—my own place to grow, to change, to come back carrying something new in the way I stood.

I kept the photo in my hands, studying every detail, imagining what that kind of distance could do for me.

Back in Colombia, my days felt small in comparison. Junior year at the Catholic school had turned into a routine of jokes, pranks, and a loud confidence I didn't always feel. I kept playing the role of the funny one, mostly because it was the easiest way to stand out. Grades meant little to me then; reactions meant everything.

In the middle of that routine was Julia.

She was a happy girl—always smiling, always saying something sweet, always reaching for my hand or my attention without hesitation. There was an innocence in the way she expressed affection, as if she had never learned to hold anything back. Raised mostly by her mother, with brothers living in the U.S. and a father who moved like a distant shadow in her life, she poured a lot of her world into me without realizing it.

Our relationship became intense without either of us planning for it. She'd lean close and say, "You are everything to me," and at first it felt good—warm even—to be seen like that. But there were moments when I caught the weight behind her words, the unspoken expectation that I could fill the spaces left by the people who were supposed to guide her. I cared about her, and I wanted to be there for her, but sometimes her affection settled on me with more force than I knew how to handle at that age.

After returning to Pereira from the school's spiritual retreat, and following the priest's advice to break up the relationship, I decided to talk to Julia outside my house. She came over the way she always did—smiling, ready to talk—but the moment I told her I needed some space, everything inside her collapsed at once.

"Why? Why?" she asked, her voice shaking.

Before I could explain, she rushed past me into the bathroom. I followed a few steps behind, unsure whether to go in or stay out, and heard her sobbing. She dropped to the floor beside the toilet, gripping the ceramic as she began throwing up between broken breaths.

"Julia... let me help you," I said from the doorway, feeling completely unprepared for what I was seeing.

"Don't leave me. Please, Fede... please," she repeated.

The noise brought my mom and Estelita to the hallway. They looked into the bathroom, taking in the scene. My mom didn't hesitate.

"You are an ass," she said, staring at me like I had crossed a line she couldn't ignore.

Estelita stood beside her, shaking her head with quiet disapproval.

Between their reactions and Julia's collapse on the floor, the pressure closed in fast. I couldn't see her like that—I cared about her too much to stand there while she fell apart. Whatever clarity I had gained at the retreat vanished under the weight of that moment. I knelt beside her, put my arm around her shoulders, and told her it was okay, that I wasn't leaving, that we would figure things out.

The words came out quickly, more out of fear and instinct than decision. They weren't true—not fully—but I needed to calm the chaos, and I needed her suffering to stop.

Still, when the house finally quieted, the truth stayed with me. The decision I couldn't voice had already formed inside me days earlier, even if I wasn't ready to face it.

A few weeks later, I was in the school bathroom when two boys walked in talking quietly. I stayed inside the stall, not wanting them to know I was there. One of them inhaled sharply—a quick, rough sound I had heard before at neighborhood parties. Then one asked, "Where did you get it?" and mentioned a street I recognized immediately.

That afternoon, I walked to that same street by myself. It wasn't about Julia or anything happening at home. I had always been curious about things I should have avoided, and now the opportunity was right there. I bought a small bag, tucked it deep in my pocket, and walked home feeling the weight of what I'd done settle in slowly.

The first time I tried it, the tension I carried didn't disappear, but it softened enough for me to notice the difference. My thoughts stopped pushing against each other. Everything felt more distant and easier to ignore. I didn't use often at the beginning, but enough to see changes in myself. My humor got sharper, my patience shorter, and I took risks I would've stepped back from before.

We went to the school together to pick up my final grades. The secretary handed me the envelope, and I opened it before we even reached the parking lot. The first page showed all my classes stamped with "Passed." I felt a rush of relief and threw my fist in the air, celebrating like I had pulled off something impossible.

My dad took the papers from my hands, smiling a little when he saw the same page. For a second, everything felt normal—like we would get in the car, drive home, and leave the school year behind us.

Then he noticed a second sheet stapled to the back, one I hadn't seen.

He flipped it over and read it without saying a word. We kept walking across the parking lot until he finally stopped and showed me the page. His voice was steady, but there was a weight in it I hadn't heard before.

"They're not accepting you back next year."

I looked at the bold line beneath it:

"Due to his influence as a negative leader."

There was no anger in my dad's face—just disappointment mixed with disbelief, as if he was trying to understand how things had gotten to that point without him noticing. Standing there between rows of parked cars, the noise from the street in the background, the words didn't feel dramatic or unfair. They felt direct, almost clinical.

Negative leader.

My celebration ended as quickly as it had begun. I had been in that school since kindergarten; every hallway, every field, every teacher felt familiar in a way I didn't question until that moment. I only had one year left. The idea of not graduating with the same friends I had grown up with didn't make sense to me at first. It felt like I was being cut out of a life I thought was mine by default. Standing there in the parking lot, holding the letter, I didn't know what to say or how to react. I just knew that everything I expected for the next year had disappeared in a single sentence.

A few days after I found out I wouldn't be returning to the school, it was my brother's turn to graduate. The ceremony was held in the main auditorium, the same one where we had held all our events—donation banquets, Mother's Day celebrations, and the afternoons we practiced choir under the rhythm and direction of the priest who ran the school, his accordion leading every song. The space had always felt formal and familiar, a place tied to years of routines and traditions. Seniors lined up in neat rows, dressed in the same traditional suits everyone wore for the occasion—except for him.

He walked in wearing a sharp suit with a white jacket, the kind of choice that immediately separated him from the rest. His ponytail was tied back as usual, but that day he had a thin lace hanging from it, subtle but unmistakably intentional. It wasn't loud or rebellious; it was simply him, refusing to blend in.

As he took his place among the rows of students, a few priests exchanged looks—not angry, just surprised, maybe even uncertain about what to make of someone who didn't fit neatly into their expectations. He didn't seem bothered by any of it. He stood tall, relaxed, carrying himself with a maturity that made the outfit feel deliberate rather than showy.

When he stepped onto the stage, standing slightly apart from the rest in that white jacket, something clicked for me. He wasn't trying to send a message, but the way he carried himself—different, unafraid of being out of sync with the line—made the idea of graduating somewhere else feel less like a failure and more like a possibility. Almost like his confidence opened a small door in my mind, a reminder that finishing in a different place didn't mean finishing wrong. It just meant finishing my own way.

Getting expelled didn't give me a break. It sent me straight into a very different world: Colegio General Rafael Reyes, a school built on a military concept where discipline was enforced by a retired lieutenant who treated every formation like a small parade. The switch was abrupt, but there was one thing I liked immediately—unlike my old Catholic school, this one wasn't all boys. Seeing girls in the hallways made the place feel less insular and more like the real world.

I didn't arrive there planning to prove anything, but the moment classes began, something in me shifted into focus. I studied, listened, and pushed myself in ways I never had before. My mom noticed it before anyone else. One afternoon she opened my backpack, expecting to see the usual notebooks and textbooks. Instead, she found random books that didn't even belong to my courses. I barely used any of them. I didn't study the way people expected; I simply paid attention in class and filled pages of notes I actually understood. She was surprised that I could perform so well without even using the textbooks required for the classes.

My grades climbed quickly after that, and soon I was competing for first place with another kid who had also been kicked out of my previous school. He and I kept trading the top spot on the rankings; the competition made us closer, and having a familiar face there made the transition easier.

I joined the school band and played the bass drum, the deep beat that carried across the courtyard and echoed during rehearsals. The school took its band seriously—we marched in civic parades, school events, and neighborhood competitions where the lieutenant demanded precision and charm. The uniform, the cadence, the synchronized steps, all of it made me feel part of something structured and visible. Even so, the only thing that earned me a real privilege was my grades. Because of them, I was chosen to raise the Colombian flag every morning during formation before the day began. It wasn't lost on me that a kid who had just been labeled a negative leader was now standing at the front of a military-style school, lifting the flag in front of everyone.

My discipline didn't suddenly improve. I still got into trouble—talking back, bending rules, showing up late to formation—but being the top student balanced things out. Teachers respected the academic part of me, even when the rest of me didn't quite match the image.

During the day, I looked like I had everything under control. At night, the version of me that the school never saw came back. I didn't use often, but I used enough to keep a distance from everything I didn't want to feel. It wasn't excitement or rebellion. It was habit, curiosity, and the quiet belief that I could manage both sides of my life without anyone noticing.

The acceptance letter for the exchange program didn't arrive like normal mail, because mail rarely came. So when a man on a bicycle stopped at our door and handed over a large white envelope with my name on it, all three of us—my mother, my father, and I—looked at it with surprise. My dad happened to be there visiting, just getting back to the city from his daily trip to the farm, still carrying a small bag of oranges and limes.

We opened it in the living room. My dad took the envelope first; he was the only one at home who could read English. My mom and I watched as he unfolded the papers.

He read the official part quietly, then moved to the introduction letter from the host family.

"They live in Wisconsin," he said. "The father teaches religion at a private Catholic school, and the mother is the superintendent for the school district in Marshfield."

He paused for a moment, as if noticing how neatly those details matched the world I was coming from. It almost felt arranged that way, a path opening exactly where it needed to.

The photo showed them standing on a wooden porch with their little boy, all three smiling naturally. There was something steady in the way they stood together, a kind of calm that felt unfamiliar but inviting.

My reaction wasn't simple. It was a mix of relief, fear, and the quiet hope that maybe this was the chance to step into a version of myself that didn't exist yet. I had spent years in the same neighborhoods, the same routines, carrying choices I didn't know how to outgrow. Suddenly, there was a doorway leading somewhere else.

I showed the letter to Julia later that day. She tried to smile, but the sadness behind her eyes was immediate. She held the page gently, as if accepting something she wished she could stop. I didn't know what to tell her; I barely understood what the letter meant for me.

Leaving meant stepping away from everything—my friends, my family, Julia, and a life that had started to feel too small for who I wanted to become. The trip represented something I hadn't felt in a long time: hope. It was the chance to rebuild myself in a place where none of my bad choices followed me, a clean break from the pressures and patterns I kept falling into. More than anything, it felt like the right moment to step away from it all and give myself the space to start again.

Eduardo, my youngest brother, watched all of it with a kind of hopeful envy. He didn't say much, but the way he followed every detail made it clear he was already imagining the day it might be his turn.

This was my first real Walk Away, even if I didn't have the words for it then.

Chapter 10

Becoming Fred

Stepping into Newark Airport felt like walking into a rush of movement and noise. It had been many years since I last set foot in the United States—long enough that everything felt new again, familiar only in the way distant memories are.

Our group was diverse—students from different cities across Colombia, men and women, each headed to a different state after our week of orientation on Long Island. As we moved through the terminal, I could feel my thoughts of home slowly fading, pushed back by the anticipation of what waited ahead. It felt selfish in a way; a part of me knew Julia was probably back home wondering where I was and what I was doing, while my mind was already being pulled toward this new world opening in front of me. The newness of everything kept my emotions open, ready for whatever this experience would reveal.

People walked with a kind of urgency, all of them trying to meet their flight schedules in such a vast airport. Travelers from all over the world crossed paths there, and that alone made our arrival feel special—already rich with culture before we had even stepped outside. I moved through the terminal distracted, caught between watching people and trying to make sense of the signs and the fast speaker announcements echoing above us.

I had taken English classes at an institute in Colombia for several months, but hearing the language here felt completely different. It was intimidating—fast, fluid, nothing like the slow, careful phrases from the textbooks. I had expected to understand more, but instead I felt a quiet disappointment settling in. The classes back home had made it seem much easier.

Jaime, our program coordinator, clapped loudly to get our attention. "All right, young people! Welcome to the beginning of your adventure." With that, he guided us toward the bus waiting to take us to the campus at the University of Long Island.

The ride to the university felt strangely quiet. The chatter that had filled the airport faded as soon as we settled into our seats, replaced by a soft, collective silence. One by one, we turned toward the windows, taking in the bridges, the wide highways, and the endless rows of cars that moved with a rhythm so different from home. The city opened around us in layers— industrial buildings, clusters of houses with identical roofs, and patches of trees that appeared and disappeared like quick snapshots. No one said much. We were all breathing it in, letting the new reality settle over us, each of us wondering in our own way what waited on the other side of this ride.

Orientation was like being dropped into a movie. The campus stretched out with perfectly cut grass, wide gardens, and long walkways lined with American flags. Everything looked larger, cleaner, and more carefully maintained than anything I had seen back home. What struck me most were the dorms—actual buildings where students lived. In Colombia, universities didn't have that. The idea of sleeping on campus made the whole experience even more foreign, like stepping into a different version of what education could be.

For the first time, I could sense anxiety tightening in my stomach—an odd, persistent discomfort that wouldn't go away. Maybe it was just nervousness altogether. Very soon I would be leaving for Wisconsin, and the last trace of my Colombian friends would blur into nothing. I knew I would have to face the reality of a completely new and unfamiliar world on my own.

As the days unfolded, one session stood out above the rest. A speaker wrote two words on the board: Adaptation and Growth. "You will feel out of place," he said. "You will miss home. You will make mistakes. But the discomfort—listen carefully—that is where the growth happens." I took it as an early revelation, as if the next year could be summarized in just those few words.

Later, in the evenings, the campus softened. Groups of students from different countries gathered on the lawns, talking in clusters, comparing stories, and laughing at the small things we all found strange or familiar. It was a moment of spontaneity, the kind that sneaks up on you. We started forming real connections—quick, genuine bonds that felt deep even though we knew they wouldn't last. In just a few days, those friendships would scatter across the country, each of us heading to a different state, leaving these early connections behind almost as quickly as they appeared.

But just as rapidly as the magic had begun, the final morning of our orientation arrived. The days had flown by, and we were now huddled together near the buses, exchanging hugs and promises to stay in touch. There was an unspoken understanding among us that this part of the journey was ending, but we all knew it was just the beginning of something much bigger.

Jaime was there, offering his steady presence as always. He handed out final reminders, his voice calm yet encouraging. "Remember," he said, his words firm but kind, "you are representing Colombia. Show them who you are, and don't be afraid to learn who they are."

When it was my turn to board the bus, Jaime clapped me on the shoulder, his smile reassuring. "You're going to do great, Fred," he said. "I know it."

It was strange how a few simple sentences could offer so much comfort. I nodded, a lump forming in my throat. As the bus pulled away, I looked out the window at the campus fading into the distance. My excitement for meeting my host family was tempered by a bittersweet feeling. I had only known this small group of students for a short time, but it felt like we had already shared so much. And now, I was leaving that behind.

The smell of jet fuel lingered in the air as I stepped off the plane in Wisconsin. My carry-on bag was slung over my shoulder, and my heart raced with a mixture of excitement and nerves. I'd come a long way from the familiar comfort of Pereira, and now I was stepping into a new life. A family stood waiting near the gate, their smiles wide and welcoming. The woman at the front waved enthusiastically, wearing a light summer dress that carried a kind of casual authority. "Fred!" she called, her voice warm and familiar despite the fact we'd never met in person before.

I felt a flutter of nerves in my stomach, but I walked toward them, my legs moving on their own. The family was here, and I was here. This was my new reality.

I dropped my bag and hugged them tightly. I had promised myself I'd call them "Mom" and "Dad," and I did, the words coming naturally as though they'd always been there. My host mom smiled, her voice light and genuine, and she patted my back. "You're already part of the family," she said, her smirk radiating kindness. Her words eased the tightness in my chest, and I felt a little of the tension melt away.

My host dad, quieter but no less kind, shook my hand firmly. His deep blue eyes were calm, steady, and warm, the sort of eyes that made you feel like you were exactly where you were meant to be. Their little boy peeked out from behind his mom's legs, wide-eyed and curious, his front tooth missing in a way that made his smile even more unforgettable. His gaze was innocent and filled with wonder, and I could almost feel his thoughts racing— who was this person? What was I like?

Their house was cozy, a quaint suburban home with the kind of warmth that comes from a family that actually lives in it. What struck me first were the gardens—simple, well-kept, and clearly cared for. Tools rested neatly along the side of the house, next to a small excavation that was meant to become a pond for birds to drink fresh water. Spruce trees lined the backyard, forming a natural border instead of the concrete walls I was used to in Colombia. There were no metal guards on the windows either, something that felt almost unreal to me. And then there was the garage. They had left the door open when they went to pick me up at the airport— intentionally, without worry. Inside were expensive tools, equipment, and even a door that led straight into the house. It was a different kind of trust, the kind that quietly told me I was very far from home.

Inside, they walked me through each room with easy excitement, enjoying the moment of showing me my new home. "This is where we spend most of our evenings," my host mom said as we stepped into the living room, pointing toward the fireplace sitting quietly at one end of the room. "We'll light it when the cold comes." My host dad added, "And if you ever need anything, don't hesitate. Everything here is yours as much as ours."

Their voices carried a lightness that eased something inside me. My room was in the basement—spacious, private, and arranged with just enough furniture to feel welcoming while still leaving room for me to make it my own. I stood there in the dim light, taking it all in, everything felt right. This space, this house—it felt like a retreat, a place where I could think, adjust, and slowly become someone new.

Over the next days, my host family took the time to introduce me to a few senior-year students who lived in the neighborhood, kids who could help me navigate the school system and make me feel less like a stranger. We spent afternoons talking, shooting hoops in driveways, and sharing the kind of small conversations that start shaping early friendships. By the time school was about to begin, I felt a little more oriented, as if I had at least one foot on familiar ground.

But even as I adjusted to this new environment, the challenges of fitting in at school loomed large. The first day, the hallway felt like chaos. Lockers slammed shut, voices carried in all directions, and students rushed past in a never-ending tide. I clutched my schedule tightly, trying to make sense of the maze of room numbers and the unfamiliar bell codes. The odd/even day system was completely foreign to me, and by the time I stumbled into the auditorium for what I thought was study hall, I realized I had made yet another mistake.

"Fred," the teacher called out, his voice echoing through the cavernous space. "You're in the wrong class."

The room erupted in laughter, and my face burned with embarrassment. It wasn't the first time I'd gotten lost, but it was definitely the most humiliating. Still, I reminded myself that I had to keep going. One foot in front of the other. This was just another step in the journey. I stood up, muttered an apology, and shuffled out of the room, hoping the next step would be a little smoother.

***

The cafeteria buzzed with clattering trays and loud chatter. I sat with a group of girls I'd grown close to—funny, bold, and full of the kind of confidence I wished I had.

"Fred," one of them said suddenly, grinning. "You'd look good with an earring."

"An earring? Me?"

"Yes! Totally," she said, eyes bright. "It'd make you look… edgy."

The others chimed in immediately. "Do it!" "You'd look awesome!"

I laughed awkwardly. "Isn't it painful?"

"Oh, don't be a wimp," another teased.

Before I could escape, one girl pulled a small stud from her ear and held it up like a trophy. "Let's do it now."

"Right now? Here?" My voice cracked.

"Why not? It's just your ear."

Their excitement was a wave I couldn't fight. "Fine," I muttered. "Do it."

They cheered. She wiped the earring with a napkin—questionable hygiene at best—and reached for my ear.

"You're not using a needle, right?" I asked.

She smirked. "Trust me."

I didn't, but it was too late. She grabbed my earlobe, positioned the stud, and said, "This might hurt a little."

It hurt a lot.

She shoved the earring in, and a sharp, burning pain shot through me. I gripped the table, knuckles white, as she twisted and pushed like she was tightening a bolt.

"It's not going through!" she complained.

"Because that's not how it works!" I hissed.

With one last brutal shove, it finally popped into place. I slumped back, clutching my ear while the table erupted in applause.

"You did it!" she said proudly.

"My ear is bleeding," I groaned. "I think I'm dying."

"You'll live," she said, waving me off.

I wasn't convinced. By the end of lunch, they'd told at least five dramatic retellings of my "bravery," each more exaggerated than the last.

When I got home, my host mom took one look and narrowed her eyes. "Fred... what happened to your ear?"

"Peer pressure?" I said, half-smiling.

She sighed. "Only you."

That night, I went to bed with an ice pack pressed against my swollen ear, laughing at my own stupidity.

Later, in history class, I stared at the list of events the teacher had scrawled across the whiteboard. Louisiana Purchase. Emancipation Proclamation. The New Deal. Each term felt foreign, distant, like it belonged to someone else—someone who had grown up in this world. I sat there, pen hovering over my notebook, unsure of where to start, what to write, or even what the teacher was saying. The words floated around me, just out of reach, like a language I was still learning to speak.

I had learned how to fake it well enough. Nod along. Pretend to understand. Smile when everyone else did. But today, I felt it more acutely than ever—the overwhelming knowledge that no matter how hard I tried, I was never going to be the student I was back home. The comfort of my native language, of knowing the rhythm of each lesson, had been replaced with this strange, alien world.

Gym class became my refuge. The squeak of sneakers on the hardwood floor and the rhythmic thud of the basketball felt like a language I could understand. It was one thing I didn't need to translate. I started working out, eating better, and feeling my body change. The extra time spent lifting weights, riding my bicycle, and even just pushing myself harder than I ever had before—it all started to pay off. By the time I glanced at myself in the mirror one morning, the lanky boy I had been was gone. Each day, my reflection showed a slightly different version of me—less boyish, more solid.

It wasn't just my body that was changing. I had found strength in movement, in pushing through discomfort, in going the extra mile. In the chaos of new surroundings, gym class became a space where I could just *be*, a place where I didn't need to worry about speaking the right words or fitting into a new social structure. I could simply focus on improving, becoming something new.

Woodshop became my creative outlet. The smell of sawdust and the hum of machinery grounded me, and I learned to shape rough planks into polished creations. There was something satisfying about seeing a piece of wood take shape under my hands—something raw and primal about transforming a simple, messy block into something functional, even beautiful. I had never worked with my hands like this before. It was the kind of skill I never imagined I'd develop, but it felt right, like it was always meant to be a part of me.

Photography opened a different world—capturing moments I couldn't quite put into words but felt deeply. I started carrying my camera everywhere, clicking the shutter to freeze fleeting moments of beauty in a world that felt so chaotic. Whether it was the angle of the sun on a crisp morning or the curve of a leaf caught in the wind, there was something about capturing the world that helped me understand it in a new way.

Back at our house, the snowstorm hit overnight, leaving the driveway buried in a thick blanket of white. My host dad handed me a shovel, his breath visible in the crisp morning air. "Let's get to work," he said with a grin.

We cleared our driveway first, and I leaned on the shovel, expecting to go back inside. But my host dad pointed toward the neighbor's house. "Let's do Mrs. Smith's driveway," he said, already heading over.

"She didn't ask us to," I said, confused.

"She doesn't have to," he replied without missing a beat. He plunged his shovel into the snow, working with the same quiet determination I'd come to admire. By the time we finished some of the houses on the block, my arms ached, and my fingers were frozen, but I couldn't help but smile. This was a lesson in kindness.

I didn't realize it at the time, but in that simple act, my host dad had shown me more than I could have learned from any textbook or lecture. It wasn't just about doing what was asked of you; it was about doing more, about reaching out and helping others without expecting anything in return. It was about embodying the idea of community, something that I had grown to appreciate in a way I never had back home.

The letters, though—they were a different story. Julia's handwriting had been a constant in those days of my life. I used to rush to the mailbox after school, eagerly tearing into her letters, her words like a bridge back to the world I'd left behind.

But lately, the box held only silence—bills, flyers, and the hollow weight of absence. Every empty-handed walk back to the house left me fraying at the edges, though I clung to my excuses like brittle leaves: *She's busy. The mail's delayed. It's nothing.*

Then, one afternoon, the ordinary turned extraordinary. The mailbox—usually a dull metal void—gleamed under the sun, and inside, like a whisper against the silence, lay a single envelope. Pale, pristine, unmistakable. My pulse kicked hard, a wild drum of hope. Even from steps away, I knew. The slope of her *J*, the flourish of her *y*—her cursive was a language only I could read, a language that had always meant *home*.

Fede, I don't know how to say this...

Each sentence carved deeper into me. I met someone. The distance is too much. I can't pretend anymore.

My breath hitched. This wasn't happening. Not after all the promises, the late-night calls, the way she used to whisper, *"Te extraño, mi amor."* The memories flashed—her laugh, the scent of her perfume lingering on old letters, the way she'd trace hearts beside her name. Now, those same hands had written *goodbye.*

I'm sorry.

The apology meant nothing. Sorry didn't unkiss her. Sorry didn't undo the years. Sorry didn't stop the hollow ache spreading through my ribs, like someone had reached in and ripped out every hope I'd clung to.

I squeezed my eyes shut. Breathe. But the air felt thick. The letter in my hand was already wrinkled from how tightly I'd been holding it. The last words she wrote blurred every time I looked at them.

The sun slipped behind the clouds, stretching shadows across the pavement. My legs were numb, but I couldn't move. If I stayed still long enough, maybe none of this would be true. Maybe the world would give me one more second before everything changed.

But the paper in my fist was real.

A drop hit the page. Then another. Rain? No—my cheeks were wet. I wiped them quickly, frustrated with myself. Crying wouldn't undo anything. Yet the tears kept falling, steady and hot.

How could she?

The question circled in my mind, sharp and insistent. Had I not called enough? Not cared enough? Or had I simply been the boy she waited to replace?

Then another thought crept in, quiet and honest and undeniable. This must have been what she felt that day back in Colombia, the day I tried to end things. That terrible emptiness that appears when love abandons you was finally something I understood. It settled inside me in the same way, hollow and unforgiving.

A gust of wind scattered dead leaves across the pavement. I should've felt cold, but I didn't. I felt nothing except the quiet collapse of something I thought was unbreakable.

Slowly, I folded the letter. Her perfume still lingered on it, faint and familiar, a warm, slightly sweet smell that felt like her.

I slid it into my pocket and pushed myself upright. My knees trembled. The mailbox ahead sat silent, its emptiness echoing the exact feeling inside me.

When I finally walked inside, the warmth of the house wrapped around me like a blanket. My host mom stood in the kitchen, stirring a pot on the stove. She glanced up, her expression shifting the moment she saw my face.

"Fred," she said, concern lacing her voice. "Are you okay?"

I held up the letter, managing a weak smile. "I just got dumped."

Her brows knit together as she put down the spoon and crossed the room. Without a word, she pulled me into a hug, her arms firm but comforting. "I'm so sorry," she murmured, her voice soft against my ear. "Do you want to talk about it?"

I shook my head, pulling away gently. "Not right now."

She nodded, her hand squeezing my shoulder before letting me go. "I'm here if you need me."

That night, I lay in bed with the letter resting on my chest, the ceiling above me blurred by unshed tears. The ache was real, but there was something else—something quieter, like a door creaking open. Julia had been my world, my anchor to home, but now that tether was gone. And although deep down, when I left Colombia, I had a feeling that our relationship might fade naturally with time and distance, I never imagined I'd be replaced. That part—being replaced—hurt far more than I was prepared for. It wasn't just about losing her. It was about realizing that someone else had taken the place I once held in her heart, and that pain settled in deeper than I ever thought it would.

Chapter 11

When Fear Meets the Gaze of Strangers

I barely slept. When morning finally showed up, it felt like an intrusion. The sunlight pressed in through the curtains, blunt and uncaring, like it didn't give a damn about the state of my heart. I blinked into it, eyes burning, throat tight. Maybe this was what moving forward looked like—just standing still and letting the light in, even when it didn't feel like it belonged to me anymore.

The letter was tucked away now. Out of sight, but not out of mind. I could still feel the creases on my fingertips, the echo of her words wrapping around my thoughts like ivy. *I met someone.* The sentence repeated itself in the back of my skull like an unwelcome song on loop.

But "forward" didn't feel like something I could see yet. I was still carrying a strong feeling for her, still trying to understand how to move through the heartache.

That's probably why I said yes when my friends invited me to go camping for the skip-day celebration. We'd gotten close that year, close enough that being around them felt easier than being alone with my thoughts. The idea of escaping—just for a night—was too tempting to turn down.

We hiked out to a clearing just outside Wausau, a beautiful campground tucked between tall pines and the steady rush of a creek. A paved road curved through the sites like a quiet ribbon, each spot alive with the chatter of senior students celebrating the end of the year. Someone lit a bonfire, and the flames rose with a kind of joy that made it feel like we were part of something ancient. Brandy passed from hand to hand in soda cans, a makeshift rite of passage. The warmth from the fire and the quiet of the woods settled into me, easing the breakup just enough to let me feel a little lighter.

But little by little, the night shifted. My friends settled in beside their girlfriends, whispering, laughing softly, and then disappearing into their tents one by one. Before I knew it, the clearing was quiet, and I was the only one left sitting by the fire, staring at the glow of their tents as they came alive with silhouettes and low murmurs. The stars above felt too bright, the brandy too warm in my chest, the breakup too close.

I stood up—unsteady, stubborn, and drunk enough to say out loud, "I'm going to get me a girlfriend too," as if declaring it to the trees would make it true. I started down the spiraled road, still holding my can, letting the night pull me along.

I saw two guys walking toward me, silhouettes in the dark. When we passed each other, I lifted my can and said, "Hi, guys," and kept going. They took a few more steps before turning around, their flashlight snapping on and cutting through the darkness.

"ID?" one of them barked.

At first, I thought it was a prank. Someone playing around. But the way the voice carried—stern and practiced—and the way two figures emerged from the darkness, belts heavy with gear, badges catching the firelight... There was no mistaking it. Cops.

I froze. For a second my mind just... stalled, like it couldn't catch up to what was happening. Then everything hit at once—flashes of ruining my whole year in the U.S., of being sent home, of all of it ending right there on that spiraled road. The fear landed so hard it knocked the drunk right out of me. I dropped the can on the spot and ran.

I don't remember making the decision. It was like my body took over, instincts screaming louder than logic. One second I was standing there, and the next I was in the woods, branches whipping across my face, threatening to rip my shirt as I tore through them.

"Stop! Stop right now!" they shouted behind me.

I ran harder.

My sneakers slipped on the mossy ground, roots rising like traps. Somewhere in the scramble, I realized how stupid it was—running only made it worse. But by then, it was too late. I could hear them getting closer. The flashlight beam bounced wildly through the trees, then caught my shoulder for a split second. I veered left, heart crashing against my ribs.

Then everything snapped.

My foot hooked under a thick root, and I hit the ground hard. The air shot out of my lungs in a gasp. I tried to push myself up, but before I could even shift, a weight slammed onto my back. Hands pinned my arms, dirt grinding against my cheek.

"Got him!" one of them grunted.

I struggled, reflexively, stupidly. But they were trained, efficient. One arm twisted behind me, another knee dug into my spine. The other officer came up, flashlight casting everything in blinding contrast. I could see the fog of his breath in the cold air, his face hard.

"You thought you could outrun us?" he said. Not a question. A scolding.

"I... I didn't..." My voice cracked.

The one on top of me let out a breath that was half laugh, half snort. "Yeah, sure. You didn't."

They hauled me up, and my knees buckled slightly. My palms stung where I'd caught the fall. As we stumbled back through the woods, the fire appeared like an island of heat and light in a sea of cold fear. But they didn't take me toward it. They kept walking past the clearing and straight toward the patrol car parked near the campground entrance.

"ID," one of them demanded again.

I couldn't answer. My throat locked. All I could see in my mind was the worst possible outcome—getting sent home, losing everything I'd built that year, all because of one dumb night. The fear paralyzed me. Not defiance— pure panic.

They opened the back door and pushed me inside. The plastic seat was hard and cold, the metal partition in front of me turning the space into a kind of cage. The door slammed shut, and suddenly it was just me, my heartbeat, and the sound of their voices outside.

"Name?" one of them asked through the grate.

Nothing came out. I was terrified that saying anything—anything at all—would trigger the end of everything I'd fought to hold together that year.

Their voices blurred. The adrenaline drained. My head grew heavy, the brandy still warm in my system, and somewhere in that fog, I fell asleep.

I woke to Randy's voice.

He was standing outside the car, talking calmly to the officers. I couldn't make out the words, but his tone carried something steady, something reasonable—something they were actually listening to. After a moment, the door opened, and cold air hit my face.

They guided me back toward the fire. I felt the eyes of everyone before I even saw them—shock, confusion, a little fear.

"This one tried to run," the officer said, giving me a final shove. "Not a smart move."

A heavy silence hung over the clearing.

Then Randy stepped forward, firelight flickering across his face.

"Look, officers," he said calmly, "he's new here. He doesn't know the rules. It's his first time drinking. Let's cut him some slack, huh?"

The officers exchanged a look. One scratched his chin, thinking it over, then sighed.

"We'll let it go this time," he said. "But if we catch you again..."

He didn't have to finish. The silence did the rest.

They turned and disappeared back into the trees.

The moment they were gone, the tension snapped.

"Fred, man, you ran like a deer!" someone laughed, slapping me on the back.

Another voice chimed in. "Dude, I thought you were gonna vanish into the woods like Bigfoot or something."

Laughter rippled around the circle.

I tried to laugh with everyone, but my hands wouldn't stop trembling. My palms still carried the sting from the fall, and my shoulder throbbed where the officer's knee had pressed me into the ground. The fire looked softer than it had before, settling into embers now that no one was tending it.

Randy must have noticed. He told me to crash in the back of his Bronco, away from the circle of eyes and questions. I climbed in and lay on the blankets he kept spread over the floor, beside him, both of us staring up at the ceiling, letting the quiet settle.

It didn't last.

A group of college guys had gathered near the truck—too close, too loud. Their voices cut through the dark, filling the small pocket of quiet around us. After a while, Randy exhaled, sat up, and stepped out to ask them to keep it down.

I stayed inside, watching through the window. At first it was just talking—hands moving, shoulders loose. Then something in the way they stood changed. Bodies angled in. The space around Randy seemed to shrink.

The urge to help got me moving before I'd really thought it through. I pushed the door open and stepped out.

I didn't make it two steps.

A fist came out of nowhere—no warning, no words—and crashed into my face. The ground rushed up and the night disappeared.

When I woke up, the sky was pale and the campground was quiet. I was curled around the metal fire pit, my arms wrapped around it like it was the only warm thing left. The coals from the bonfire still held a faint heat, just enough to keep the cold from biting all the way through. My face ached. My body felt heavy, off-balance. I hadn't found a girlfriend, but I'd definitely found something to cuddle with.

People started stirring not long after. Tent zippers, car doors, the clatter of coolers—it all blended into a low morning noise. It was time to pack up: sleeping bags rolled, fires doused, gear shoved into trunks. I climbed into the Bronco with the others, and we drove back to Marshfield. My head pounded with every bump in the road, but the silence in the car felt like a kind of mercy.

When I walked into the house, my host mom was in the kitchen. She turned, took one look at my face, and froze.

"What happened to you?"

I kissed her on the cheek, trying to play it off.

"We were messing around," I said. "Playing football."

She didn't believe me—I could see it in her eyes—but she let me walk past her without another question.

Time softened the bruises faster than it softened my restlessness. The story of that night by the fire slowly turned into something we could laugh about, at least on the surface. I told myself I'd be more careful, but I was still a teenager, still drawn to anything that felt like escape.

There was still the pull of the thrill, the magnetic force of new experiences my friends would come up with. It never took much to get us going—just an idea, some enthusiasm, and a dash of mischief.

A few weeks later, on an evening that started out harmless, the air was cool and clean. Weather like that made everything feel a little more awake—the quiet brush of leaves, a dog barking somewhere down the block, the full moon laid over the neighborhood like an excuse to stay out longer than we should. The neighborhood felt calm, almost sleepy, but to us it felt wide open.

We gathered at my friend's house on a whim, no real plan, just the usual group of teenagers who liked to get into trouble together. We weren't doing anything stupid—just hanging out, chatting, enjoying the time. But as always, our conversations meandered, and before we knew it, someone had brought up an old grudge, a petty annoyance with a kid.

"You know what we should do?" someone asked, their voice light, casual, yet laced with mischief. "Let's TP his house."

The suggestion hung in the air for a moment, almost like a dare, before the laughter spread across our group. It was one of those ideas that seemed so absurd that it became irresistible. We weren't serious—at least, not in the way most people would think—but the thought of sneaking into someone's yard and covering it in toilet paper was just too ridiculous not to entertain. And as I glanced around at my friends, I could see they felt the same excitement bubbling beneath their calm exteriors.

There was no heated argument, no raised voices. We all simply agreed without much discussion, and in a matter of minutes, a simple late-night conversation had turned into a full-blown plan.

The kid we were targeting wasn't exactly an enemy; he was someone my friends had clashed with a few times. Nothing major, just those petty high school squabbles that seem important when you're a teenager, but that you laugh about later in life. We didn't want to cause real harm, so it felt good to have a harmless way to get back at someone like him. We wanted to make a statement in a way that wouldn't cause lasting damage.

As the night deepened, the streetlights flickered on, casting pools of yellow light onto the quiet, suburban streets. The houses along the cul-de-sac were dark. The neighbors were asleep, unaware that a small group of teenagers were plotting their next act of harmless rebellion.

We crouched down behind a row of neatly trimmed bushes at the edge of the yard, our hands clutching rolls of toilet paper, ready to strike. The yard before us was still, the house looming like a sleeping giant, untouched by the chaos we were about to unleash. I could feel my heart thumping in my chest—not from fear, but from the excitement of the prank. My friends were just as giddy, their eyes darting between the house and each other, trying to hold back their laughter.

"Okay," someone whispered, "Everyone knows the plan. We hit the trees first. Then, the mailbox. And no getting caught."

There was a low murmur of agreement. The rules were simple: be fast, be quiet, and don't get caught. We'd made sure to wait until the house was empty—there were no cars in the driveway, no lights on inside. We were in the clear.

When the coast was clear, we moved.

The first roll left my hand and curved over the yard. The paper unrolled in the air with a soft hiss before it landed on the roof and hung over the edge like an accidental decoration. The streetlights caught it just right, making the white streamers glow against the dark sky.

"Got the roof!" someone whispered, barely able to contain their excitement.

One by one, we followed suit. Toilet paper sailed into the trees, caught on branches, and danced in the breeze like confetti. Another roll hit the mailbox, wrapping around the post like a paper lasso. The yard transformed before our eyes—what had been a simple, manicured lawn was now a mess of fluttering white paper.

We were quick, but not without our fair share of clumsiness. One of us tripped over a loose patch of grass, another got tangled in the toilet paper trailing behind them. The laughter was impossible to contain. It wasn't just the thrill of pulling off a prank; it was the sheer ridiculousness of seeing their house draped in toilet paper, it was undeniably absurd.

"Got the trees!" someone whispered, pride evident in their voice. Another roll soared through the air, unfurling as it flew. It landed in a beautiful arc, draping over the branches of the nearest tree like an accidental work of art.

We kept moving, trying not to get caught in the hilarity of it all. The toilet paper hung from the trees, swaying gently in the breeze. The entire scene felt surreal—a strange, temporary installation of white against the dark backdrop of night.

But then came the moment of panic.

The porch light flickered on.

Someone inside had woken up, and we froze.

The warm glow of the porch light bathed the front of the house, and I could feel my heart drop into my stomach. We'd been caught—or at least, it seemed like it. Someone had noticed. Maybe they were just getting up to grab a glass of water, but we couldn't risk being seen.

Without a word, we scattered.

We dashed in every direction, each of us running off into the darkness, our laughter muffled by the sudden surge of adrenaline. We split up, ducking into nearby yards and alleyways, trying to stay out of sight. My breath came in sharp, excited gasps as I ran, my sneakers slapping against the pavement. The thrill of the chase was far greater than any fear of getting caught. We had just pulled off a perfect prank. Now, we had to escape without anyone finding out we were the culprits.

Later, when I thought back on it, I knew it was stupid and childish, but that was part of why it stuck with me. No one got hurt, no one's life changed, no one carried it for longer than it took to clean the yard and curse our names. In a year filled with breaks and bruises that went much deeper, this was one of the few things that didn't leave a scar.

THE WALK AWAY

Chapter 12

Bringing the World Home

Leaving Marshfield hurt more than I expected. Saying goodbye to my host parents felt like someone was carefully pulling up roots I hadn't realized had grown so deep.

The house was quieter that last morning. The kitchen, the heart of our days together, felt almost like a memory already. I stood in the doorway, watching my host mom move around like she always did, wiping the counter that was already clean, checking the oven twice even though it was off. My host dad carried one of my suitcases to the door, the way he always carried things: without complaint, like it was simply what you did for family.

Little flashes of the year kept popping up in my mind, one after another, like someone flipping through a photo album too fast. All of us in the kitchen on weeknights, each with a different task—someone chopping vegetables, someone stirring a pot, someone setting the table. No shouting. No tension. Just jokes, stories from the day, and that low, steady murmur of people who knew how to love each other well.

I thought about Sundays, especially. Waking up early to go to church together, the quiet of the morning broken by the sound of the coffee maker and soft voices. After the service, we'd always pick a different restaurant for breakfast, sitting around a table full of pancakes and eggs, talking and laughing like we had all the time in the world. Then we'd head back home, change clothes, and everyone would pitch in—cleaning the house, working in the garden, fixing whatever needed fixing. No one had to be begged or pushed. You just helped; in that family, everyone quietly did their part.

Their relatives lived in Iowa, most of them farmers. On special occasions we'd drive out to visit. They showed me farming the American way—tractors, barns, fields that seemed to stretch forever. After the work was done, everyone would gather around a long table. Before anyone touched the food, we prayed, giving thanks first to God and then, one by one, to the people who had helped prepare the meal, which, in some way, was almost everyone there. It was simple, but it felt big. Right. Whole.

In that home, I had seen what it looked like to live under the care of a truly functional family. Love wasn't something they talked about—it was in everything they did. It was in who got up early to make breakfast, who quietly did the dishes, who noticed when someone was having a hard day and sat beside them without asking for details. For the first time in my life, I got to be part of that kind of everyday peace.

Standing by the door with my suitcases at my feet, I realized how much I didn't want to let it go.

My host mom hugged me first, her arms wrapping all the way around me, holding on longer than usual. My host dad stepped in next, his hug firm and brief, but his eyes were wet. We took a quick picture together in the driveway, all of us forcing smiles that didn't quite match what we were feeling.

"Don't forget to write," she said.

"Take care of yourself out there," he added.

"I will," I said, but the words caught a little in my throat.

When I finally climbed into the car, I looked back one last time. They were still standing there in the driveway, side by side, waving. That image burned into me: two ordinary people who had loved me like a son for a year, and a little boy with a wide smile who treated me like an older brother.

They had changed my life.

A couple of hours later, in Appleton, I finally climbed onto the bus that would start the long trip home. This time there was no cheering, no excitement—just the scrape of suitcases, the hiss of the doors, and a few quiet goodbyes. Most of us didn't know each other. We were a random mix of exchange students from different towns and schools, suddenly grouped together for one last route: a week in Minneapolis with new host families, another week in Detroit, and then Long Island, where the program would officially come to an end. After that, it would be Colombia—the home I hadn't seen in more than a year.

The bus hummed steadily beneath us, gliding down long stretches of Midwest highway. Fields blurred past in green and gold, like someone was smudging the paint on a landscape. Inside, the mood was heavy. Some students whispered in low voices, others stared out the window with their headphones on, lost in their own thoughts. I leaned my head against the cool glass and let it all settle inside me—gratitude for what I had lived, sadness for what I was leaving behind, and the quiet uncertainty of what waited for me back home.

Ahead of us were two weeks, two cities, and then the end.

I didn't know it then, but Minneapolis would change something for me.

We had a group gathering there—a casual get-together at the home of a generous local family. The place buzzed with laughter, plates of food being passed around, and that tentative energy of people who didn't know each other yet but knew their time in this country was running out. I was hovering awkwardly near the snack table, half-heartedly sipping a can of soda, when I saw her.

Elena.

She stood across the room, her blonde hair catching the light like spun gold. Her face had this soft, almost glowing quality, but it wasn't just that. It was the way she stood—confident without trying to be, relaxed but full of quiet energy. She laughed at something someone said, and just like that, the noise in the room seemed to dim. I didn't even notice I was walking toward her until I was already halfway there.

I don't remember what I said to start the conversation. Something generic, probably. But once we started talking, it didn't matter. Her voice had this delicate musicality to it, Swiss with a hint of something else. We talked about everything and nothing, from our host families to the weirdness of American school lunches and what we missed most from home.

"I miss Swiss chocolate," she said, grinning, her eyes lighting up.

I laughed. "I'd trade all the chocolate in the world for some Colombian arepas."

She laughed back, warm and easy, and just like that, we fell into a rhythm that felt both new and completely familiar.

The rest of the evening disappeared. One moment we were talking by the kitchen, the next we were outside by the grill. The air smelled of charcoal and sizzling hot dogs and burgers, people shuffling around with paper plates, passing ketchup and mustard, laughing in small groups. But for me, none of that really registered. It was her—just her. The way she brushed her hair behind her ear, how she leaned in a little when she listened, like what I said mattered.

I asked for her phone number and address so we could stay in touch. It felt like the safest way to hold on to something without saying more than I was ready to say. She took a pen and carefully wrote everything on a napkin, her handwriting neat and a little tilted. I folded it and slipped it into my pocket like it was something fragile.

When the night finally wound down and it was time to go, we walked to the door together. We hugged, said we would write, and then I stepped away and lifted a hand in a small wave. She smiled back, and for a second it felt like the noise around us faded. On the way back to my host family's house, I kept slipping my hand into my pocket to make sure I hadn't lost that napkin.

After Minneapolis came Detroit.

That week was memorable for a completely different reason. My host sister there was white, but the school she attended was mostly Black. From the moment I walked into the building with her, I knew I was stepping into a world I had never experienced before. The energy in the halls was louder and faster than what I was used to in Marshfield or back home in Colombia. The place felt alive. People moved with a kind of style and confidence I admired but didn't quite know how to copy.

My host sister moved through the crowd like she belonged there, stopping every few steps to say hi to someone. I stayed close, feeling both curious and out of place at the same time. Students looked at me with open curiosity. Some asked where I was from. Others just nodded or gave a quick

"What's up" as they passed. It wasn't unfriendly, just new—to them, I was the unfamiliar one.

The classrooms were no different. The teachers were direct and energetic, and the students didn't hesitate to speak up, joke, or push back on ideas. I spent most of the day quietly observing, trying to take everything in. It was still the United States, but inside that school it felt like another version of the country, one I never would have seen if I had only stayed in Marshfield. That day in Detroit opened another window for me into how many cultures exist inside the same borders.

I felt out of place at first, like an outsider. There I was, the foreign exchange student with a thick accent and an unsure smile, as if everyone else had already learned the rules of a game I was just seeing for the first time. But my host sister was a pro. She moved through the crowd with ease, introducing me to her friends, translating slang I didn't quite understand, and making sure I felt included.

The students seemed genuinely curious about me, their questions coming fast and full of humor. "Colombia, huh?" one boy asked, raising an eyebrow. "Do you ride a donkey to school?"

The group around him burst into laughter, and I couldn't help but grin. I knew the stereotype was coming, but it didn't bother me. In fact, it felt kind of fun. "Only on Fridays," I shot back, and they all nodded approvingly, laughing even harder. There was something in the way they welcomed me with humor and curiosity that made me feel more comfortable, like I was already part of something.

In one of the classes, I think it was history, the teacher suddenly turned to me and asked if I could share a little about Colombia. My stomach tightened. I hadn't prepared anything, and for a second I just stared back at her.

Then I started with what I knew best: coffee.

I told them how, in the mountains back home, people woke up before sunrise to pick the coffee cherries by hand, how the sacks were carried on mules along narrow, muddy paths, and how the whole town could smell the beans drying in the sun. I talked about the fruits too—how we had lulo, guava, maracuyá, mango, things you couldn't just grab at any supermarket there in the U.S. Some students raised their eyebrows when I mentioned that in my hometown many schools separated boys from girls, and that most of our houses shared walls with the neighbors instead of sitting in the middle of a big yard with grass all around.

At first my words came out shaky, but as I kept talking, the room grew quiet. They weren't just being polite; they were actually curious. A few hands went up with questions. Someone asked what lulo tasted like. Another wanted to know if I had ever picked coffee myself. By the time the bell rang, I didn't feel like the strange foreign kid as much. For that one class, it felt like I had brought a small piece of my world into theirs.

As the day came to a close, I found myself reflecting on the experience. The school was unlike anything I had ever seen before, and yet, it felt oddly familiar. The students were full of life, unapologetically themselves, and open to new ideas. It was a reminder of how big the world is, and how small it can feel when you start to connect with people who are different from you.

The bus ride to New York after that last day was bittersweet. As we headed toward Long Island, my final stop before flying back to Colombia, I stared out the window at the fields and small towns blurring past and thought about the boy who had first left home almost a year earlier. Back then, my world had been so narrow—Colombia was everything: my home, my culture, the people I loved. It was all I knew. I carried my assumptions about the world like a shield, believing that the way I lived was simply how life was. But this year abroad had shattered that narrow perspective. My world had stretched far beyond what I ever imagined, and suddenly it didn't feel small at all.

Throughout the year I had met people from all over the globe. I thought about Elena from Switzerland and how easily she talked about her mountains and her chocolate, how her laugh made me feel close to her even though our lives had been so different. I remembered the German student who once sat beside me on the bus, explaining how reliability and discipline were almost like family traditions for him. I saw again the Brazilian exchange students, loud and warm, their energy reminding me of Colombia but with a different rhythm.

Little by little, people like them had chipped away at the invisible walls I didn't even know I carried. I stopped seeing the world so much as "us" and "them" and started seeing it more as a mix of stories, each one adding something. The more I got to know people from other countries, the more I realized how much we shared under the accent, the food, and the habits.

Being an exchange student hadn't just been about learning English or getting used to a new country. It had taught me to borrow other people's eyes for a while, to look at life from their side of the table. And after a year of doing that, I knew I would never see the world the same way again.

But now, as I sat in that bus full of students returning from their exchange programs, everything felt different. Not because the world had changed—but because I had.

The bus rolled to a stop outside the orientation center in Long Island. The building was buzzing with energy. Friends who hadn't seen each other in months were embracing like siblings. You could see it in our eyes—we weren't the same kids who had first landed in the U.S. months earlier. People who had seemed so different at the start now felt like part of our lives.

I spotted a few other Colombians from my original group. We hugged tight, speaking fast in Spanish, our words crashing into each other as we tried to catch up all at once. Almost right away we started laughing at how different we all looked. Everyone seemed taller, more muscular, more defined, like each of us had gone through our own private transformation. We joked about what supplements the others had taken, who had spent more time in the gym, who had changed their haircut or style. Everyone looked fantastic, like upgraded versions of the kids who had left Colombia a year earlier.

Still, amid all the noise, my thoughts kept drifting back to Elena. I finally spotted her across the parking lot, near the buses, surrounded by friends, moving from one hug to the next, laughing and talking in quick bursts. I thought about walking over, but every time I took a step in her direction, someone else reached her first. After a while I drifted back toward my Colombian group, pulled into our own circle of stories and jokes. At one point she looked up, her eyes moving over the groups scattered around the lot until they landed on me. She paused, lifted her hand halfway in a small, shy wave that could have been either hello or goodbye. I raised my hand too as I walked backwards with my friends, and then the buses and bodies shifted and she disappeared from view.

Then came the final night.

That last night we had a talent show in the auditorium. One thing led to another and somehow I ended up on the list to perform. A few hours later I was onstage in front of what felt like the whole camp, dancing to rap and lip-syncing "U Can't Touch This" by MC Hammer. I had learned the lyrics almost perfectly and did my best to copy the moves I'd seen on TV, but standing there under the lights, with hundreds of students watching, my stomach felt like it was trying to escape through my throat. Some people clapped and cheered, others laughed, but I kept going until the track ended. When I walked offstage, my face was burning, half from embarrassment, half from the rush of having actually done it.

After the show, everyone spilled out into the hallways and common areas, taking pictures, trading addresses, signing flags and yearbooks. I floated between groups, saying goodbye, accepting hugs, promising to write. It all felt a little unreal, like the night was moving faster than I could hold on to it.

I didn't sleep much.

And then, just like that, it was morning. The bus to the airport waited, engines running. I climbed aboard, found a seat by the window, and watched as the orientation center, the parking lot, and the clusters of waving students grew smaller. The city slowly gave way to highways and sky. Long Island faded behind us, but inside I felt strangely alert, as if my mind refused to close its eyes on the year that was ending.

After a short connection in Bogotá, the final plane dipped over the mountains toward Pereira. When we landed and the doors opened, a wave of warm air rushed into the cabin. By the time I walked past baggage claim and into the arrivals area, the sounds hit me all at once—taxi drivers calling out, families shouting names, kids running in circles, announcements echoing over the speakers. It felt loud, messy, familiar.

And then I saw her. My mom, waving frantically from behind the crowd. Her eyes sparkled with tears as she rushed toward me, but for a second she just stopped and stared. I must have looked like a different person—long blond hair, three earrings in one ear, baggy pants and an oversized T-shirt straight out of a rap video.

She pulled me into a hug so tight it squeezed the air out of my lungs. My dad stood just behind her, arms crossed, looking me up and down with a half-smile.

"What happened to my son?" he asked, his voice thick with emotion and pride.

"I told you you wouldn't recognize me," I said, grinning back.

Chapter 13

Into Their Hands

The draft didn't start with the lottery. It started at the San Mateo army base, in a cold room where ten of us at a time stood completely naked in a horizontal line.

The doctor, an army officer with a clipboard under his arm, walked slowly in front of us, checking knees, backs, chests, eyes. Nobody knew where to look. The only sound was the squeak of his boots and the occasional nervous cough. Then he stopped, glanced at the line, and barked a single word:

"Stretch."

Everyone lifted their arms and got on their tiptoes. I, for some reason, heard something else. I grabbed my penis and literally stretched it, thinking that's what he wanted us to do. The doctor froze, staring at me like he couldn't believe what he was seeing. The other guys tried not to laugh, their faces turning red from the effort. My own face burned so hot I wished the floor would just open and swallow me whole.

After that, the rest of the process felt almost easy. We got dressed, handed over our ID cards, and watched the clerks copy our names onto the army lists. When my turn came, the clerk wrote my name and number in a cramped line, then grabbed a rubber stamp and slammed it down on the page. A red watermark appeared over my details: APTO—fit for service.

If there was ever a day my mother might have wished a doctor would find something wrong with me, it was that one. I still had six months of high school left after coming back from the U.S., but from the moment that stamp hit the paper, the rest of the year felt like borrowed time.

On the morning of the lottery, they lined us up outside the school and marched us onto the buses. I grabbed a seat by the window. The ride into Pereira buzzed with nervous energy—knees bouncing, fingers drumming on the metal rail, someone in the back snapping his backpack buckle open and closed on a loop. Short bursts of laughter flared up too loud and died just as fast. It felt like the whole bus was holding its breath, waiting for someone on a stage we hadn't seen yet to decide the next year of our lives with one small colored ball.

The theater in Pereira was already filling when we arrived. We were the only ones in uniform—our school's strict dress code stood out against the jeans, T-shirts, and random hoodies of the other boys' schools that hadn't gone that far yet. We filed into the empty rows in the middle and dropped into our seats. Some guys leaned forward with their elbows on their knees; others sat rigid, hands clasped. Down by the stage, under the bright lights, a few officers moved around a table and a large cloth bag, arranging papers and talking quietly, as if what was about to happen was just another item on their schedule.

The officers took their time, calling out names one by one. Every time someone walked up to that bag and turned around with their hand closed, the room seemed to lean forward. Those who opened their fist and found a red ball looked like the floor had dropped beneath them. The ones who picked "yellow" walked back trying not to smile too much, as if showing relief might tempt fate to change its mind.

I sat there, waiting for my name, feeling unusually calm. My mind wasn't fixed on avoiding the draft the way most of my classmates' were. Part of me actually wanted to be selected. I didn't see the military as something to fear; it felt like a chance to grow stronger, more disciplined, maybe even to open doors I couldn't reach any other way. In the back of my mind, one thought kept repeating: if I made it in, maybe I could apply for the Multinational Force and Observers in the Sinai Peninsula. I didn't just find that mission interesting—I wanted it.

When my name was finally called, I stood up and walked to the stage. My legs felt a little looser than I wanted them to, but I forced myself to keep a steady pace. Reaching into the bag, I fumbled briefly, my fingers brushing against the different balls inside. Finally, I pulled one out.

It was yellow.

I felt the weight lift off my shoulders, but instead of a feeling of total relief, there was something else. A sense of disappointment washed over me. I had just avoided mandatory service, but at that moment, I realized that my vision of joining the MFO and experiencing something beyond the ordinary was slipping away. I had imagined it so vividly—being part of an international mission, serving alongside people from different countries, and possibly even traveling to places I would have never seen otherwise. But now, that chance seemed out of reach.

I sat down, trying to process my feelings. Everyone around me was either celebrating or consoling one another, depending on the color of their ball. But I was in a daze. It wasn't relief that I felt, nor was it joy. Instead, I felt a deep sense of ambivalence, like I had just been given the chance to escape one thing, but in doing so, I had missed out on something else.

The longer I sat there, the stranger it felt to know my turn was over. My name was off the list of those who "owed" a year, but it didn't feel like I'd been spared; it felt like I'd been pushed out of the only line I actually wanted to stand in. If a random draw could take the MFO away from me that easily, maybe I shouldn't be leaving this to chance. The idea came quietly at first, then settled in with more weight than anything else in that room: if the army wasn't going to choose me, then I would have to choose it.

When the lottery was over, the room began to empty. Laughter and low voices drifted through the aisles as students headed back to their schools or homes—some already making plans, others walking out in silence with their hands shoved deep in their pockets. A few stayed seated for a while, staring at the stage as if the bag might come back out and someone would say there'd been a mistake. I stayed in my seat, letting the rows clear around me. My name was on the safe list, but it didn't feel safe at all. Somewhere between the stage and my chair, I had already made the decision that would change everything.

A few of the officers had started gathering papers, organizing clipboards, and talking among themselves. I watched them, my mind racing but weirdly calm. My mom's words that morning were still loud in my head—*"If you get the chance to avoid this, take it. Don't go looking for trouble."* And yet, trouble—or whatever this was—was exactly what I'd just walked into.

After I spoke to the sergeant major and confirmed my decision to volunteer, he told me to wait. He scribbled something on a form, then called over another officer who looked at me like I'd lost my mind. "You know this isn't like a field trip," the second officer said, half-joking, half-serious.

"I know," I said. But in truth, I didn't *really* know what I was stepping into. All I had was a strong pull, like a compass pointing toward something unknown but important.

While I stood there waiting for further instructions, a few guys—clearly from another school—nudged each other and glanced in my direction. One of them eventually approached and asked, "Did you just volunteer?" I nodded. He looked confused, maybe even impressed. A few minutes later, he did the same. Then another. I hadn't meant to start a chain reaction, but apparently I had. Still, I wasn't doing this for anyone else.

By the time I left the theater, I walked out with a nervous, insecure kind of pride in my heart. I had walked in with a future wide open—college, travel, maybe even a return to the U.S.—and walked out with a commitment to serve.

On the way home, I rehearsed what I'd tell my mom a hundred different ways. But none of the versions felt right. I could already picture the look on her face. So I lied.

When I told her I got the red ball, her reaction was immediate. She went still, her hand rising to her mouth as if she were trying to hold something in. Her shoulders sagged, and her eyes filled so fast it was like the tears had been waiting there all day.

She didn't say much at first. She just pulled me into a tight hug, then sat down and stared at the floor for a long moment. When she finally spoke, her words came out soaked in frustration and fear. "We've worked so hard to give you a different life, and with all the violence in this country, you still end up in this terrible thing? This is so dangerous," she said.

I let her believe the story. I let her be angry at the system, at the military, at fate itself. I stood there quietly, accepting her sadness as part of the cost of my choice.

The next few days passed in a strange haze. While other students were celebrating their freedom or dealing with their forced enlistment, I moved in silence. I didn't tell my brothers the truth either. I let them assume I was one of the unlucky ones. They cursed the system on my behalf, and I kept my mouth shut. On the outside, I looked like someone who'd been dragged into this; on the inside, I knew I had raised my own hand.

Part of me started to wonder if I'd made a mistake. I had imagined something noble, something adventurous. But now the reality of military life was starting to take shape in my mind—early mornings, endless drills, strict discipline. This wasn't going to be a movie. At the same time, another thought slipped in beside the fear: maybe this was my chance to see if the army—and the idea of becoming an officer—really had anything to do with the person I wanted to be. A year of service felt like a way to look inside that world without committing to full military school, a test not just of the institution, but of myself.

The idea of serving in the MFO was still the biggest stake in all of this. But even if I never reached that mission, I began to see everything else as a kind of consolatory purpose: a chance to measure who I was against the life I thought I wanted. Without that meaning, all I would have been left with was a lie, a disappointed mother, and a future I couldn't yet picture.

Months passed, and then the day came—the day I had to report for duty. My parents came with me to the local sports coliseum where the new recruits were being processed. The place buzzed with tension and quiet goodbyes. Families filled one side of the bleachers, clutching small bags, water bottles, and each other. On the opposite side, we—soon-to-be soldiers—stood in loose groups, waiting for instructions.

It didn't feel real. The whistle of the wind through the open arena, the squeak of shoes on the concrete, the occasional sob from a mother in the stands—it all blurred together. Then the sergeant major appeared, his voice firm and commanding, breaking through the buzz of the coliseum.

"Volunteers, move to the left!"

I froze. Just for a second. My eyes flicked to the stands. I scanned for my mother's face, praying she hadn't heard those words. But she didn't react. Maybe she didn't catch it, or maybe she didn't want to believe it. Either way, I turned and walked left, joining the small group of volunteers.

Then came the final moment—the chance to back out.

"If any volunteers want to change their mind," the sergeant said, "do it now."

A few stood up quietly and stepped away.

I didn't move.

When it was time to say goodbye, I moved down the line of faces that had come to see me off: my father with his hands in his pockets, Estelita holding back tears, Eduardo trying to look composed, my new girlfriend forcing a smile that kept collapsing at the edges. I hugged each of them, but when I reached my mother, everything else faded. Her arms wrapped around me with a desperation I could feel in my bones, her tears soaking my shoulder. "Take care of yourself," she whispered. "Be strong."

She still thought this had happened to me, not because of me.

As I climbed onto the bus and looked back one last time, I saw all of them standing there, but my eyes went straight to my mother. The weight of both truth and love pressed down on me. I had chosen this, and there was no turning back now.

**

The first night at the military base felt wrong in a way I hadn't expected. Everything I had imagined about this experience—traveling abroad, being part of something bigger—didn't disappear, but it suddenly felt far away. In front of me there was no adventure, just noise, confusion, and a cold, unfamiliar routine beginning to form. The place was nothing like I had pictured. It wasn't a mission yet; it was disorder trying to organize itself, and I was standing in the middle of it.

After we unloaded our bags, they moved us into the main square of the base. It was a plain, gray concrete plaza surrounded by dull brick buildings. Beyond the perimeter, rows of coffee trees climbed the hills, blending into the familiar green landscape of Armenia, Quindío. I'd grown up seeing that mix of brick and countryside before—schools, factories, neighborhoods—but here it felt different. Inside the fence, everything was rigid and colorless; outside, life went on as usual. There was nothing glamorous about this place. No rush of excitement. Just an empty, functional space where it was suddenly clear that whatever was coming next would be on their terms, not mine.

The lieutenant who had insisted on pulling me off the Cali battalion list and placing me under his command stood before us now, completely transformed. Gone was the kind, friendly man who had met my family before we boarded the bus. In his place stood someone whose very presence commanded attention. His posture was rigid, his face hard, and the authority in his voice was unmistakable.

"You're mine now," he shouted, his voice booming and echoing off the cold, concrete walls of the base. "No more mommy. No more daddy. No more girlfriends. From now on, you do as I say. And you do it fast."

I had heard yelling before—mostly from my mom when I was late for school or from a teacher reprimanding me for something I hadn't done—but this was different. This wasn't just yelling. It was controlled chaos, the kind that stripped away your identity and replaced it with something else entirely. In those few words, he made it clear that we were no longer individuals, just soldiers bound by the rules of a new life.

I tried to take it all in, sitting there in the cool night air, feeling the weight of what I had done. I had volunteered for this. I had willingly chosen this path, and now it felt like I was watching myself from the outside, as if someone else had made that decision. What had seemed like a noble cause just weeks ago now felt like a decision I would never be able to take back.

And then, of course, I made a mistake.

While the lieutenant was talking, I couldn't help myself. The night sky was so clear, the stars so bright, it was hard not to be distracted. It took me straight back to the farm, to those nights with no electricity when I'd sit outside for hours staring at the sky, spotting satellites and shooting stars against the pure black. I caught a glimmer of movement now—maybe it was a satellite, maybe just my imagination—but it was there, and it was beautiful.

It pulled my attention away from the lieutenant's harsh words, and I whispered to the guy next to me, "Look, a satellite."

Big mistake.

The lieutenant's eyes locked onto me immediately. "What's so important, Private Botero, that you can't listen to me?" he snapped, his voice like a whip. My stomach dropped. The other recruits fell into an eerie silence, every pair of eyes turning to me. "Stand up!" the lieutenant barked.

I scrambled to my feet, my heart pounding. I could feel every pair of eyes on me, and it was enough to make me feel like I was suffocating.

The lieutenant circled me like a predator, his eyes scanning me up and down. I could feel my face flushing with embarrassment, the heat of humiliation creeping up my neck. Then, as if I hadn't been embarrassed enough already, he leaned in closer—too close.

He stopped in front of me and his sharp eyes zeroed in on something I had completely forgotten about until that moment: the holes in my ears. Two tiny punctures from when I had worn earrings as an exchange student in Wisconsin. I hadn't worn them in months, but the small holes were still there—barely noticeable, but visible enough.

"Well, well," the lieutenant sneered, stepping back to let the rest of the recruits see. "Look at this one. We've got ourselves a pretty boy! Wrong battalion, huh? You sure you didn't sign up for the dance squad?"

The recruits erupted into nervous laughter, some chuckling under their breath, others full-on laughing at my expense. I stood there, frozen, wishing I could disappear. The humiliation was unbearable.

But it didn't stop there. The lieutenant unhooked the long keychain he wore on his belt, a jingling mass of keys, and handed it to me. "Here," he said, swinging his hips in an exaggerated, mocking gesture, making the chain whirl in a circle. "This is what you're going to do. Swing this chain around like this while I finish my speech. And make sure you put your hips into it."

My mind was screaming, *Please, no*. But I had no choice. I had to do what he said. So there I was, standing in front of a group of strangers, swinging a chain around like a fool. My hands trembled as I held the chain, trying to ignore the heat of embarrassment spreading across my face. I swayed my hips, just like he said, for what felt like an eternity. The recruits watched, some staring wide-eyed, others snickering, and I was trapped in that moment, unable to escape.

I wanted to disappear. My face burned with shame as I gripped the chain in my hands. For fifteen painful minutes, I swung it in circles like some kind of joke while the lieutenant continued yelling at the others.

When it was finally over, I sat down, still clutching the chain so tight it left marks on my palm. I kept my eyes on the ground, replaying everything in my head. What did I get myself into? Is this really what I signed up for? My heart told me to push through, but my mind screamed that I'd made a huge mistake.

That night was worse.

The barracks were freezing, the bunks hard and uncomfortable. I had met David on the bus ride to the base, and we'd quickly bonded. Together, we chose a bunk—me on top, him on the bottom.

We were whispering to each other in the dark when the lieutenant shouted, "Silence!"

I didn't stop fast enough. The room went quiet, but my voice kept going for two more words.

The lieutenant stormed in, his boots slamming against the floor. Before I could move, he climbed onto my bunk, grabbed my face, and shoved the barrel of his gun into my mouth.

"You think I'm playing with you, Private?" His voice was low, but his anger burned like fire. "Open your mouth again without my permission, and I'll blow your teeth out."

The metal tasted bitter and cold. My heart pounded so hard I thought I'd pass out. For the first time, I realized—*this is real*. This wasn't some adventure. The military wasn't a game. These men would break me if they had to.

When he finally pulled the gun away, I gasped for air. He jumped down, yelled at the rest of the room to "get it together," and walked away.

No one spoke. The silence was so thick you could hear every creak of the bunks, every rustle of fabric. None of us were able to sleep that night.

I lay there, staring at the ceiling, wondering if I'd survive this place.

***

The next morning arrived with the same intensity—blaring trumpets, shouting drill sergeants, and the usual haze of confusion and dread. The cold, sterile air hit me like a slap to the face as I stumbled out of bed, grabbing my towel and soap with clumsy hands. I was already shivering, not just from the chill, but from the knowledge that I was about to face another round of humiliation and dehumanization.

As we shuffled toward the showers in silence, I could hear the grumbling of my fellow recruits. Some whispered to each other in quiet voices, trying to comfort one another, while others kept their heads down, avoiding eye contact. We were all in this together, but it felt like we were each battling our own private war.

When we reached the shower room, the chaos erupted. Superiors barked orders, pushing us in and telling us to hurry up, driving us through the doorway in one tight, messy line. There were no formalities, no second thoughts. The showerheads stood like silent sentinels, waiting to deliver the same cold, unyielding pressure.

I took a deep breath and undressed quickly, trying not to think too much about how many of us were crammed into that narrow room. The other recruits moved with the clumsy urgency of people who knew they were being timed—soap on, water on, water off, done. The water came in short, freezing bursts while the sergeants shouted for us to hurry. There was no talking, no joking, just the slap of bare feet on the wet floor. For most of them, it looked like something they could push through on instinct. For me, it felt like being thrown under a harsh light with nowhere to hide.

The cold water hit me almost immediately, and I winced, trying not to let my body react too much to the shock. I kept my head down, determined to get through it without attracting attention. I focused on washing as quickly as possible, barely feeling the water as it ran over me, the weak pressure doing little to clear the mix of fatigue and tension already settled inside me.

But then, as I reached for the bar of soap, I felt a sharp bump against my side. A recruit who had been inching his way closer to the water had inadvertently brushed up against me. It was a simple mistake, an accident, but it felt like an invasion. My body went rigid, and I swallowed hard, trying to shake off the surge of discomfort. The sheer closeness to so many strangers was one of the most jarring parts of it all—a quick, brutal lesson that personal space didn't really exist here.

I took another quick glance around the room, hoping to avoid further contact. It didn't help. I saw some recruits laughing as they tried to maneuver into the water streams. They seemed comfortable in their discomfort, as if the chaos and vulnerability of the situation didn't affect them. But I wasn't like that. I wasn't comfortable being exposed like this.

As the minutes dragged on, I could feel the pressure building. The sergeant's voice boomed through the room, his command to hurry up echoing off the walls. My heart raced, not just from the anxiety of being in this cold, crowded space, but from the knowledge that the smallest misstep could lead to punishment. Every second counted.

I finished as quickly as I could, rushing to rinse off the soap before the next order to move came. I grabbed my towel and stepped out of the water, drying myself in quick, rough strokes. As I pulled my clothes back on, I glanced around at the others—some already dressed, some still under the weak streams, all of us moving fast, like the clock in that room was always a few seconds ahead of us.

When I finally made it out of the shower room and back to the barracks, I felt drained. Not just from the cold water and the rush, but from the sense that the morning had already started shaving off small pieces of who I was. We weren't "Federico" or "Carlos" or "Andrés" anymore; we were last names shouted across patios, numbers on lists, voices answering "¡Presente!" on command. It wasn't only the lack of privacy or the constant discomfort. It was the first clear sign that the life I'd brought with me was being pushed to the back, and the version of me they wanted was moving to the front.

Breakfast didn't offer much respite. We had a dry roll, a slice of cheese, and coffee that tasted like burnt tar. I had barely taken a bite when the announcement came over the loudspeakers—this time, it was about the haircuts.

We were all supposed to report to the barber shop. At first, I thought it was no big deal. A haircut was just a haircut, right? I had short hair already, and I assumed they'd just trim it down to a regulation length. But when we arrived, I realized I had severely underestimated what was about to happen.

The barber shop was nothing like I imagined. It was a cramped room, with only a handful of chairs. The air smelled like a mix of old clippers and aftershave. The sound of buzzing clippers filled the space, and I felt an involuntary knot form in my stomach. The other recruits lined up, waiting their turn, some chatting, some silent, lost in their own thoughts.

When it was my turn, I sat down in the chair, trying to steady my breath. The barber, a man with a rough, no-nonsense demeanor, didn't say a word. He switched on the clippers, and their vibration climbed straight into my skull as he ran them over my scalp. I couldn't help but flinch as the first strands of hair slid down the cape and onto the floor. The steady buzz filled my ears, and the touch of the metal against my skin felt like an intrusion.

I kept my eyes fixed on the ground, trying not to think about what was happening. It was just a haircut, I told myself. Just a haircut. But it wasn't just that. It was the loss of control, the stripping away of something that had once been mine. I had always kept my hair a certain length, had taken pride in it, and now it was disappearing in front of my eyes. The barber didn't care. He was just doing his job, moving on to the next recruit as soon as he finished with me.

By the time he was done, my scalp felt raw, exposed. I didn't recognize the guy in the mirror. It was just a haircut, but it drew a clear line: there was the boy who had walked into that room, and the recruit who was walking out.

Standing up from that chair, I understood that this was the first real cost of the choice I'd made in that theater. I was being pushed away from the life where I decided how to look, how to move, what to do with my days—from the small freedoms, pride, and dignity I'd taken for granted. They needed someone they could shape and control, and I had been the one who volunteered to step into their hands.

Chapter 14

They Won't Break Me

The sun hung low over the soccer field, casting long shadows that stretched like fingers across the dry grass. The heat was still thick, pressing against our uniforms. Dust swirled up with every step. We'd just wrapped up another long, punishing training session. Most of us were half-dead from exhaustion, sweat clinging to our backs like glue. I thought that was the end of it for the day.

Then I heard my name.

"Private Botero, stay behind," the lieutenant said. The conversations around us thinned out as a few guys turned to glance at me, their expressions unreadable, and a knot pulled tight in my stomach. Maybe some felt sorry for me. Maybe not. Either way, no one said anything. They just kept walking back toward the base with the others.

I stayed where I was, alone on the field with him.

The lieutenant paced slowly in front of me, arms crossed behind his back. He wasn't calm by nature—he usually raised his voice with purpose, commanding attention through volume and force. But not this time. This time, he didn't have to. His eyes never left my face, tracking me as he moved around me, steady and unblinking. The weight of his silence was louder than anything he could've shouted.

"You know, Federico," he said, using my first name like we were friends, as if whatever was coming next wasn't exactly official, "I haven't practiced my martial arts in a while."

I didn't respond. I didn't know what to say.

He kept going. "I don't have a punching bag around here... so I thought I'd practice with you."

His eyes held mine. No emotion. Just a flat, almost detached expression. My mouth went dry. I stood frozen, trying to convince myself he was only trying to scare me, that he'd stop before it went too far. Then he took a step back. "Stand right there!" he ordered.

I did. My legs were stiff, a tight pulse hammering in my upper body. I had no idea what he was about to do, or which part of me he'd aim for, but every instinct I had was telling me to run. Too late. He launched forward without warning. One second he was standing still, and the next he was airborne— his body twisting, a blur of movement. The kick came fast, hard, and straight into my chest. Pain exploded through me. My feet left the ground. I slammed into the dirt, choking on the sudden loss of air. I gasped, hands clawing at the grass, my lungs refusing to work.

"Get up!" he barked.

I tried. Every breath stabbed at my chest, but I forced myself up.

"Stand right there. Do nothing."

He moved again—faster this time. Another flying kick, right into the same spot. The pain doubled. I went down again, coughing, my head spinning.

"What? You can't take a little kick?" he said, circling me like I was something less than human.

I felt the sting of humiliation more than the pain. I wasn't even allowed to defend myself. Not even a flinch. Just stand there and take it.

I got back up. My body protested. Every part of me wanted to quit. But I couldn't. I didn't know what would happen if I stayed down too long—and I didn't want to find out.

He gave me one last look. Then he spun, and his leg snapped out like a whip. This time, the kick hit my upper arm, right near my shoulder. The impact felt like a steel bat. I didn't fall, but my knees buckled. I caught myself, barely.

"Better," he muttered.

He didn't praise. He didn't smile. He just gave a small nod like he was talking to himself.

Then, without looking at me again, he waved his hand. "That's enough for today. Go join the others." He walked off, and it was over.

I turned around and started walking. My arm throbbed with each step, and my chest felt like it was caving in. I didn't look back. I didn't want him to see the way my face twisted from the pain or how badly I wanted to collapse.

The walk back felt longer than usual, each step landing like a quiet reprimand for even being there. I had volunteered my time and my life to serve a country that was paying me back with kicks and blows I had done nothing to deserve. In the distance, small clusters of soldiers stood around on break, their shapes shifting as a few heads turned in my direction and bodies angled slightly, pockets of space opening in their circles as they noticed me coming.

When I finally reached the base and rejoined the others, no one said a word. They could see it—the exhaustion carved into my face, the way I cradled my arm close to my ribs, trying to dull the pain. I thought about telling the other soldiers what had happened, but I held back. In a place like that, nothing stayed quiet for long, and if the lieutenant ever heard his name wrapped inside a rumor, he would only make sure the next round hurt more.

Nights in the barracks were the only time we got a break from the constant yelling, the endless drills, the humiliations. But sleep didn't come to me that night. My ribs ached with every breath, each inhale pulling at the spots where his kicks had landed. My body was sore all over, and the pain mixed with a tightness inside me—a steady unease that something was not right—keeping me wide awake in the dark.

I wasn't wrong.

A shape moved through the dim barracks, slow and deliberate. One of the dragoneantes. They were first-class privates, promoted not because they inspired anyone, but because they enforced orders without asking questions. Men with a small slice of authority and a green light to act like little tyrants, always looking for someone to land that power on.

This one stopped at my bunk. His shadow stretched across me like a curtain being drawn.

"I saw you had a little attitude this afternoon, soldier," he said. His voice wasn't loud, but it had that calm, dangerous tone that never meant anything good.

I blinked up at him, trying to stay calm. "What are you talking about, First Private? I didn't—"

He didn't let me finish.

"Oh, so now you're talking back?" His mouth pulled into a thin, satisfied line. "Meet me in the bathroom."

It was happening again. The whole room went quiet. A couple of guys turned their heads slightly, eyes flicking between us. But no one said a word. They wouldn't. They knew what the consequences were. This was my moment to endure. Or break.

I climbed down from my bunk slowly. My legs felt disconnected from me—heavy and stiff, each step an effort. Every movement sent a pull through my ribs. I followed him to the bathroom, trying to keep my breathing steady and my face blank.

Inside, the light buzzed faintly overhead. The bathroom was cold and smelled of damp tiles and bleach. On the right side, a half-wall separated the showers. On the left, a long urinal, and past that, toilets lined up in a row— each with thin partitions, no doors. There was no privacy here.

The dragoneante stepped onto the urinal, used it like a ladder, and perched himself up on the half-wall between the urinal and showers, watching me from above. His face was lit in the harsh light, and he wore that same smirk I was starting to hate more than the pain.

"Take off your clothes," he said, cool and commanding.

I hesitated. Just for a second. Then I obeyed.

Piece by piece, I stripped. Shirt. Shorts. Underwear. The cold air hit my skin all at once. I stood there, shivering, trying to hold onto some piece of dignity, though I knew I had none left in that moment. He didn't blink.

"Get under the water," he ordered, pointing toward the shower.

I walked over and turned the faucet on. The cold water crashed over me, stealing my breath. I gasped but said nothing. He threw a bar of soap on the floor. I didn't wait for the command—I picked it up and lathered my body as he watched.

"Turn off the water," he said.

I turned it off. My skin still slick with soap, the air biting.

"Sit on the floor."

I sat down slowly. The tile was freezing, and the soap made it even more slippery. He waited just long enough for the tension to stretch tight between us.

"Now give me fifty crunches."

I hesitated for a second, then dropped to the floor and started doing crunches.

Each crunch felt worse than the last. My back slipped every few movements, sliding on the soapy floor. I kept trying to brace myself, but there was no grip. My muscles burned. My ribs pulsed. He laughed from above, taking his time, watching me slide and flail on the tiles.

"Keep going!" he yelled when I paused.

I kept going. I had to. I locked my eyes on the ceiling, letting my mind drift to somewhere else. Anywhere else. Somewhere far away where I wasn't naked, bruised, and crawling across soap and tile.

When I finished, I looked up, breathless, praying it was over.

"Back in the shower," he said. "Soap up again. Now fifty push-ups."

I could barely stand. But I went back to the shower, turned it on, lathered up again. My arms trembled as I lowered myself to the ground.

Push-ups. On soap. On slick, cold tile.

Every push sent a sharp strain through my arms. My palms kept slipping. I fell once, hard, my chest smacking the tile. I could sense his enjoyment, like I was putting on a show. I gritted my teeth, forced myself back up, and kept going.

I kept pushing until my arms simply refused to lift me anymore. He let the silence hang for a moment, then finally spoke. "Go take a shower. Then get to bed." That was it. No reaction, no comment, just another order to follow.

I rinsed off as fast as I could. I pulled on my boxers and T-shirt, still damp, and walked back to my bunk. In the dim light, I could see a few of the other privates still awake, their eyes following me along before they turned back to their pillows. They had been waiting to see what version of me would walk back out of that bathroom.

That night, I didn't sleep. I couldn't. I just lay there, staring into the dark, the ceiling above me barely visible. Somewhere in the barracks, someone sobbed quietly, the sound buried in a pillow. Listening to him, it struck me that whatever they had done to me had also dragged his own torment back to the surface, another reminder of the small hell we were both captive in.

I didn't cry. Not because I didn't want to. I just couldn't. Something inside me had locked up tight.

My mind wandered back to the bathroom. That place. I remembered what I'd heard—the rumors passed in hushed tones. A private had ended his life in there. Right in that same space. He used his rifle. No one talked about it openly, but everyone knew. It was the bathroom where men were stripped down, not just physically, but mentally. Broken.

And he hadn't made it.

I thought about him a lot that night. I wondered how many nights he lay in the same bunk, with the same aching ribs, staring at the same ceiling. I wondered what pushed him to that edge. I wondered how close I might one day get.

And then, I made a promise to myself.

They might keep beating me. They might keep dragging me into showers, into fake punishments, into real pain.

But they wouldn't break me.

At least, that's what I told myself.

***

The morning after the dragoneante humiliated me in the bathroom, I felt like a target painted across my body. His eyes followed me through every drill, every line-up, every movement. He didn't bother to hide it. The way he stared—it wasn't casual. It was calculating, like he was waiting for the smallest flicker of rebellion so he could crush it. After one of our mid-morning drills, he came strutting up, the smirk already on his face. His voice was just loud enough to make sure others nearby could hear.

"You got a problem with me, soldado?"

I stood in front of him, hands locked behind my back, eyes fixed on his. I drew a slow breath before answering.

"I just don't understand why you're so obsessed with me," I said, my tone flat and steady. I didn't raise my voice or look away.

His grin deepened, eyes flashing with something close to pleasure. "Oh, you didn't like it? Good. Then we'll do it again. Every night. All week."

And he meant it.

Every night, after lights out, I heard the sound of boots on the tile floor. They always stopped at my bunk.

"To the bathroom. Now."

He kept his promise. Night after night, the same cold tiles, the same commands, the same routine that stripped a little more out of me each time.

Days weren't much better. The meals were barely edible. The food tray looked more like slop from a pig trough than anything meant for human consumption. Sometimes it was gray meat in a puddle of grease. Other times, watery rice or mashed vegetables that smelled like they'd expired months ago. But Fridays were special. That's when they served red beans and rice.

At first, it felt like a treat. The smell was better than usual. It looked edible. Then you'd see them—the tiny black bugs floating in the beans, legs curled in the boil. The first time I noticed, I nearly threw up. I pushed the plate away, appetite gone. But hunger is a strange thing. It wears you down.

By the second week, I was picking through the beans, trying to separate out the bugs. By the third, I gave up. I ate it all. Every last bite. I told myself they were just extra protein, that I'd survive. Soon I was finishing the leftovers of others who couldn't stomach it. The shame faded quickly; my mind adjusted fast to whatever my body needed to keep going.

We each had our own plate—metal, dented, and chipped. The paint on mine was peeling, and the side had a crack that leaked if I wasn't careful. We kept them in little drawstring bags tied to our bunks, like prized possessions. Before each meal, we'd line up to grab them, dragging ourselves down the stairs and across the yard to the mess hall.

After we ate, the ritual continued. All of us would shuffle to the back of the building where a long concrete sink stretched under a rusting awning.

The line moved slowly. We'd scrape food bits off our plates with our fingers or whatever we had handy. The faucets barely worked, and the water trickled out in thin, reluctant streams. There was no soap. It wasn't provided, and the people in charge didn't care enough to change that. A few guys managed to buy or steal a bar, but those were rare. When soap did appear, it was hoarded like gold, passed quietly from hand to hand and sliced into thin pieces to make it last. After scraping my plate clean as best I could, I stared at the faucet, the grease still clinging to the metal. The water alone wasn't enough. Then I saw it—mud, thick and dark, collecting at the base of the sink pillars where water pooled before draining away through the grass.

Without thinking, I reached down and scooped up a handful. It was gritty, heavy. I smeared it across my plate and started scrubbing. The dirt cut through most of the grease and grime, leaving the metal dull but no longer slick. Sometimes it was hard to even find a patch of dirt that felt "clean" enough to use—one that hadn't just been spat on or rinsed over with toothpaste and whatever else ran off those sinks.

I kept using that method every day. Rub the plate with mud. Rinse. Dry it with the edge of my shirt. Tuck it back in the bag. Some of the others started doing the same. No one said anything—we just adapted. That's what we had to do.

The whole process was a reminder of how far we'd fallen. I used to live in a world where soap was just there, where a clean plate was the minimum, where eating didn't mean swallowing bugs or scrubbing with filth. It felt as if my real life had been put in parentheses, and inside that narrow space all that existed was physical hardship, mental endurance, and humiliation.

Here, mud was soap. Insects were food. And silence was safety.

One afternoon, as we headed back to the barracks to grab our plates before lunch, the lieutenant was waiting at the top of the stairs. He stood there like a checkpoint, a red bandanna tied tight around his forehead, the knot sticking out in the back. He wasn't shouting or giving orders yet; he just watched us come closer, and the way he held himself made it clear something was about to happen.

But it wasn't the bandanna that had everyone's attention. It was what he held in his hands.

A wooden bat.

It looked handmade, carved crudely from a bunk bed board. The edges were rough, the shape uneven, but it had weight. He spun it slowly in his hands, a small name etched into the side. Probably a girlfriend's, though none of us believed it meant anything. It was all for show—just another piece of his act. But the menace in the way he twirled it said everything we needed to know.

"Line up," he shouted, his voice snapping over the noise.

We fell into a column at the bottom of the stairs and started moving up, boots scraping on the concrete, hands brushing the rail as we climbed. At the top, he stopped each of us with a hand on the shoulder and gave the same order: pull your pants down, bend over, brace yourself. Then came the crack. The sound hit hard and quick, a small noise with too much force behind it. In front of me, one guy cursed under his breath. Another let out a short cry and bit it back. A few tried to force a laugh, but it died as soon as the bat landed.

"Next!" he barked after every swing.

When it was my turn, I clenched my jaw and stepped forward. I didn't look at him. I didn't say a word. I just pulled my pants down, leaned forward, and braced for it.

Crack.

The pain flared instantly, like fire spreading across my skin. I wanted to flinch, to wince—but I didn't. I stood up straight, pulled my pants back on, and walked away without a word. Just another humiliation in a place full of them.

By lunchtime, the barracks were buzzing. Everyone had an opinion about the lieutenant's stunt. Some thought it was hilarious—military hazing at its finest. Others were pissed off, quietly stewing. Most of us, though, didn't say much. We just ate in silence, the sting from the bat still fresh, the shame lingering deeper.

The food didn't help. That day it was the usual: flavorless rice, overcooked plantains, and a bit of gray meat that may or may not have come from a cow. I shoveled it down anyway. It felt like when they tap your arm before a shot—the sting from the bat had already dulled whatever protest I might have had about what was on the plate.

That afternoon, during formation, the captain stepped forward with an announcement. His voice was stern, but the message was clear.

"We need dogs. Guard dogs for the base. Anyone who can bring back a dog will get the weekend off to retrieve it. That's two full days."

When he said we could get two days off base, it snapped me awake. Two full days away from that madness, two days where I could finally breathe. My hand shot up before I even thought about it, and he chose a small group of us on the spot. I had no intention of losing that golden opportunity.

When the weekend came, I left the base with a feeling I hadn't felt in weeks—relief. The air outside the gates felt lighter. My shoulders didn't feel so heavy. I didn't look back.

At home, my mother and girlfriend greeted me with tears and tight hugs. I stood in our small, familiar space, thankful just to be breathing the same air as them again. Yet everything around me—the furniture, the walls, even their voices—seemed slightly off, as if the house had stayed the same while I no longer fit inside it the way I used to. After a short visit, we were already back out the door, my brief time at home turning into a search mission for a dog I could take back to the base.

We drove to a poor neighborhood on the edge of town, the kind of place where stray dogs roamed freely and people didn't ask too many questions. I kept my eyes open, scanning yards, corners, alleys. That's when we saw her—a little old woman walking a miniature pinscher down the street.

We pulled over.

"How much for the dog?" I asked.

She looked me up and down, eyes narrowed. "Why?"

"He's going to the army," I said. "He'll be taken care of."

She hesitated, holding the leash a little tighter. I saw the concern in her eyes, but after a moment, she named her price. It wasn't much. I paid her in full without arguing.

The dog was tiny—barely bigger than a shoe box. His ears stood up like radar dishes, his body lean and twitchy. He looked up at me, unsure but curious. When the weekend was over, I carried him back to the base like a prize.

At the gate, the guards burst into laughter.

"That's the dog you brought? Captain's gonna love that!"

They weren't wrong.

The next morning, at formation, we all stood in line with our "guard dogs." The others had brought big ones—German shepherds, Dobermans, pit bulls. Real muscle. Then there was me, standing there with my nervous little pinscher, who kept sniffing the ground and twitching at every sound.

The captain walked down the line. When he got to me, he stopped.

"What do you think this dog is going to do, Private Botero?" he barked.

I didn't flinch. "Sir, this dog is here to boost morale. For the troops."

There was a pause. Then snickers. Then laughter.

The captain stared at me for a long moment. I thought he was going to lose it. But then he gave a short nod.

"Fine. He can stay."

Just like that, my little dog became part of the platoon.

The pinscher never guarded anything. He ran through formations, chased after boots, barked at shadows, and slept wherever he found a bit of sun. But he made us smile, and in a place like that, even a few seconds of laughter were worth more than another shouted threat. Keeping him there felt like a small act of resistance, a reminder that they could control our schedules, our bodies, our food, but not everything inside us. They still hadn't broken me.

Chapter 15

Desert Peacekeeping

It was a Sunday, supposed to be a break—a day to breathe, to feel like a real person again. In a place that worked every day to break us down, that one day off was the only thing that reminded us we had lives before the army. My mom never missed those visits. She always came with a smile and food that smelled like home. My girlfriend sometimes came along too. Those moments with them reminded me of who I was outside of my uniform.

I waited near the barracks, pacing slowly. I kept one eye on the clock and the other on the road. Any minute, I thought. I could almost picture them walking toward me, my mom holding a little bag with food, my girlfriend waving from beside her.

But then, out of nowhere, the new captain called us all together. He had only been with us a few weeks, but we all knew the type. He was strict, cold, and always looking for a chance to prove something. His eyes lit up when he said it—mandatory training at the shooting range. No warning. No way out.

My heart dropped. The range was deep in the restricted zone. No families allowed. That meant I wouldn't see my mom and girlfriend that day.

I stepped forward and tried to explain. I told him my family was waiting. He didn't even look at me. Just waved his hand and said, "They'll have to wait." Like they didn't matter. Like I didn't matter.

I was angry. Furious, even. But I couldn't do anything. If I pushed back, it would only make things worse. So, I stayed quiet and volunteered to go first. I just wanted it to be over.

The captain's drill was something he called "action and reaction." His voice sounded too excited as he described it. We'd start at the 500-yard line, lying flat. Fire. Then sprint forward to the 300-yard line. Fire again. Crawl under a table. Hide. Fire again. All while he shot real bullets around us. Not blanks—real, live rounds. He said it was to "keep us sharp." But to me, it felt reckless—way too risky, especially since none of us really knew how good his aim actually was.

I crouched at the starting line, holding my rifle. My hands were already sweating. The captain stood nearby, putting on his ear protectors, lifting his weapon, and giving me a short nod.

Go time.

I dropped flat at the 500-yard mark. Aimed. Pulled the trigger.

Then his shots started.

Real bullets flew over and around me. The ground exploded beside me as the rounds hit. Dirt flew in my face. My ears were ringing. I didn't even feel like I was in training anymore—it felt real. Like war.

I started crawling forward, pushing toward the 300-yard line. My elbows dragged across the grass. I knelt and took another shot, then heard more bullets—closer now. My body tensed. Every nerve felt on fire. I was breathing so hard I could barely keep the rifle steady.

I moved again. Crawling. Dragging my body to the 200-yard line. My arms shook. I could barely hold myself up. The captain had moved closer. He was circling me like a predator. Still firing.

Then my rifle jammed.

My fingers scrambled to clear it as I lay flat on the ground. Bullets were hitting so close now that dirt pelted my back; some impacts felt just inches away. All I could think was that if I moved in the wrong direction for even a second—one unplanned twitch—one of those rounds could end up in my head.

I finally fixed the jam. Fired once. Then I ran.

The table was just ahead. I dove under it, panting and shaking. I thought it was over.

But then the captain climbed on top of the table above me and started firing again. The noise was so loud it felt like my chest was going to crack. The

113

gunfire echoed in my skull. Every time I tried to stick my head out from under the table, he fired a burst into the ground right in front of me, so close that dirt exploded into my face and eyes, forcing me back under and keeping me pinned there.

I was stuck there, helpless. My heart was pounding so hard I thought it might stop. I wasn't exactly terrified, but my body was locked tight, my ears ringing, my cheek bruised from the rifle stock and my shoulder already aching. Finally, after what felt longer than a few minutes, he stopped shooting. I crawled out from under the table, moved up to the last firing position, squeezed off my final shots, and finished the drill.

"You're good," he said like it had all been normal. "You're dismissed."

"Yes, sir. Thank you, sir," I said, more relieved it was over than anything else. I slung my rifle, turned, and started walking uphill toward where the families waited, hoping my mom and girlfriend were still there.

My uniform was covered in dirt. My face was smudged—not exactly how I wanted my girlfriend to see me.

And then I saw them.

My mom and girlfriend were standing with the other families. But my mom didn't smile. She didn't wave. She didn't run to hug me like she always did.

She stood still. Her eyes looked different—darker, sadder. She didn't move until I got close.

Then she spoke.

"You lied to me," she said, her voice tight, full of pain. "You didn't get the red ball. You volunteered."

I froze.

I didn't know how she found out. Maybe another soldier told her. Maybe she overheard something. Maybe someone slipped up. But it didn't really matter. I had always been taught that God finds a way to set things straight—and that's exactly what had just happened: the truth prevailed.

"You don't care about me," she said, her voice breaking. "You don't care how much I worry. You don't care about anyone but yourself."

I opened my mouth to explain, to say something—*anything*—but she didn't want to hear it.

114

She handed me the little food bag, the same kind she always brought. She used to do it with so much love, like it was her way of still taking care of me. But this time, she just gave it to me and turned away.

My girlfriend gave me a quick look—sad, understanding—but she followed my mom. They didn't stay. They didn't say goodbye. I just stood there, holding the bag, feeling empty and embarrassed, wondering if they would ever understand the reasoning behind what I'd done. In my mind, volunteering was also a way to keep moving forward in my own cleanup process after the addiction I'd been trapped in back home. If my mother could see that this was part of staying away from that life, maybe she wouldn't feel so betrayed. But that was a subject I didn't want to talk about with anyone yet.

In the weeks that followed, she didn't come back.

No more visits.

No more Sundays.

The base became colder. Quieter.

That night, in the bottom of the food bag, I found a small bundle of money. Not much—but to me, it felt like I'd just become a rich man among the rest.

We were paid almost nothing. Two dollars a month. Barely enough for the basics—shoe polish, toothpaste, the cream we used to shine our belt buckles. That little bit of money from her was like hope in my hands.

That Monday, the sun sat straight over our heads, heavy and unforgiving. The air shimmered over the asphalt, and the heat turned every step into work. We were on the training field, tired from the drills, sweat staining our uniforms in patterns we'd stopped noticing weeks ago. That's when we heard it—*ding ding ding*, the cheerful chime of an ice cream cart. The sound didn't belong; it drifted through the formation like a children's song inside a prison yard.

The ice cream man came by every so often, pushing his dented metal cart with its sticker-covered sides—bright colors in a place that had none. He always wore the same wide smile, like someone who refused to let this place turn him gray. Most of us never had money. Ice cream might as well have been something totally unaffordable.

But that day, I had cash—thanks to my mom. That little bundle she'd left in the food bag the day before felt like treasure. I dug into my pocket and waved the man down. He came over, his eyes lighting up with surprise. I pointed to a lime popsicle and handed over the money. Cold sugar met my tongue and I swear, for an instance, I felt human again. I stood there, sucking on the popsicle like a kid after school, not a soldier in training.

Then I felt eyes on me.

"Hey!" a soldier called out, walking over. "Can I have some?"

I hesitated. It was one of those moments where saying no would set you apart in all the wrong ways. But before I could respond, another guy chimed in.

"Yeah, me too. Let me have a lick."

They were joking. At first. But one took the stick from my hand and actually licked it. Then, I passed it to another. And another. I watched, stunned, as the popsicle went from hand to hand, mouth to mouth. Each one took their turn like it was some sort of ritual, some shared joke.

It reminded me of being a kid at school. I hated it when other kids asked to drink from my soda bottle. I'd purposely drop crumbs or bits of lunch inside so no one else would want it. I didn't like sharing things that touched my mouth. I had already hit a low point eating other soldiers' leftover red beans—with the bugs and all—but this took it to a new level.

After it had made its rounds—probably twenty mouths in total—someone handed it back to me with a smirk. "Here. Finish it."

What I held now wasn't the treat I'd bought. It was something else. A melted, soggy stick coated in layers of other people's saliva. I wanted to throw it away. Everything in me screamed not to eat it. But I knew better. Throwing it away would make me look like I thought I was better than them. Like I was soft.

So I took a deep breath, closed my eyes, and finished the popsicle.

It was disgusting. But also, weirdly, unifying. That single moment, gross as it was, taught me something the drills and lessons hadn't. We were in this together. We shared heat, pain, boredom—and now a popsicle.

***

Later that day, as the sun dipped behind the trees, we were called into the common area. On the bulletin board there was a new sheet posted. It announced the results of the prequalification to travel to Bogotá and take the English proficiency test for the MFO mission in the Sinai. I stepped closer and scanned the list. When I saw my name, a sense of relief and excitement invaded me. For an instant, the dream of joining the force felt closer to becoming real. Right beside my name was one more: López. He was a good guy, said he spoke English pretty well. We looked at each other, grinned, and shook hands.

The next day, I packed quickly. I was excited—nervous, too, but mostly focused. I hadn't prepared specifically for this test, but my year as an exchange student in Wisconsin had given me a quiet confidence in my English. I knew only one of us would be chosen. The army didn't need two translators from our base, just one. If neither of us passed, we'd both be back to square one.

López and I boarded the military vehicle that would take us to Bogotá. It was a long ride—hours of hills, winding roads, and dusty stops. We made small talk. At one point, I asked him about his experience with English. He told me he had taken classes at a vocational school in town and felt he could manage the basics.

We didn't switch to English on that ride, but from the way he described it, I could tell his level was limited. Mine wasn't perfect, but my year as an exchange student in Wisconsin had given me more than vocabulary; it had taught me rhythm, slang, and confidence. Deep down, I knew I was the stronger candidate.

We finally arrived at the army base in Bogotá where the testing center was located. Soldiers from several battalions around the country had been sent there. We socialized for a while, trading stories about our experience with the language. From those conversations, I could tell I had a competitive edge over most of them.

The test began.

First came the written section. Grammar, vocabulary, reading comprehension. I flew through it. Then came listening. Fast conversations, tricky accents, idioms meant to trip us up. I focused, took notes, and answered every question like it was the key to unlocking my future.

Then came the part I was waiting for: speaking.

They called us into small interview rooms one by one. Inside, a panel of three officers asked questions in rapid English. Some were about military terms. Others about politics, daily routines, or personal stories. I answered everything confidently. I even cracked a small joke when one asked what I missed most about civilian life. "My mom's food," I said, smiling. One of them laughed. It felt good.

Outside, I saw some of the other soldiers walking out, shoulders slumped, eyes low. I could tell many hadn't done well. López came out of his room, shrugged, and gave me a look that said, *I did my best.* We both knew what that meant.

Me? I felt good. Real good.

After the test, there were no immediate results. No triumphant announcements, no comforting certainty—just a quiet instruction: return to base and wait. That was all. The waiting, I was told, could take days, maybe weeks. We weren't given answers, just silence and suspense. So López and I climbed back into the same worn-out military vehicle that had brought us in and headed back to our base, hearts heavy with tension and uncertainty.

By the time we finally reached the base, the sun was long gone, and I was completely drained—physically and emotionally. But despite the exhaustion, a flicker of hope still lived in me. The possibility of being chosen was enough to keep my spirits afloat, even in the uncertainty. Now, all that was left was to wait. Wait for the decision that could change the trajectory of my life.

The days that followed were agonizing. I went back to my regular duties on base, but the test stayed in the back of my mind. A loose formation here, a call to report there; each time, I couldn't help wondering if this was when they'd finally say something. Weeks passed, and nothing came. Not a word.

The tension between López and me grew thicker by the day. He knew his chances were slim. I could see it in the way he avoided eye contact and started talking less as time went on. I felt a flicker of sympathy, but I couldn't let guilt distract me. This was my dream, my future, and I was determined to see it through.

Then, one evening, around 6 PM, it happened.

The lieutenant walked into the barracks. His presence always brought tension, but this time it felt different. His face was unreadable, that same emotionless stare that had become his trademark. When he called out my name—"Private Botero, come here"—my first thought was that he had come up with some new late-evening punishment for me. His voice carried no clues. Just cold authority.

As I followed him down the corridor, I kept watching his face, trying to read him and at the same time wishing he would just spit out whatever was coming. This was the same lieutenant who had been giving me hell for months—extra drills, extra duties, public reprimands—so I naturally expected the worst. We stopped at the end of the hallway, away from the others, and he turned to me with that familiar, condescending smirk that usually meant trouble.

"You lucky bastard," he said.

I stepped closer, unsure if I had heard him correctly.

"What's going on, Lieutenant?" I asked, my voice tight, cautious.

"You've been selected to go to the Sinai. You lucky bastard," he repeated.

I paused, looked up, and breathed the reality in. "Gracias, Dios mío," I thought. I had done it. I was going. Against the odds, despite everything, I had been selected.

A thousand emotions surged all at once. Relief. Pride. Joy. I felt like I could float. A grin broke across my face, uncontainable. "Really? That's great!" I said, trying and failing to keep my excitement in check.

He gave a small nod. "Yes, but don't get too comfortable. You leave tomorrow for Bogotá for pre-deployment training."

"Tomorrow?" I asked. "Can I at least go tell my mother and my girlfriend?"

The lieutenant sighed, clearly irritated by my enthusiasm. "If you're going to do that, you'd better leave now and be back here tomorrow morning. I'll sign your leave slip."

I didn't waste a second. I threw together a small bag with the essentials and was out the door, moving faster than I had during any drill. I wanted to see my mother. I wanted to tell her that everything I had fought through wasn't in vain, that this opportunity was real and already on its way.

The road to the highway was steep—almost a mile and a half of gravel cutting through the coffee plantations—but I barely felt it. The smell of the coffee plants had never seemed richer, and the stars hadn't looked that bright in a long time. I just wanted to reach my mother's door, look her in the eyes, and tell her what was happening. My girlfriend, too—I wanted to see her before I left and say goodbye properly. I was stepping into an adventure I had envisioned for myself for a long time, one my family still wasn't sure I could actually make happen.

Finally, I reached the highway and managed to flag down a bus heading toward Pereira. It was an old, rickety machine, nothing comfortable about it. No bathroom, no reclining seats. But none of that mattered. I found a seat near the back, wedged between two strangers, with the faint scent of sweat and the strong smell of a floor mopped with diesel hanging in the air.

As the bus lurched forward, my mind was still racing, still high on what felt like one of the biggest triumphs of my life and on the path that was suddenly opening ahead of me.

That's when it hit me. A sudden, sharp cramp in my stomach. Deep and insistent. My body tensed. I started to sweat, the excitement and nerves and maybe something I'd eaten all crashing together at once.

I needed a bathroom. Fast.

Panic crept in as I looked around. No rest stops. No buildings. No small tiendas on the side of the road. Just miles and miles of coffee fields and cattle pastures rolling past the windows. Nowhere to go. And the pain was getting worse.

I tried to hold it in, but the pain was too much. It wasn't just discomfort—it was fire twisting through my gut, clenching me from the inside out. I couldn't sit still. I couldn't think straight. I rushed to the front of the bus, gripping the seatbacks for balance as I begged the driver to stop.

"Please! I need you to stop. I need a bathroom!" I blurted out, barely keeping my voice steady.

He looked at me like I was overreacting. "There's no bathroom here, kid," he said, his voice flat with indifference, as if he failed to see how urgent my need really was.

"Then just let me off," I pleaded. My hands were shaking, my forehead slick with sweat. The urgency in my voice was unmistakable. I wasn't going to make it.

He stared at me for a moment, annoyed but maybe sensing the desperation in my eyes. Finally, he relented and pulled over to the shoulder.

"Go on without me!" I shouted, waving him away as I jumped off the bus. There was no dignity left to preserve. I just needed to disappear.

I sprinted across the road and scrambled over a low wire fence into a cattle pasture. The field stretched out under the darkening sky, nothing but uneven ground, cow trails, and patches of grass, silent except for a few distant moos and the sound of my own labored breathing. I found a spot behind a thick bush, dropped to a squat, and tried not to think too much about the full humiliation of what was happening.

There I was, in the middle of nowhere, relieving myself in a cow field with nothing to clean up but a few rough leaves. It was the lowest moment of my life. I had just received one of the best news I'd ever heard, and now here I was—sweating, crouched in a field like some half-wild animal. The irony wasn't lost on me. My triumphant moment had been reduced to a desperate, degrading mess.

When it was over, I cleaned myself up as best I could and walked back to the highway, scanning the surroundings as discreetly as I could, hoping there hadn't been any human spectators. The shame still clung to me like sweat. I stood by the roadside in the fading light, praying that another bus would come soon.

Eventually, one did. I flagged it down, climbed aboard, and kept my head low, hoping no one would ask questions. No one did. I sat in the back, silent and shaken but still driven. My resolve hadn't changed—my pride had taken a hit, but my purpose was intact.

When I finally made it to the city, I caught a taxi to my mother's house. I didn't call ahead—I wanted it to be a surprise. When she opened the door, she froze, then her face lit up.

"Federico! What are you doing here?" she asked, a smile spreading across her face.

I stepped inside, already smiling, my chest full. "Mom," I said, "I've been selected. I'm going to the Sinai. I'm going to be part of the Multinational Force and Observers."

Her expression softened instantly. She pulled me into a tight hug. I could feel her pride and relief, but also the fear sitting underneath. With tears in her eyes and a small smile, she said, "This is what you wanted, right? I suppose it might even be safer over there than here, with all these mafia wars and the guerrilla."

She was happy for me, but I knew her well enough to sense the sadness behind the comment. I was her son, and I was about to leave again—this time farther than ever before.

That night, she helped me pack a few things for the journey ahead. I explained that I would be going back to the base the next morning, and from there they would send me to Bogotá for pre-deployment training and then on to Egypt. It was all moving so fast, and I wasn't even sure if we'd get another chance to see each other after this visit.

As I lay in my old bed that night, staring at the ceiling, it finally hit me in full: this was happening. I was about to leave everything behind—the routine, the pain, the familiarity—and step into something unknown and full of possibility. I wasn't scared. I was ready.

The next day was a blur. I spent a few final hours with my mother, my girlfriend, my father, Estelita, and my brother Eduardo, soaking up their faces and their words of encouragement. Then it was time to go. I made my way back to the base, my emotions a mix of excitement and gratitude. López, the other soldier who had taken the test with me, didn't make the cut. I tried not to gloat, but the difference in our paths was clear. While he stayed behind, I was heading toward something greater.

***

When I arrived in Bogotá, I reported to the designated army base. The facility was enormous, sprawling with rows of old buildings and soldiers moving like ants through a maze of order and duty. But bigger didn't mean better. If anything, the conditions were worse.

The barracks were packed—hundreds of bunks lined up with barely any room between them. Privacy didn't exist. The bathrooms were brutal: 20 toilets in a row, no partitions, no curtains. Just you and the guy next to you, trying to pretend it wasn't the most uncomfortable situation imaginable. It was strange to have casual conversations while sitting there, shoulder to shoulder, trying to ignore the reality of it. I thought I had seen the worst of military life in Armenia, but this... this was next level.

The food didn't help either. Uninspired and barely edible, it made me long for the sad, bug-infested red beans we'd been served back at the battalion. Still, I kept my spirits up. I reminded myself that this was temporary—a checkpoint on the road to something far more important. I'd made it this far, and I wasn't about to be brought down by bad soup and open toilets.

Despite everything, the atmosphere at this base had its upsides. The treatment here was noticeably better. Officers spoke to us like we were human. They seemed to respect that we were part of an elite selection, not just another batch of grunts. And I met interesting people.

Some came from military families, sons and nephews of generals. Others had earned their place through merit in combat. I had my own bit of prestige—my father's cousin, General Botero, was the Minister of Defense at the time, the last military officer to hold the role before it became civilian. But I didn't flaunt that. I barely mentioned it. I didn't know him personally, and even if I had, I didn't want my name to be what got me ahead. I wanted to earn everything myself.

And in that strange, crowded barracks, I found a small tribe of brothers. Ricardo—an old friend from my exchange year in Wisconsin—was there, and reconnecting with him was like finding a lifeline. We fell into friendship easily, like no time had passed. Then there were Alejandro and Julio, two cousins with serious military blood. Both had gone through the infamous Escuela de Lanceros, Colombia's version of the Rangers. Their stories were intense—jungle missions, endurance trials, things that earned them immediate respect. They were calm, serious, and always composed.

Rafael from Montería rounded out the group. Together, we found solidarity in the madness, a makeshift family in a place where comfort was rare.

And as hard as things were, there was a shared sense of purpose among us. Many of the men here had already faced combat. Some had medals, scars, and stories that bordered on legend. They spoke of firefights, narrow escapes, and losing brothers in the line of duty. For them, this mission was more than a reward—it was a kind of closure, or maybe a stepping stone to something better.

And for all of us, it was a financial breakthrough. In the Sinai, we'd be earning $470 a month. That kind of money changed lives. Soldiers came back and bought homes, started businesses. For most, it was a ticket out of poverty.

For me, though, it was something else. It wasn't about the money. It was the chance to see beyond the horizon, to do something that mattered, to live a life that most could only imagine.

Chapter 16

The Mission Begins

The day of our departure finally arrived. Everything had been carefully arranged by the army. We were all dressed in brand-new suits—elegant and almost unrecognizable from the recruits who'd been grinding through the same dirt a few weeks earlier. Our hair was freshly cut, and on our feet we wore new dress shoes the army had issued, polished the night before with wax, a little water, and the rounded bottom of a glass soda bottle. Even our bags were new, the emblem of the Colombian Battalion and the number of our rotation stamped on the side. Suddenly, for the first time in months, my shoulders felt lighter.

We stood tall in formation, side by side, our bags at our feet, nerves and excitement bubbling beneath our serious faces. The major, a small man from Boyacá with a kind voice, stood before us. He gave a short but moving speech. He thanked us for our effort, for surviving the intense training, and for being chosen for such an important mission. He reminded us that we weren't only fighters; we were ambassadors of Colombia, a piece of our homeland in a faraway place. He would be traveling with us as second commander of the battalion. The first commander, a colonel also from Boyacá, was already at his post in the Sinai.

Then the vehicles rolled in: cargo trucks for our duffel bags and buses for us. We loaded the bags, took our seats, and the convoy pulled out toward El Dorado Airport. Soldiers on motorcycles sped ahead, clearing traffic. We didn't stop at red lights. We didn't slow down.

The closer we got to El Dorado, the more a quiet mix of nerves and excitement settled in. I knew my family would be waiting. My aunt, who lived in Bogotá, had told me my mother was planning to come to the airport to say goodbye, together with my girlfriend, Diana. It had been more than a month since I'd last seen them. I missed Diana's energy, those eyes bright with mischief and love. She had this incredible way of lighting up any moment. No matter how serious or stressful things were, she could crack a joke, make someone laugh, or come up with a wild solution to a problem. She was bold and brave.

When we stepped off the bus, my family rushed toward me. I hugged my mother first and kissed the tears on her cheeks. Her face had that look only a mother can have in moments like these - a mix of helplessness and surrender, as if she were offering her son to destiny and to God's protection. She placed her hand on my head and gave me her blessing: "In the name of the Father, the Son, and the Holy Spirit." "Amén," I whispered, and hugged her again.

Diana went straight to sarcasm, joking about how I was leaving her alone again, but her eyes were already turning glassy. There wasn't much time— just that blur of hugs, a few kisses, and hurried words before we were ordered to move toward a secure area of the airport. It struck me how far my mother and Diana had traveled for such a brief goodbye. Their sacrifice was just one more example of how far these two women could go when they were together.

Once we crossed into the restricted part of the terminal, the major called us back into formation. That's when the big introduction came. The commander of the National Army, General Óscar Murillo, stepped forward to address us, offering a few words of encouragement before we headed on this peacekeeping mission. Standing there in front of one of the highest-ranking officers in the country, I felt like I grew a couple of inches.

When the briefing ended, we were ordered back into formation and told to start walking toward the aircraft. The walk was long, and I could feel the last brushes of Bogotá's cold on my cheeks. I stayed near the back of the line, stretching every step, trying to catch one last bit of eye contact with my family. The plane was parked in a distant corner of the airport, far from the main terminals and traffic. Military police and security lined our path, and no one else was allowed near. It didn't feel like an airport anymore. It felt like a controlled corridor between one life and the next.

Just before I reached the stairs, I turned my head and saw her again. There she was, my girlfriend, laughing with a security guard like she'd known him forever. Typical Diana, finding a way to charm even the most serious people.

I was just stepping onto the plane when I heard it.

"¡Fedeeeerico! ¡Fedeeeerico!"

I turned, and there she was—running across the tarmac toward me. It felt like a scene from a romantic soap opera, just without the slow-motion speed. I could not believe it.

She kept coming, straight through the restricted area, as if none of the rules applied to her. She slipped past the guards, past the barriers, like she had every right to be there. You could see the confusion on everyone's face— the soldiers, the flight attendants, even the ground crew getting the plane ready—trying to figure out how she had gotten that far with so much security around. And still, I wasn't surprised. This was the same girl who once walked more than thirty blocks just to bring me an afternoon snack at work before I joined the army, and the same girl who had played a joke on me outside one of my mom's stores, gathering a whole crowd as she stood on the roof and shouted, "If Federico doesn't love me, I'll jump!"

She reached the plane, breathless but smiling, and started up the stairs like she was climbing onto her dad's private jet. Inside, the cabin erupted in laughter and cheers. My fellow soldiers immediately jumped in with jokes, shouting, "Botero, she's following you to Egypt!" and "Marry her before she invades the base!"

I was half-embarrassed, half-awestruck. I couldn't believe what was happening.

She came straight to me and pressed a small folded letter into my hand, the paper soft and warm from her grip. Before anyone could pull her away, I wrapped my arm around her and kissed her in front of the entire plane. The cheers got even louder. For a moment, it was just the two of us standing there on those metal steps, with a whole battalion as our audience.

Then they gently escorted her back down, and I watched her walk away, letter in my hand and a stupid smile on my face, knowing she had crossed a line no one was supposed to cross just to say goodbye.

We finally settled into our seats. The turbines on the wings came alive, the wheels left the runway, and Colombia began to shrink below us.

I opened my hand and looked at the letter she had given me, still warm from her fingers. A simpler truth followed me up through the clouds: this hadn't come cheap. To get here, I had swallowed pride, doubt, and fear—and more than once, I'd had to choke down the kind of bitterness that comes with paying for a dream in installments—one humiliation at a time.

That letter reminded me of what I was leaving behind. The seat beneath me reminded me of what I was chasing.

We were flying toward Egypt, to a whole new mission in a different world. And for the first time that day, it wasn't the goodbye that filled my mind, but the quiet certainty that every hard step so far had been part of the road to this moment.

***

The long flight passed in a haze of plastic meals, cramped naps, and anxious thoughts about what my new assignment was going to be. We had been told that once we arrived and settled in, our formal postings would be announced at the next morning's formation. I had heard that being the translator for the commander or the second commander were the best assignments—also the ones with the most responsibility. I was quietly wishing for one of those two. By the time we landed in Cairo, cleared immigration, and collected our bags, daylight was already slipping away.

That night, Cairo received us with noise and movement. From the bus window I watched taxis fighting for space, buses stopping wherever they could, and people crossing the avenues in the middle of the traffic as if it were just another part of their routine. Horns didn't follow any pattern; they were more like a constant background sound. Shop signs in Arabic hung over narrow sidewalks, small food stands smoked on the corners, and every few blocks a minaret rose above the roofs. In many ways, the chaos wasn't so different from Bogotá or Cali at rush hour, but the language on the walls and the clothes on the people reminded me with every block that I was very far from home.

We were taken to a hotel in the heart of the city. After weeks of base food and early mornings, the luxury of crisp sheets and warm lighting was overwhelming. Dinner that evening was a full display of Egyptian hospitality. The meal was a feast—rice spiced with cumin, roasted meats, fresh breads, and sweet tea with mint. And then came the belly dancers.

They moved with such grace and control that it seemed like the music obeyed them, not the other way around. The soft chime of the finger cymbals, the deep rhythm of the drums—it pulled us in. I caught Julio shaking his head in disbelief, muttering, "*Esto sí que es otro mundo.*" I couldn't agree more.

The next morning, we left behind the bright lights of Cairo and began our journey to the North Camp in Sinai. It would be a five-hour drive, east across Egypt, through places most tourists would never see. At first, the landscape was lush—the Nile Delta stretched wide with fields of green, small farming villages clustered by the road, children waving at our bus as we passed.

But slowly, almost imperceptibly, the green began to fade. Palms thinned out, houses became fewer. And then the land opened wide into golden nothingness. The desert.

Crossing the Suez Canal was a moment I won't forget. It felt like the border between two worlds—between the known and the unknown. The bridge was immense, spanning calm, blue water that had once been fought over by empires. On the other side, Sinai awaited us—vast, dry, and echoing with silence.

When we finally pulled into North Camp, I was struck by how serious everything felt from the very first moment. Fellow Colombian soldiers climbed onto the bus and went row by row checking everyone's passport. The guards looked impressive in their orange berets and bulletproof vests, with 9 mm pistols hanging from their belts. Outside, more Colombian soldiers moved around the bus with rifles, checking the undercarriage with long mirrors.

I had heard North Camp was "nice," but I had never imagined a place this big. Once we cleared the gate, it looked less like a camp and more like a small city in the middle of the desert. There were paved roads, long barracks, offices, recreation areas, and even two big movie theaters. Despite the heat, everything seemed to run with a kind of quiet efficiency.

After we got off the buses, they lined us up in a small Colombian battalion square behind the command offices. The sun hit us straight on; feet planted, backs straight, nobody talking. The commanding officer stepped forward. He was short, compact, with the same clipped Boyacá vowels as the major who had flown with us.

"*Buenas tardes, soldados,*" he said, his voice cutting clean through the heat. His beret sat rigid on his head, his uniform without a wrinkle, and his eyes moved slowly down the formation, taking the measure of each of us standing there in our civilian clothes.

"This is not a combat mission," he began. "After the Yom Kippur War in 1973, when Egypt and Israel fought over this same land, the countries involved agreed someone had to watch the limits of that peace every single day. That's why this force exists."

He paused, letting his eyes move slowly down the formation.

"You're not here alone. Soldiers from twelve countries serve in this mission. Some handle logistics, some aviation, some communications, some military police. Our role as a Colombian battalion is clear: we provide security for North Camp and several checkpoints and observation posts in this sector. We'll be at the gates, in the towers, on patrol, and in the convoys when needed. Your presence here is what reminds both sides that someone is paying attention."

I looked at my friends—Ricardo, with his easy grin even under pressure; Julio, always quiet, always thinking; and Alejandro, the strongest among us, and the one the officers seemed to notice a little more than the rest. Our looks sealed a quiet pact: whatever assignments we got, we'd work hard— and we'd still find ways to have fun.

The colonel began reading the list of assignments. First, he called the names of the soldiers who would join Commando Company—radio operators, drivers, escorts, translators. After that came the rest of the companies, whose soldiers would rotate through guard posts around North Camp: the perimeter, the gates, the small airstrip, the control centers, and the temporary observation points along the border.

When my name finally came up, it was in that first group. I took a step forward. The colonel looked at me and said, "Translator for the second-in-command, Major Morales. Commando Company. You had the second-highest English score in the battalion—don't make me regret this decision," as he handed me a sheet of paper. I nodded and said, "Understood, Colonel," then returned to the line thanking God in silence.

Translator for the second-in-command. It looked straightforward on paper. In real life, it meant that when Major Morales sat across from officers from other countries, I sat there too—inside every sentence. I had to deliver his meaning the way he meant it: firm when it was firm, diplomatic when it needed to be, never sloppy. A single mistranslation could create a problem difficult to fix.

Julio and Alejandro, my closest friends since training, were also assigned to Commando Company in support roles. That gave me a wave of comfort. Knowing they would be nearby, facing similar challenges, mattered in a place that still felt foreign. Ricardo was placed in communications. He probably had the third-best score of all of us.

We were lucky. While some soldiers were posted to more repetitive tasks—manning the camp's gates, rotating through distant observation posts under the sun—we'd been placed where things moved fast and demanded sharp thinking. The commando unit had a reputation for being elite. We knew it meant long hours, unpredictable tasks, and little room for error. But it also meant we'd be in the thick of things—right where we wanted to be.

Our living quarters reflected that privilege. We were assigned to one of the best barracks in North Camp, a one-story building with smooth tiled floors and, in the desert, the rarest gift of all: air conditioning. I still remember the first rush of cold air on my face when we stepped inside. The rooms even had a TV and a VHS player, small comforts that suddenly felt enormous out there.

Each room had two beds, wooden closets, and just enough space to personalize a small corner. The shared bathrooms down the hall were clean, stocked with basic supplies, and far better than we'd expected. Best of all, our building was near the center of the camp—close to the dining hall, the gym, and the recreation area.

Later that day, we lined up again, this time to receive our orange berets—the symbol of the MFO. When it was placed in my hands, I just stared at it for a moment. The color was bright, almost unreal, but it carried deep meaning. It was more than a uniform accessory—it was a symbol of unity. Soldiers from twelve nations wore it. It meant that despite our different languages, flags, and faces, we shared a single mission: peace.

As the sun climbed higher, we unpacked, settled into our rooms, and began to meet the rest of the company. That's when the reality of the multinational environment really hit me. On a short walk around camp, I passed Fijian guards laughing in their native language, a group of Dutch MPs organizing their patrol schedule, an Italian helicopter crew checking their equipment, and a group of American logistics officers wheeling crates toward a warehouse. Each one had their own job, their own routine—but all of them were part of the same greater purpose.

That evening, I sat on the edge of my bed, the steady hum of the air conditioner filling the room. I unfolded the assignment paper once more and read my name next to "Translator, Commando Company."

Around me, the room slowly settled into order. Bags were unpacked, clothes folded, routines beginning to take shape. Voices drifted in and out, calm now, familiar. Alejandro glanced my way and gave a brief nod.

"We made it, hermano," he said.

I nodded back.

Yes. We had made it. And what lay ahead was no longer abstract or imagined. It had a place, a role, and a responsibility—and it had begun.

Chapter 17

North Camp Nights

Life at North Camp felt different from the army back in Colombia. The chaos, punishments, and dehumanization were gone. Here it felt more like a job.

Most mornings started early. Around five, we gathered at the small square for PT in shorts, T-shirts, and tennis shoes—PT uniforms made in the Colombian flag colors, like a soccer team kit. Each of us held one bottle of water, warm already from the desert air.

The colonel stepped in front of the formation. He lifted his own bottle, took a measured pull, then lowered it and pointed down the line like he was counting us with his eyes.

"Half," he said.

Plastic caps snapped open. Bottles tilted. Nobody drank like they were thirsty—we drank like we were budgeting.

"Move."

We broke into a run and stayed out for nearly an hour, chanting running songs through dry mouths, our shoes thudding against sand-packed ground as the sun climbed higher. When we finally came back, we re-formed in the same square, lungs burning, sweat cutting lines down our faces.

The colonel walked in front of us again, calm as ever. He raised two fingers, then closed his fist.

"Finish it."

We tipped the bottles up and drained what was left. After that came showers, then breakfast in the dining hall—buffet style.

From there my day moved to Major Morales' office. I helped with his duties and sat in on meetings with battalion commanders from the different countries that made up the force. I translated what was said, but I also had to keep up with the pace, the tone, and the way things were handled between ranks and between countries.

One day, at a force-wide briefing in an auditorium, the Force Commander sat at a table in the center of the stage with other high-ranking commanders. He was from New Zealand, and his Kiwi accent could be hard to catch—sometimes even for native English speakers from other countries. The briefing wasn't routine, either. We were going over critical safety issues—camp security updates, gate procedures, and precautions to take with the region still on edge after the U.S. war in Iraq had recently ended.

At one point he gave Major Morales a specific instruction, and I missed it. The major turned to me, waiting for the translation. I opened my mouth—and what came out started to sound vague, like I was trying to read the future off a deck of cards. I panicked and defaulted to something safe, something flattering about Colombia doing a great job. I could see it in Morales' face immediately: that tight look of frustration, like he knew I'd just failed him in front of everyone.

I didn't know exactly what I'd gotten wrong until later. A plane requested access to the airstrip, and the Colombian soldier responsible for authorizing entry denied it. Minutes later, Major Morales got a call: the order had been given in the meeting to grant access. That's when it clicked—whatever the Force Commander had said, it was probably about airstrip security and gate operations. And I had let it slip right through my hands.

Evenings at camp had their own routine. After dinner, the lights at the bars came on and the music started drifting across the sand. The Colombian bar filled fast. So did the U.S. Army bar, the Dutch MP bar, and the Uruguayan bar. You could walk the camp and hear the accents change from one doorway to the next.

On some nights the mood stayed light. On others, it didn't take much. A drink bumped out of someone's hand. A comment said too loud. A stare that lasted one second too long. You would see a circle form, chairs scrape back, voices rise. Most fights didn't start because someone was evil. They started because the desert had been cooking us all day. Heat, boredom, homesickness, and testosterone. Alcohol didn't create the problem, it just removed the lid. I used to think of it as "Sinai pressure."

The Dutch MPs had their own complications. Some of the women sunbathed topless inside their barracks yard, and a nearby guard tower had a clear line of sight. It should have been a non-issue—private space, clear boundaries—but a few guards treated it like entertainment with binoculars. Later, you'd see some of the same guys trying to introduce themselves at the bar, confident and clumsy at the same time. It didn't always end with conversation. More than once it ended with Dutch MPs stepping in, pushing someone back, and fists coming up.

I remember one night in particular. A tall American soldier squared up with a short Colombian, the kind of size difference that should have ended the story before it began. The Colombian didn't back away. He unhooked his thick regulation belt, wrapped it around his hand, and took a step forward. Someone grabbed his arm. Someone else pulled the American back. The circle broke apart, but the energy stayed in the air long after the music resumed.

The next morning, we stood in formation under the sun, trying to look fresh and disciplined. The colonel looked down the line and spoke in a calm voice that carried.

"I have learned that my little Colombian soldiers like to go beat up soldiers from other contingents," he said. "They have banned you from visiting their bars."

No one laughed in formation. But you could feel it moving down the line—men biting the inside of their cheeks, staring straight ahead, sneaking quick side glances to see who would crack first. That night, the Colombian bar was packed.

The friends I made there, Alejandro, Julio, Ricardo, and Rogelio, stopped feeling like coworkers and started feeling like my inner circle. Out in Sinai, you learned quickly who you could count on, not just on duty, but in the long hours when the desert made everything feel repetitive and far from home.

We even turned drinking into something official. We had our own "order of the day," drafted like a real schedule, except the roles were ridiculous.

There was always a "drunk on duty," whose job was to be available if any of us decided that was the night to get wasted. There was an "environmental officer," responsible for setting the mood, decorations, and making his room available as the headquarters. A "light and sound engineering officer" handled the music and the lighting, hanging his red PT uniform over the lamps to create a cabaret effect. And the next morning there was the "hangover officer," the man in charge of getting the "not feeling well" note to the right people before jogging formation.

Everybody had a role. If you tried to disappear, they would find you. The Johnny Walker nights happened so often they stopped feeling like special occasions and started feeling like part of the routine.

Yeah, about that "not feeling well" note. It didn't always work. One morning my name was on it. I felt sick, but I was still in bed when someone started knocking hard on the door. I cracked it open slowly, hoping it would be one of my friends. It was not.

A couple of MPs pushed the door the rest of the way open and Major Morales stepped in behind them. The room was exactly as it had been decorated for the night: my red PT uniform and another one from one of the guys hanging over the lamps to tint the light, and the center pages of Playboy magazines taped to the walls like we were running some cheap strip joint in the middle of the Sinai—and seeing it through his eyes made my stomach drop. The major didn't say much. He took one look around and started pulling the posters off the wall with a serious face. Then he looked at me and said, "How disgraceful. You're late for running."

He turned around and walked out.

I ripped the uniforms off the lamps, threw on my PT clothes, and ran after them, my stomach turning, fighting the urge to throw up and betray every bit of evidence I had consumed the night before.

Sinai gave us good conditions, decent pay, and a level of respect I hadn't known in Colombia. But once the workday ended, we only had each other to keep our minds from drifting into the same loneliness that lived out in those dunes. Back in Colombia the conditions were worse, but at least Sundays came with the hope of a visit, a face you loved, a reminder that your life still existed outside the base.

Diana's letters became my steady reminder of the love waiting at home. Through her words, she stayed close enough to steady me when solitude found its way in. Once a week, the mail would come in, and we'd pack into that cramped room shoulder to shoulder, shouting our names over each other while the guy sorting tried to find the right envelopes. Her letters always stood out, scented, kissed, full of color. She'd write to me every day, sometimes just a paragraph, sometimes pages and pages, then send them all at once. I'd read them slowly, stretching them out over days.

The guys used to tease me. "What did she write this time, *Botero*? A poem? A sonnet? A marriage proposal?" They were relentless, but good-natured. I laughed with them. Deep down, I appreciated Diana more than I could say. She loved me completely—unconditionally. But as her letters grew more emotional, more intense, something inside me shifted.

I started to realize that while she was pouring herself into us, I was drifting. I cared for her—respected her deeply—but I didn't love her the way she loved me. I kept telling myself I just missed home, that I was overwhelmed, that the pressure of the mission was making everything feel distant. But the truth was harder.

Love is a strange thing. You can't command it into existence. When it's real, it moves on its own, like water in a creek, finding its path again and again, persistent and stubborn. With Diana, what I felt was not that. It was gratitude, comfort, familiarity, and the quiet pressure of knowing she loved me more than I could return.

So I made the hardest decision I'd made in months. I sat down to write her a letter and kept stopping, staring at the page, wiping at my eyes, trying to find words that wouldn't bruise her more than the truth already would. I thanked her for everything, told her how much her letters had meant to me, how they had carried me through the long weeks. But I also told her I couldn't love her back with the same fire, the same intensity, the same devotion. She deserved someone who could meet her there, and I wasn't that person.

It was painful, yes. But necessary. She had given me everything, and the only way I could honor that was to stop taking what I couldn't give back.

I sealed the envelope and sent it. After that, time started moving one week at a time. Every mail call became a gamble. Half of me braced for her silence. The other half prayed for a line that said she'd be okay.

Chapter 18

The Sweater

Two weekends later, some of the guys suggested we get off base and take the MFO shuttle to Jerusalem. I said yes. I needed a break from the routine, from the perimeter, from the office, from the same sand and the same faces. We'd heard about a cave-like dance club with great music and gorgeous girls. Sounded like a fun plan.

The club was called *Underground*, and the name wasn't a joke. It sat beneath the street in an old stone basement, packed tight with people and loud music that made the walls feel like they were breathing. There were Israeli soldiers mixed in with civilians, uniforms on, rifles still with them, as if it were the most normal thing in the world.

That had already hit me once before in Tel Aviv. I'd seen a soldier walking along the beach with his rifle slung over his shoulder, his boots tied together by the laces and hanging from the other shoulder, his pants rolled up, barefoot in the sand, holding his civilian girlfriend's hand. It was the same feeling now in Jerusalem. It unsettled me because back home a rifle in public changed the temperature of a place. Here the rifles stayed in the room while people danced, flirted, and laughed, as if nothing about it was unusual.

And then I saw her. Maya. Her light blue eyes and black, silky hair were striking. She danced with a seductive ease that seemed to pull the room toward her, and she wasn't drawing just one stare.

When she stopped dancing, I made my way over and started talking to her. I don't even remember what I said. Something lame, probably. But she didn't laugh at me. She laughed with me. That night we danced, talked, drank, and when the music got too loud, we walked out onto the empty cobblestone streets of Jerusalem. I remember how cold the air felt compared to the heat of the club, and how, when I brushed my hand against hers, she didn't pull away. That first kiss, we didn't rush it. We stood there long enough for me to feel it settle in, clear and undeniable: I was falling for her.

We exchanged numbers. She lived just outside the city, serving her own time in the Israeli forces. Over the next few days, we talked. Nothing too serious, just updates and plans to meet again. I couldn't see her the next weekends because of base duty, but we kept in touch. And in the gaps between messages, I started building a story in my head. Not just about a second date, but about continuity. About something that could hold.

The problem wasn't hope. The problem was that I was writing the future alone.

It was a quiet evening when it all unraveled. I'd just finished a long shift at the main gate and was sitting alone in the camp movie theater, hoping to forget the world for a couple of hours. That's when one of the guys from our battalion walked in, just back from Jerusalem. He sat beside me, still buzzing with excitement. We chatted, and after a couple of minutes, he started gushing about this club called Underground. I laughed, told him I'd been there not long ago, that it was a wild place.

Then he started describing a girl he'd met.

"She was incredible, man," he said. "Like, unforgettable. Short black hair, piercing blue eyes, Israeli." He stretched his arms out in front of him, holding the sweater by the shoulders so I could see it. "She gave me her sweater after we kissed."

That's when my stomach dropped. I knew the sweater. I'd seen it wrapped around Maya's shoulders that night, soft grey wool with a tear near the hem. He kept talking, not realizing the ground beneath my feet had started to shift.

"We hooked up in the alley beside the club," he said, lowering his voice like he was sharing something sacred. "It was intense. Like, real chemistry. Crazy passionate."

My alley. Our alley. The same cobblestones. The same cold night air. The same kiss. It was like watching someone replay your memory—but with the wrong person in it.

I stayed calm on the outside, said nothing. But inside, I was unraveling. I told him we should go back to his room, that I wanted to hear more. When we got there, he opened his backpack and pulled out a small photograph she had given him. It was her.

Maya.

"The girl's name," he said, "is Maya."

I don't know how I stayed composed. But I did. I looked at the photo, nodded slowly, then said, "That's my girl."

He stared at me, stunned. "Wait—what?"

"That's Maya," I repeated. "I met her two weeks ago. Same club."

He couldn't hold my eyes after that. His words came out in short bursts, then stopped. He kept rubbing the back of his neck, shifting his weight like he wanted the floor to open up. When he finally spoke again, it was only to say he hadn't known. He hadn't meant to hurt me. And I believed him. It wasn't his fault. I didn't blame him. I blamed her, for making what we shared feel real when it clearly wasn't.

That night, I didn't sleep. I kept replaying it all in my mind. The look in her eyes when we kissed. The warmth of her voice on the phone. The way she'd made me feel like I mattered.

The next day, he brought me lunch, tried to apologize again. I accepted. I smiled. I even joked about how he had better luck than I did. But beneath the smile, I was fractured. Something in me had cracked. I had allowed myself to hope again, and that hope had turned to ash.

Still, I needed closure. I called her.

She answered, cheerful at first. But her tone shifted when she realized why I was calling. I asked her about him. About the sweater. About the alley. She went quiet.

"I didn't know he was your friend," she said, her voice smaller than usual. "I swear I didn't. If I had known, I would never have... I didn't mean to hurt you."

I held the phone tighter. "You did."

She went quiet for a moment, then said, "Federico, I'm sorry. I didn't think you and I were anything serious. Not yet. It was one night. I didn't understand what it meant to you."

"It meant something to me," I said.

"I know," she replied, and I could hear her swallowing. "And I'm sorry. Truly."

I told her it was over. Not as punishment. As a boundary. I didn't want explanations or promises or more confusion. She said she understood. She said she was sorry again. And that was the last time we spoke.

My friend never wore the sweater.

Chapter 19

Guard These with Your Life

When I look back, I realize that love and heartbreak aren't the only forces that shape your life. Sometimes, it's the people you meet. On my base, no one did that more than the major. He was an enigmatic figure. Stern and reserved.

He wasn't chatty, and he didn't invite familiarity. Even off-duty—out of uniform, in an informal setting—he carried the same gravity that made people choose their words carefully. Beneath the hard exterior, though, he sometimes let a human moment slip through: a restrained smile, a brief look of approval, never more than that. With me, it stayed strictly professional.

That changed one day because of the most unexpected thing—a bag of ants. The major received a package from Colombia, and I happened to be in his office delivering paperwork when it arrived. For a man who kept his emotions locked down as tightly as his uniform, the reaction was immediate. He set the papers aside, glanced at the door as if checking who was watching, and then reached for the package with unmistakable anxiety. "You won't believe what this is, Botero," he said, his voice almost youthful as he ripped open the box.

His hands, usually so composed, fumbled with anticipation. At last, he pulled out an unopened crinkled plastic bag filled with *hormigas culonas*—roasted, salted leafcutter ants.

"These are my favorite," he said, grinning as he held the bag aloft like a trophy. His voice was reverent. "You ever had these?"

I hesitated, not wanting to admit I'd tried them as a child and wasn't a fan. But the major's enthusiasm was contagious. He tore open the bag, popped a few ants into his mouth, and chewed with obvious delight. Then, he offered one to me.

"Come on, try it," he said, his sternness giving way to a rare note of friendliness.

I picked up one of the ants, its glossy, roasted body glinting in the light. It wasn't exactly appetizing, but the major's expectant gaze left no room for refusal. I bit into the rounded abdomen—the part everyone said was best— and to my surprise, it wasn't bad. Crunchy, nutty, salty; not so different from roasted peanuts.

"It's good, right?" the major said with a smirk, clearly pleased with my reaction.

"Yes, sir," I said while nodding. "It's... different, but good."

He talked about the ants with surprising enthusiasm. He told me they were a delicacy in Santander, how people collected them, roasted them, and salted them, and that they were best with a beer or a shot of aguardiente. For a few minutes, he wasn't the guarded, unreadable officer I knew. It felt like stumbling onto a hidden chapter of someone I thought I'd already figured out.

As the conversation wound down, the major handed me the bag with a solemn look. "Guard these with your life," he said. "Don't let anyone touch them while I'm gone."

He was leaving for an event in Cairo with the commander. I assured him I would protect his precious ants.

At first, I was resolute. I tucked the bag away safely in his office, telling myself I wouldn't give it another thought. But as the weekend wore on, temptation crept in. I kept thinking about those ants—the crunch, the odd, addictive flavor, the memory of home hidden in every bite. It was ridiculous, I told myself. Who would miss just a few?

On Saturday, I went back to the office.

It was empty. I slid open the wooden drawer in his desk and took the bag out. I held it for a second without doing anything. The plastic sounded loud in my hands. I listened down the hallway, then unfolded the rolled seam at the top just enough to uncover the opening.

Three ants dropped into my palm. Salt dusted my fingertips. I ate them one at a time, slow, the crunch too loud for how silent the room was. Then I rolled the top back down along the same fold, pressed it flat, and put the bag back in the drawer and left.

A few hours later, I returned. This time I didn't hesitate. My fingers went straight to the fold. I tipped out four ants and ate them faster than the first time. I rolled the top down tighter than before and set it back.

The next visit wasn't planned. I found myself there again, already pulling the drawer open. I unfolded the seam and poured five into my palm. I didn't count them until they were already there. I ate them standing there, eyes on the doorway, chewing fast. Then I rolled the top down and pushed the bag deeper into the drawer.

Only afterward, with the drawer closed again, did I realize I had crossed the line. The promise I had made him was already gone.

By Sunday night, I didn't have to open it to know. When I picked it up, it sat flatter in my hand. The weight was wrong. The shape was wrong. I folded the plastic neatly, smoothed it flat, and tucked it back where it belonged, relying on neatness to hide what was missing. Then I stood there for a beat, staring at the drawer, already knowing he would notice.

Monday morning came too quickly. I heard the major's voice—sharp, echoing down the corridor. "Botero!"

My heart sank. I walked into his office, doing my best to look calm. The bag of ants sat on his desk, wrinkled and half-empty. His eyes met mine, disappointment clouding his features.

"What happened to this?" he demanded, gesturing to the sad remains of the bag. His tone was harsh, but underneath it I heard something else—a mix of hurt and disbelief.

I hesitated, reaching for an excuse. Nothing came. "I don't know, sir," I said, but my eyes dropped before I could stop them.

He leaned back in his chair, studying me in silence. "Botero, these were special to me. Do you know how hard it is to get these here?"

I nodded, shame burning in my cheeks. "I'm sorry, sir. It won't happen again."

The silence between us was reprimand enough. He studied me briefly, then gave a small shake of his head. "Dismissed," he said, controlled and final.

I walked out of the office and closed the door behind me, my face still hot. It wasn't just the ants. It was my word. In the chain of command, that was all I had. He hadn't handed me a meaningless task; he had placed something he cared about in my hands, a rare personal gesture from a man who offered very few. I had used my access to cross a line I knew better than to cross, and I had made him regret it.

For weeks afterward, everything between us cooled. The small rapport we'd been building evaporated, replaced by strict formality. He stopped offering the occasional joke or scrap of wisdom. Our interactions became brief, practical, and impersonal. And I beat myself up over how something so small had been enough to damage what little trust I'd earned.

I refused to let regret take over. I started showing up early, taking on extra work, and carrying myself with steady respect. I looked for every chance to serve him well, because I wanted to earn back what I'd damaged.

Slowly, almost imperceptibly, the frost began to thaw. The major's tone softened. He started to ask for my opinion again, sometimes even offering a quiet, approving nod. We never spoke directly of the ants, but a new, more measured understanding grew between us—a tacit agreement to let the past lie where it fell.

Today, I can laugh at it. At first, the shame was immense, and the lesson stayed with me. Trust is fragile. It breaks easily, and sometimes a small pleasure is enough to crack it. To this day, when I see a bag of roasted ants, I think of the major and the rapport I damaged. It reminds me that forgiveness, when it comes, is usually earned the same way trust is rebuilt: little by little.

Chapter 20

The Key to Jerusalem

The Israel tour had been on my mind for weeks. It was five days on the itinerary—Jerusalem for one night, then Bethlehem, Masada, the Dead Sea, and the Jordan River. I was going as translator for the second commander—the major—traveling with about twenty-five soldiers.

I had always wanted to see the places connected to Jesus with my own eyes—like a seed the man made of stars had planted in me early in life. A quiet curiosity to learn more about Him, and maybe even connect deeper through whatever each place would awaken in me as I visited.

Before we left, the instructions were clear: stay in the hotel at night, do not wander, and take no unnecessary risks.

We reached Jerusalem late, and when our bus pulled up to the hotel, I just sat there staring, my face full of admiration.

A vast edifice of cream-colored stone rose in front of us, towering like a castle at the edge of the ancient city. The light moved across it and laid a warm gold over the façade, catching the arches of its windows and the weather-stained walls. It didn't feel like a hotel. It felt like a place borrowed from another century.

Inside, the air was cool and faintly fragrant, the kind of clean scent that comes from marble that's been polished again and again. At the reception desk, we were greeted with polite smiles. The concierge set a box of room keys in front of us and explained the room assignments to the major and me.

He opened the box and went through the assignments, point by point. The soldiers would share rooms. The corporal would have his own. The sergeant major would have his own. Then he paused and reached for a single key, holding it up a little higher than the rest. He tilted his face slightly to the side, leaned forward, and said it was for the major—a special suite.

I translated, but not the way he said it.

"Alright," I told the group, keeping my voice flat. "The soldiers will share rooms. Corporal and sergeant major, you'll share a room." They looked up, surprised, but nobody challenged it. Then I nodded at the major. "Sir, you have your own room."

While they started sorting themselves out in the lobby, I slipped the suite key into my pocket. Curiosity did it—along with the part of me that likes to test the edge. If Jerusalem was a dream, the room should match it.

As soon as I opened the door, I stopped and just stared. It was unbelievable—the most beautiful room I'd ever had the chance to sleep in. There were two spacious sitting rooms, a king-size bed draped in flowing curtains, marble floors, and ceiling frescoes that reminded me of a Renaissance chapel. The furnishings glowed under the warm light, every detail deliberate—the gilded frames, the intricate mosaics, the kind of old-world grandeur you only expect to see in museums.

I completely lost myself. I was like a kid, jumping up on the bed and laughing as I bounced, letting the mattress swallow me up. I wandered everywhere—marveling at the luxury, touching marble, staring at the ceiling frescoes, then drifting to the windows to look out at the city glittering beyond the glass.

Outside, Jerusalem called to me. The city's heartbeat pulsed outside the hotel walls, and I couldn't stand the idea of staying cooped up inside, rules or no rules. I called around, hoping to recruit a partner in crime. Most of the guys hesitated, wary of breaking protocol, but Arturo, tall and easygoing as ever, finally agreed.

"I know a place," I said. "It's called Underground. The music is insane—and it's full of beautiful women."

We slipped out into the night, winding through ancient streets until we found the entrance. Then we started down—step after step—dropping beneath street level until the air cooled and the bass hit us in the chest. The dance floor was packed, bodies moving shoulder to shoulder in the half-dark.

Arturo leaned in close so I could hear him over the beat. "You weren't lying, Botero," he shouted. "This was totally worth the escape."

The women were unforgettable—midnight hair, sharp, magnetic eyes. Arturo and I scanned the room, quickly drawn to a table where two women sat alone. I gathered my courage and introduced myself.

Her name was Leah—a white girl from Be'er Sheva, with wild black curls and a smile that made me relax instantly. Her friend was a blonde British student, and Leah was visiting her for the weekend.

Leah and I clicked right away. Conversation came easily, laughter slipping in between sentences, and before long we were on the dance floor, moving with the music until we lost track of time.

When the disco finally closed, Leah's friend invited us back to her apartment to keep the night going. Arturo and I exchanged a quick glance—a silent pact formed between two tired men willing to sacrifice sleep for the possibility of something extraordinary.

At the apartment, we sank into the mismatched living-room cushions and poured drinks, trading stories that moved back and forth between English and broken Hebrew, with a little Spanish slipping in now and then. We chatted into laughter, and the laughter into wordless looks. We found other ways to communicate—smiles, touch, and the simple comfort of being close.

Dawn pulled Leah and me closer. Her head rested on my shoulder, and my arm went around her, almost shyly. In that suspended quiet, words felt unnecessary. It wasn't a promise or a plan—just a real moment between two people who were genuinely drawn to each other.

Suddenly, reality came rushing back. I glanced at the clock—6 a.m. Panic jolted me upright. Our bus was leaving the hotel at seven. "Arturo!" I called out, my voice slicing through the sleepy hush. He stumbled out of the bedroom, hair wild, shirt half-buttoned, wearing the dazed grin of a man who'd made similar choices.

We said a quick goodbye—a hug, a few words, one last look—then Arturo and I were moving. We hurried down the stairs, caught a cab, and made it back to Notre Dame with fifteen minutes to spare.

Back at the hotel, I barely had time to shower before someone knocked—firm, impatient. I knew it immediately. I opened the door with a towel still around my waist, keeping the gap narrow.

The major leaned in, and I tightened my grip on the door, trying to keep the opening small. He didn't need more than a second. His eyes slid past my shoulder—over the marble, the height of the ceiling, the space, the quiet luxury of it—and then came back to me. You could see it landing in real time: whatever room he'd been given, it wasn't this.

His mouth opened like he might say something about the suite, about the key, about the obvious mismatch. He didn't. His jaw set, his gaze held on mine a beat too long, and the accusation sat there without words.

"You're late," he said. "Downstairs. Now."

As soon as he turned away, my mind started racing. How had he even found me? The only thing I'd done differently was make calls from that room the night before, trying to recruit someone to go out with me. Maybe one of the guys let something slip. I didn't know. I only knew it wasn't luck—somewhere, the suite key had stopped being my secret.

I fumbled into uniform and sprinted to breakfast, while adrenaline and guilt competed against the halo of the previous night. When we loaded ourselves into the bus, and finally had a moment to relax, all I could see was Leah. I could feel the bend of her smile, the fall of her curls, how she just easily had entered into my mind. The morning chaos faded, replaced by the memory of her.

That day, we visited the most important places in Jerusalem first. At each stop I found myself slowing down, taking it in, trying to let it sink past the noise and the schedule. I wanted to stay longer, to stand there in silence and reflect, but I couldn't drift too far into my own thoughts—I was the major's translator, and every few minutes someone needed me to be present, to listen, to speak, to keep the day moving.

After that, we went to Bethlehem and then to Masada. We hiked past the crowds to a quieter edge of the Dead Sea, and the water did what it always does—it turned grown men into kids. At some point the whole group gave up on modesty. Underwear came off, and we started floating naked, laughing at how impossible it was to sink, letting the salt hold us up.

I drifted away from them without meaning to, toward the Jordanian side. The hangover and the lack of sleep from the night before finally caught up with me, heavy and delayed. I lay back, staring at the sky, and the next thing I knew I was waking up still floating—too far from the group. Nobody noticed. Good. I was a strong swimmer. I rolled onto my stomach and started swimming back, stroke after stroke, until I was close enough to blend in again as if I'd never disappeared.

Jericho was next. In the Jordan River, the major found his sense of humor again. "Come here, Botero," he called, wearing a mock-solemn priest expression. Before I could protest, he waded into the shallows, gripped my shoulders, and dunked me beneath the surface. "I baptize you!" he proclaimed, laughter ringing out. I surfaced, sputtering, but there was a strange awe in the moment—baptized in the same waters where history itself was shaped. It was surreal, humbling, and unforgettable.

Even as the tour kept moving—up to Tiberias, then Capernaum and Nazareth, where we spent the last three days before returning to Sinai—I carried two separate currents inside me. One was what those places did to my faith: seeing the geography of Jesus with my own eyes, stopping when I could, taking a few seconds to reflect even while I had to stay "on" as the major's translator. Sometimes I wanted to linger, to stand there longer and let the moment settle, but the day kept pulling me forward—another question to translate, another instruction, another stop.

And then there was Leah. Not holy—nothing like that. Just real. Her face kept showing up when it had no right to: the curve of her smile, the fall of her curls, the ease of that night. The places fed something deep in me; Leah stayed with me in a different place—simple, human, and stubbornly present.

Though the major said nothing about my choices during the trip, I could tell something was brewing. The fallout from my choices came as soon as we arrived back at camp—swift and undeniable. He didn't raise his voice or drag things out with lectures. The simple finality of his decision carried all the weight. I was stripped of my translator position and reassigned to

Ayacucho—a regular company responsible for the monotonous task of guarding North Camp's perimeter, with shifts at the main gate.

Chapter 21

The Silence I Chose

The difference was immediate and jarring. There were no more commando-company perks: no more single rooms, no more insistent air-conditioning whispering me to sleep, no more pillowy beds, no more first-floor convenience that spared me the worst of the Sinai sun. My new, college-like reality was a small, run-down dorm and a roommate whose character constantly grated against mine. The air felt stale and unmoving, and the old ceiling fans only clicked and complained as they pushed heat in slow circles.

Sleep became a negotiation. My limbs stuck to the thin sheets. Every turn reminded me of what I had lost.

I knew I deserved it. I was living with the burn because I had played with fire. I told myself I should accept the new reality and do my best to make the most of it. But resignation never fit me. Time passed, and the shifts at the gate blurred together, one shading into the next. The days were a mix of dust and boredom, broken only by the vehicles coming in and out of camp—and the occasional radio crackle that reminded us we were still on watch.

One afternoon, on the walk to chow, I started paying closer attention to the officers' quarters. It wasn't some luxury world—it was basically the same building design I had lived in before the demotion. That was the point. I knew exactly what was inside. And the more I watched the traffic around that building, the more obvious something became—there were more rooms than officers, and some of them sat empty. An alternative started forming in my mind. Maybe I didn't have to accept the version of North Camp I'd been assigned after my punishment. So I paid attention, kept my mouth shut, and started planning.

The demotion hurt. It reminded me every day that I had gone too far and was being punished for it. Still, I didn't want to give up trying to find my way back to something decent. Maybe it was stubbornness, but it kept me from getting lost in the desert haze.

Later that night, I went back. The window sat low enough that I could glance inside before touching it. No gear, no boots, no movement—no one in the room. I eased it open and climbed through. The air was cool. I sat down, let it hit my skin, and decided this would be my new setup.

After that, I slipped in every night and slept there, then climbed out before dawn. It wasn't perfect, but it beat sweating through the night in the crowded Ayacucho barracks. I didn't tell anyone. All it would take was one loose comment to turn it into a problem.

I kept the routine until the day I left North Camp. It wasn't only comfort I was stealing back—it was dignity. I had lost the major's trust and my former role, but I hadn't lost my ability to figure things out on my own. Crawling through that window became my personal protest, my reminder that even in punishment, I could still find a way.

Nobody ever caught on. The officers didn't pay attention, and the other soldiers didn't bother checking where I slept at night. It was my little secret— a small victory in the midst of the chaos I had created for myself.

I laughed nervously to myself every time I crawled through that window, imagining the major's face if he ever found out. I would have been in big trouble.

The thing with Leah was complicated. We kept in touch, even with the distance. At North Camp, I could use a phone in the communications room, and I called her two or three times a week.

Both of us were eager to meet again, and after a while she invited me to visit her in Be'er Sheva, a desert city in the Negev with deep biblical roots. She helped me arrange a cheap bed in a hostel, since she still hadn't mentioned me to her parents.

Leah welcomed me in Be'er Sheva. That same evening, we went out to dinner—but it wasn't just the two of us. She had invited a small group of friends, about six. They were friendly, but they spoke only Hebrew, and I didn't understand a word.

Leah tried to pull me into the conversation, but her English wasn't strong, and translating on the spot was a struggle. Most of the time, I just sat there smiling at the right moments, a spectator at my own dinner. I kept wanting a moment alone with her—to recover what we'd had in Jerusalem—but at the table it never opened up.

After dinner, Leah walked me back to the hostel. Our hands stayed laced together as we moved through the warm night, our steps unhurried. Every so often she looked up at me with a small, shy smile, and my face softened in response.

When we reached the entrance, we slowed as if neither of us wanted to be the first to let go. We stopped under the doorway light. She stepped closer. I did too. For a second we just stood there, close enough to feel each other's breath—then she leaned in and I met her halfway. The kiss was gentle, then sure, and the romance between us came rushing back.

The following day, we met again. This time, the plan was for me to meet her parents. But when I saw her, she was clearly crying—her eyes were red. She told me her father, a Jewish police officer, had forbidden her from introducing me to the family. He didn't like our relationship because I wasn't Jewish.

A knot tightened in my chest. "Why does it matter that I'm not Jewish?" I asked.

Tears rolled down her cheeks as she explained, "It's just how it is. My family doesn't think I should be with you. But it doesn't matter to me. I want to be with you."

Her determination reached me, but it didn't solve anything. I could feel how little power I had against a father, a household, a whole world I wasn't part of. And still—standing there with her, watching her wipe her cheeks and steady her voice—I knew I was falling in love.

We spent the day together anyway, pretending we could keep the sadness at the edge of the frame. But it followed us. It sat in the pauses. It showed up every time she checked the time, every time she looked down the street as if expecting someone to appear.

155

When it was time for me to return to base, she held onto me hard. We kissed, then didn't separate right away. We stayed there a moment longer than we needed to, holding the last seconds like they could be saved—both of us acting as if we didn't know, but feeling it all the same: this might be one of the last times.

Back at the base, life moved on. Not long after my visit to Be'er Sheva, I was assigned to Control Center Three for thirty days. It was a remote post along the border between Egypt and Israel. That meant I wouldn't see Leah for at least a month.

We talked on the phone during the week before I left, and in one of those calls her voice was full of distress. Her father had found out we were still in touch and had given her an ultimatum: end the relationship with me, or leave the family.

I was shocked.

"Leah, you can't leave your family for me," I told her. "They're your family—they love you."

But she was resolute. "I've already decided, Fred. I'm leaving tonight. I'm going to Eilat. A friend of mine lives there, and she said I can stay with her."

I tried to convince her to reconsider, but she wouldn't listen. That night, she left.

About a week later, she called me from Eilat. She told me where she was staying—a small room arranged through a friend who worked at a bar. Even through the phone, I could hear the atmosphere: noise, laughter that wasn't kind, voices too loud. She said the place filled up at night with drunk, rowdy customers who didn't respect boundaries—men who leaned in too close, comments that turned crude, hands that reached as if they had the right.

All of it broke my heart. I felt guilty for being part of the chain that had put her there, and helpless because I couldn't protect her from across a desert and a schedule I couldn't escape. I started doubting everything—our relationship, our future, whether this love story, as beautiful as it felt, could survive reality.

The more I considered it, the more impossible it became. I was thousands of miles away. I had responsibilities I couldn't abandon. I didn't even know what my next month would look like, much less my next year. Leah deserved stability, and I couldn't provide it.

One night, I climbed the communications antenna at the control center. I did it when my thoughts wouldn't settle—when I needed height and wind and distance. From up there, everything looked close and unreachable at the same time. The horizon felt like a promise you couldn't touch.

And up there, with the wind pressing against me, I made one of the most difficult decisions of my life. I chose not to call her anymore. I knew what my disappearance would do: it would leave her with no reason to keep standing outside her family's door. She needed them more than she needed me.

It was the most painful thing I had ever done, but I believed it was right. I couldn't give her the future she deserved, and I couldn't allow her to sacrifice everything for me.

Several weeks later, I got a letter from her. She was back home. In the letter, she thanked me—though I didn't feel like I deserved it. She said she understood why I had done it. As much as it hurt, she didn't hate me. She told me she would never forget the memories we had shared.

That is the last I ever heard of Leah. Years later, when I was back in Colombia, I tried to trace her, but without success. Her memory has stayed with me, though. What we had was brief and intense—a shooting star: bright, beautiful, and short. And even though it broke my heart in two, I believe, deep down, that I was right to set her free.

Chapter 22

On the Mesa

Leah's memory clung to me like an open wound the desert heat couldn't cauterize. I wandered through the Sinai, trying to lose myself in duty, but heartbreak doesn't take orders—it whispers when you're alone and hits hardest when you're quiet.

Spending time at Control Center Three was an expected part of our service with the Colombian Battalion in Sinai. All soldiers had rotating shifts in isolated posts, with each obligated to serve thirty days stationed along the Egypt-Israel border at a minimum.

I still remember the drive there. The Sinai stretched in every direction— beautiful and eerie. We drove past the remnants of old wars; tanks that were sunk halfway into the sands, debris of metal and weapons that were impossible to ignore. There were signs after every corner, indicating warnings of mines along the route.

We stuck strictly to the cleared tracks. Nobody needed to tell us why— stories of those who wandered off the path and never came back had a way of circulating among the men.

Control Center Three itself was little more than a cluster of simple buildings—a handful of structures grouped around a makeshift dining area under a tin roof, a basic kitchen, and a row of mobile homes that served as sleeping quarters. Life out there felt slower, stripped down. The command staff was small: a captain, a sergeant, a corporal, and a few soldiers to keep the place running. I was assigned to the communications room, responsible for staying in constant touch with the main base and the temporary observation points (TOPs) positioned along the border.

The TOPs were lonely posts—just two or three soldiers at each, tasked with watching for anything unusual: a low-flying aircraft, an unauthorized vehicle, or the lone figure who sometimes dared the border. When something caught their eye, they'd call it in to us, and we'd relay the word to headquarters. Most days passed quietly, filled with small routines: collecting weather data, interpreting the orange wind-speed indicator, logging humidity and air temperature, checking atmospheric pressure, and estimating cloud cover and visibility. Every hour, like clockwork, we radioed North Camp to confirm everything was normal.

The other constant in this isolated place was the presence of the Bedouins. Every so often, a small group would appear at the fence, waiting patiently with the practiced confidence of those who knew we had food to spare. Our supply trucks always brought more than we needed—sometimes enough turkeys to feed twice our number.

The Bedouins would come to trade and to ask for food—sometimes offering small trinkets, but usually just hoping we'd share from our surplus and toss a bird or two over the wire. The word "Amigo!" would ring out, and every now and then, one of the women would briefly lift her veil, eyes dark and striking, flashing a smile that could melt even a homesick soldier's resolve. There was something oddly comforting about the ritual, a small reminder that even out here, people found ways to connect.

Every so often, something ridiculous would shake up the routine. Like the time I nodded off in the comms room and missed an incoming report. My captain caught hell for it, which meant I was about to catch hell too. Instead of yelling, he just gave me a look that said everything and then ordered me to collect firewood for a bonfire. Firewood—in the Sinai. As if we were camping in the Rockies and not marooned in a moonscape with nothing but a few half-dead bushes.

Orders were orders. I grabbed my Walkman, slid a cigarette between my lips, and walked out through the gate while the guard barely glanced up. The heat slammed into me. I stayed on the cleared road, knowing damn well I wasn't going to find a log—or even a proper stick—out there. It was just me, the wind, and that endless silence. I kept walking until the ground dropped away into a cliff overlooking the valley. There was nothing out there except sun and the scattered wreckage of old wars, half-swallowed by sand, but the view was almost enough to make me forget the task I'd been sent to do. I sat down, put R.E.M. on, closed my eyes, and let the music take over for a minute.

Out of nowhere, I heard a voice: "Amigo!"

The word came from behind, and I almost fell off the cliff. I turned to find a Bedouin man wearing a wide, easy smile, like we were old friends. He made himself at home, so I handed him an earbud. We sat shoulder to shoulder, listening to music, not saying a word. At some point he pulled out a bunch of herbs and rolled them into something barely smokable. He passed it to me and I gave him one of my cigarettes in return. We sat there in silence, passing the smoke between us. Two guys with nothing in common except the shade they gave each other and a moment of peace that felt like it wasn't meant for either of us.

I trudged back with a few sad twigs in hand—probably enough to start a bonfire for ants, if they were lucky. The captain glanced at them, then at me, and said, "Don't let it happen again."

Routine kicked back in, and after a few more days staring at the same four walls in the comms room, I'd had enough. I started pestering the captain to let me go out to a TOP, just to break the monotony. He kept telling me it wasn't my job, but I wouldn't let it go.

Finally, maybe just to shut me up, he let me tag along on a mission out to one of the most isolated TOPs, the kind you only get to by helicopter. The place was perched on a mesa, cliffs on all sides, with a little rectangle of rocks painted white to show the chopper where to land.

When we touched down at the TOP, the isolation hit us right away. There was nothing but rock, sand, and sky. We pitched our tent inside the faded white lines that marked our safe zone, then tried to settle in for the night. For a while, it was easy—we played cards under a flickering flashlight and traded stories to keep the nerves at bay.

But sometime after midnight, a voice cut through the stillness—close enough to feel impossible. We froze. Then the tent exploded into movement.

I grabbed my rifle, yanked a magazine, and slid it between my underwear and my lower back the way you do when there's no time to think. No pants, no shirts—just underwear, boots, and rifles in the cold desert air.

The corporal hissed, "Diamond formation," and we snapped into it outside the tent, spreading out and moving away from the safe lines in a slow, careful walk, scanning the darkness and trying to triangulate where the word had come from. It made no sense. We were on a high, isolated mesa in the middle of nowhere—rock, sand, and sky. There shouldn't have been anyone out there. That was exactly what made it so unsettling.

We swept the area in silence, listening for anything that didn't belong. One of the soldiers suddenly raised a hand. "Did you hear that?" A soft slide of dirt near the cliff edge—like a foot shifting on loose gravel. He turned his light that way, and for a split second it felt like we were about to see someone step into view. But there was nothing. Just the drop-off, the wind, and the dark swallowing everything whole.

We kept searching until the adrenaline started to sour into nerves. Nothing appeared. No footsteps, no voices, no movement—only the certainty that the sound had been real enough to pull us out of sleep and point rifles into the night. After that, none of us slept right. We lay there jumpy until morning, listening to the desert like it was listening back.

We woke to sand tapping the canvas, then hammering it. The wind built fast, turning the tent into something alive—fabric snapping, poles flexing, stakes groaning as if the ground was trying to spit them out. We lunged outside half awake, squinting into the grit, grabbing at corners and straps, but the gusts were stronger than our hands. One stake popped free, then another. The tent lurched, dragged our gear with it, and the whole mess skated across the mesa like it wanted to launch.

Packs rolled. A canteen bounced and vanished into the dust. The food boxes—heavy, squared, supposed to stay put—started sliding toward the cliff. We ran, boots scraping rock, arms out, but one box reached the edge first. It tipped, caught for a heartbeat, and then dropped out of sight. The sound of it clattering down the rock face died quickly in the wind.

We stood there for a second, breathing hard, sand in our mouths, staring at the empty space like it had swallowed our only plan. The other box sat a few feet back, wobbling every time a gust hit it.

I did the math in my head. One box wouldn't feed all of us. And I could already see it in their faces—nobody was going to volunteer to climb down for the one that had gone over. If we kept the second box safe, they'd settle for half rations and call it good. We'd be hungry, and we'd still be stuck with the same problem.

So I walked over to the second box, planted my hands on it, and shoved.

It scraped forward, bumped once, then slid clean over the edge and disappeared after the first. For a beat, everyone just stared at me.

"Now we go," I said, raising my voice into the wind. And that was it—no debate, no bargaining, no pretending we could live on less. If we wanted to eat, we had to go down and bring both boxes back up.

We found the boxes wedged on a narrow ledge below the cliff, half-buried in grit. Getting down was bad enough—boots searching for purchase, fingers jammed into cracks, bayonets stabbed into the rock like improvised hooks. But the real problem was getting the boxes back up. There was no clean way to carry them while climbing. If you tried, you'd lose your grip, and on that drop you didn't get a second chance.

So we improvised.

One of us braced himself and lifted a box. "Ready," he yelled.

He heaved it upward. The wind caught it immediately, knocking it off line. It rose just enough to give you hope, then started to fall back toward our faces like a cannonball. We moved fast—two bayonets flashed up, arms straining, trying to catch the edge of the box before it slammed into the rock and bounced away. Metal scraped cardboard. The box jerked, swung, and for a second it hung there, held by nothing but our blades and pure stubbornness.

"Pull!" someone shouted.

We dragged it toward a higher lip, shoved it onto the rock, then climbed up after it, breathing hard, eyes stinging, hands shaking from the effort.

Then we did it again.

Throw. Catch with bayonets. Drag. Climb.

We repeated the maneuver over and over, inching the boxes upward in ugly little victories, until finally the last throw cleared the edge and the box slapped onto the top of the mesa.

When we hauled ourselves up after it, we were panting and filthy, sand ground into our sweat like sandpaper. We looked at the boxes sitting there—battered, scraped, somehow still intact—and started laughing the way you do when something was too stupid to survive but did anyway.

The next day the helicopter finally circled in to pull us out, and we loaded up—battered, dusty, and strangely proud. The control center didn't exactly roll out a hero's welcome. The captain, predictably, blew his top when he heard we'd gone outside the marked safe zone, warning us about mines and a dozen other ways we could have gotten ourselves killed. But all I could think about was how alive I felt. I'd gotten exactly what I'd come for—a break from monotony, a bit of risk, and a memory that would last.

After my thirty days were up, I couldn't pack fast enough. I was desperate for a change of scenery, for anything that wasn't dust, sweat, or sand. That's when I found out about the leave—the golden ticket. Fifteen days anywhere, if you could swing it. For me, that meant one thing: Europe.

Chapter 23

Fifteen Days Anywhere

Fifteen days of leave in the middle of Sinai felt like winning the lottery. "Anywhere," they said—if you could make it happen. After thirty days of dust and radio checks, I couldn't think of anything but getting out. Not just off the post—out of the desert, out of the routine, out of my own head.

We planned it like soldiers with empty pockets: a Eurail pass, as few clothes as possible, and a promise to sleep on trains instead of paying for beds. Ricardo, Alejandro, Julio, Rogelio—and even Lieutenant Montero—were in. My pay was already bleeding from weekends in Tel Aviv and Jerusalem, and my mother sent just enough from home to keep the dream alive. It wasn't comfort we were buying. It was movement.

The only real splurge was the Eurail pass: fifteen days, first-class. Our logic was simple—sleep on the train at night, explore by day, and skip the cost of hotels. If first class ever got too quiet, we'd slip into second class for company and stories. We packed as little as we could.

My rucksack held a few clothes, a sleeping bag, and some leftover military rations—enough to keep hunger from ruining the adventure. It would be rough, and it would be cheap, but if Sinai had taught me anything, it was how to stretch the moment and make it count.

We left the desert behind by hitching a ride with the French army. They were rotating troops out of Sinai, and for a small insurance fee, we got ourselves onto a massive Hercules cargo plane. It was nothing like commercial air travel—no rows of soft seats or flight attendants offering drinks.

Just bare metal benches bolted along the walls and those stiff harnesses that felt more like something out of an ambulance than an airplane. I remember thinking, *This is the way people move armies, not tourists*. Still, none of us cared. We were Paris-bound, and it didn't matter how we got there.

Landing in Paris reset my senses, but the welcome wasn't romantic. At the airport we stepped into a borrowed civilian life, and it started with customs. They opened our bags, checked every pocket, and inspected the little canisters of 35mm film for anything illegal. Questions, stamps, zippers, hands. Then we were released into the city. We dropped our bags at the cheapest hotel we could find and didn't bother to unpack. Paris was right there, waiting for us. We were hungry for it.

It didn't take long for us to wind up exactly where every young soldier in Paris seems to go: the Red-Light District. We'd heard all the stories back in Sinai—cabarets, wild shows, places where the neon never sleeps. After months in the sand with nothing but rumors and imagination, the real thing felt almost unreal.

The streets were a blur of red and gold lights, music pouring out of every doorway, crowds packed in close, posters of women everywhere you looked. It was loud, garish, intoxicating. You could practically feel the city's pulse under your skin. We spotted the Moulin Rouge, its famous windmill glowing in the night, and started weaving our way through the crowd.

Halfway there, a guy picked us out and called out in Spanish. Instantly, we were on the same side—fellow outsiders, drawn together by a familiar language in a foreign city. He worked the door for a strip club just off the main drag and pitched us hard: ten bucks for a beer and the show, no surprises unless we started ordering more. For ten dollars, we weren't going to argue. We handed over our cash and followed him down a narrow flight of stairs into a dark, smoky basement that smelled like cheap perfume and old beer.

The place was almost empty. A few tables, a low stage, some flickering colored lights. We took seats right up front—first row, hearts pounding, trying to act like we'd done this before. The staff told us to wait; the girls would be out soon enough. So we nursed our beers, swapped nervous jokes, and waited.

When the show finally started, it was a jolt. The first dancer came out and the mood in the room flipped. We whooped and clapped, slapping the table, soaking up every minute. Then things got interesting. The dancers began leaving the stage, moving through the crowd, one by one. A woman slid up next to Julio first, leaning in close. Alejandro tried to warn him off, but Julio just grinned and nodded.

Then it was my turn. She was blonde, her English broken, her smile practiced. "Do you mind if I sit with you?" she asked, her accent heavy.

I tried to act casual, even though my heart was thumping in my chest. I shrugged and managed a smile. "Sure."

She slid into the seat across from me. For a second, I couldn't think of anything to say. I just nodded, still trying to play it cool.

A few minutes later, I glanced over and saw Ricardo getting pulled in by another woman. The rest of our crew stayed put, giving us the kind of look only good friends can—equal parts envy and warning.

She glanced at the menu, then at me. "Is it okay if I order a drink?"

I hesitated, but nodded. "Yeah, go ahead."

I figured she'd get a beer. Maybe another ten dollars, max.

Instead, a waitress appeared out of nowhere—like she'd been waiting the whole time—carrying a bucket of ice and a full bottle of champagne.

No warning. Just a practiced smile.

Within minutes, Ricardo and Julio had their own champagne buckets delivered to their tables, too. None of us questioned it. We were too caught up in the moment, clinking glasses across the smoky room. The first bottle disappeared fast, and before long, a second appeared. That's when it finally hit me—this wasn't a round of beers in Jerusalem. "How much is this?" I asked.

The waitress handed over a slip of paper. My stomach dropped—$550 for the bottle, plus the extra beers. I stared at the number, feeling like the ground had vanished from under my feet. Half my trip budget—gone, in a single pour.

Panic set in. I tried to explain I couldn't pay, but the woman next to me just shook her head and claimed I'd "touched" her, so now the bottle was my problem. Same story for Ricardo and Julio—bills in hand, no way to pay.

We tried to leave, but the club's bouncers blocked the door. Three huge guys in nothing but thongs showed up and hustled us off to a back bathroom. They went through our pockets and emptied out what little cash we had left. I'd managed to hand most of my money to Lieutenant Montero earlier, so they only got $80 from me. The others kept their credit cards out of sight. Eventually, realizing we were tapped out, they shoved us back out into the street.

We stumbled into the Paris night, humiliated. Whatever excitement we'd walked in with was gone. Nobody said a word the whole way back to the hotel. The city had taught us a lesson we wouldn't forget.

But in a weird way, that rotten night glued us together. Lying in our tiny hotel room, still processing what happened, all we could do was laugh—first at ourselves, then at the whole stupid mess. We'd been swindled, sure, but it made us closer. We'd gotten played, and now we had a story we'd be telling for years.

We had two weeks ahead of us, and we were determined not to let one disaster ruin the trip. The next morning, with the sting of the night before still fresh, we got up early, ready for a real Parisian adventure. This was the day we'd been waiting for: tickets to the legendary Lido de Paris show.

Those tickets hadn't come cheap—over a hundred bucks each—but we figured if we were going to splurge on anything, it should be this. The ticket included half a bottle of champagne and a show so famous we'd heard about it back in Sinai. We didn't have tuxedos or even jackets, so we'd booked the early show, which was a little more forgiving on the dress code.

The rest of the day was pure magic. We wandered the Louvre, jaw-dropped at the Mona Lisa and the endless halls of art. We strolled along the Seine, ducked into cafés for cheap beer, and tried to soak in as much of the city as we could.

At some point, we ducked into a little corner liquor store to grab a few beers.

That's when I saw it—the exact same champagne that had caused us so much trouble the night before, just sitting on the shelf for four bucks.

I blinked, then called out, "Hey, guys. Come look at this."

They crowded around, peering at the bottle. Ricardo snorted. "You've got to be kidding me."

For a minute, we just stood there, shaking our heads, letting out tired laughs.

"We were idiots," someone muttered.

I grinned. "Let's each buy a bottle and drink it right here."

Everyone looked at each other—and nodded. It felt like a small revenge. Revenge on the club, on our own stupidity, maybe even on the city itself. So that's what we did. We stepped out onto the sidewalk, popped open our cheap champagne, and made a toast.

"To our tour," I said, lifting my bottle.

"To friendship," Ricardo added.

"And to doing things we'd never get to do anywhere else," Rogelio chimed in.

We clinked bottles. The taste was sweet—but the laughter was sweeter. For the first time since Sinai, this felt right.

That evening was our grand night at the Lido de Paris. We went up the Champs-Élysées, dodging traffic and crowds, the whole avenue lit up. As we walked by the Arc de Triomphe with the monument gleaming in the city lights, I had to tell myself that this was really happening.

We still had some of our bargain champagne, but it was of course impossible to bring it indoors. So, we stashed the bottles under some loose boards at a construction site and went in. We made our way to the Lido de Paris, and it welcomed us to a big theater.

The theater felt like a different dimension. It had round tables, low-hung lights and waiters in tuxedos. My eyes swept around the room and saw everyone holding their breath for the curtains to rise. The anticipation in this room was unlike anything I had seen before. Our champagne arrived at the table and for the next two hours, we were pulled into the music. The sounds, the costumes, the choreography, everything was made perfect.

We slipped out after the show, collected the extra champagne we'd stashed outside, and made the night our own. We ran through the streets of Paris shouting, laughing, and living too loud. For those hours, the city belonged to us.

Eventually, the others decided to head back to the hotel. But I hadn't booked a second night—money was tight, and I figured I could sleep rough if I had to. I told them, "Don't worry about me. I'll crash under the Arc and meet you in the morning." They thought I'd lost it, but in the end, they just shrugged. Before they left, I handed my cash stash to the lieutenant—better safe than sorry.

What I didn't expect was for Julio to stick around. "You're not sleeping out here alone," he said. Despite having a paid bed waiting, he dropped down beside me, and we finished off the last of the champagne, talking ourselves into a shallow sleep right there on a ledge under the arc.

By 4 a.m., the cold woke us. Even in July, Paris can turn chilly before sunrise. "Let's find someplace warmer," I said. We found a Métro entrance, slipped into the shadows, and stretched out on a bench. The station was closed, which bought us a little privacy. We'd barely settled in when we heard keys jingling.

The janitor gave us a nudge and warned that the city was waking up—traffic would start soon, and we couldn't stay on the bench much longer.

We made our way out of the hideout and headed back to the hotel as the sun started coming up. Inside, the curtains were still drawn and the room was half-dark. My friends were sprawled across the beds, shoes kicked off wherever they'd landed. I looked around and felt something was off—the lieutenant wasn't there. I nudged Ricardo, but he only grumbled and rolled over.

"He's probably somewhere, man. Let me sleep," he muttered.

"No," I whispered. "He's not here." That got everyone up.

We pieced the story together: the night before, on the way back, they'd heard music pouring from a building. The lieutenant, always up for a little chaos, talked the guys into checking it out. The party inside was being thrown by a group of skinheads. It started out friendly enough, but when our guys tried to leave, the mood snapped. Suddenly, nobody wanted to let them go.

They shoved their way out, sprinted down the stairs and out onto the street—but the lieutenant stuck around, yelling something at the skinheads from the sidewalk. That was the last anyone saw him.

Ricardo and I hit the streets. We retraced the group's steps, knocking on doors, asking questions at bars, even checking police stations. It took hours. Finally, at one station, an officer recognized Montero's description. "We found him last night," he said. "He was in very bad shape—sent to the military hospital."

When we got there, I hardly recognized him. His face was swollen, his head wrapped in bandages, stitches peeking out from under the gauze. Still, he managed a crooked smile when he saw us.

"Montero, what happened?" I asked, trying to keep my voice steady. He blinked at us. "The skinheads jumped me outside. Smashed bottles over my head. I don't know how I made it out." The doctor wanted him to stay, but Montero just waved him off, stubborn as always.

"I'm fine," he insisted, struggling to sit up.

As we packed to leave, something nagged at me. I forced myself to ask.

"Hey... what about the money I gave you last night?" I asked Montero. He looked at me for a second and said it plainly. "They took it." Just like that, the trip budget I'd saved so carefully was gone.

Later that day, Montero caught me in the hallway, a half-smile tugging at his mouth despite the mess of bruises on his face. "Relax," he said quietly, lowering his voice so only I could hear. I stared at him, waiting. He reached under his shirt and into the waist pouch he kept hidden beneath his pants and pulled out a familiar wad of bills. "I still have your money," he said, trying not to smile too much. "Just wanted to see your reaction."

I just stood there for a second, then laughed—more from relief than humor. It hit me all at once, and I had to steady myself. I almost hugged him right there in the hallway. For all the chaos, we were still on our feet—bruised, sure, but together. I took the money, shook my head, and followed him back down the hall.

The next day, we woke up cramped in our small hotel room, hungover and checking that we still had everything. I hadn't paid for another bed, so when I showed up at dawn, one of the guys slipped me in after the front desk went quiet, and I crashed wherever there was space. We packed our stuff, stashed our bags, and hit the town. It was our last day in Paris, and by sheer coincidence, it also happened to be the final day of the Tour de France.

Paris hummed with life. Even the Tour could take over the whole city. For Colombians, this tour was legendary and I could feel the national pride swelling in me. The Champs-Élysées flowed with people, the Arc de Triomphe rising above a thousand flags and a sea of excited faces. Horns blared, hands reached into the air, and voices shouted in a wild mix of languages.

We were an odd sight in the crowd, especially with Montero shuffling along, bandaged and swollen. He tried to hide under a scarf, but nothing could dull his spirit. He was right there with us, cracking jokes, cheering as the riders crossed the finish line. For a few minutes, the bruises and troubles faded; we were just young and alive, part of something big.

When the race ended, we grabbed our bags and headed for the station— next stop: Barcelona. The train ride was a blur of tired jokes, day-old bread, and the anticipation of somewhere new. Barcelona swept over us like a rush of life. The streets pulsed with color and energy; the buildings glowed in the late afternoon sun.

La Rambla was pure theater—human statues that jumped to life when a coin landed in their jar, fire-eaters, accordion players, and a man pretending to walk an invisible dog. We strolled, beers in hand, soaking in the madness and magic of it all.

Montero was falling behind. His wounds were catching up to him, making him finally admit that he needed a break. He stayed back at the hotel to rest while we went back out. I felt a twinge of guilt—this trip was supposed to be for all of us, but for him it had turned into recovery.

Barcelona was alive, but I found myself chasing a different kind of place. Cap d'Agde. Years earlier, one of my uncles had visited and told me about it: a naturist village on France's Mediterranean coast, a town built around the idea of living without clothes and without embarrassment. Even saying it out loud made it feel unreal. I kept bringing it up with the guys until it stopped being a joke and became the plan.

The next moment you know, we're on a train to Montpellier. We caught a bus to Agde and finished the journey in the back of a cab. When we finally reached Cap d'Agde, it was like stepping into another universe. The Mediterranean sparkled under a sky so blue it almost looked fake, and the whole village radiated a kind of wild openness I'd never seen anywhere else.

Right away, we learned the rules—or lack of them. "Clothes optional" here meant almost nobody wore anything, period. Everywhere you looked, people just… existed, with no self-consciousness at all. Naked families pushed shopping carts through the market. Couples strolled arm in arm down the main street, not a thread between them. Even the guy at the bank was completely nude, waiting in line as if nothing could possibly be more normal.

Cars stopped at intersections with drivers waving to friends on the sidewalks. The beach was the same: sunbathers, swimmers, couples—everyone at ease in their own skin.

We walked around the beach for a minute. Then I thought, why hold back when we came all this way? With confidence, I took off my clothes and stepped out onto the sands. At first, I looked and felt completely ridiculous but when Ricardo did the same, the embarrassment faded.

Wandering the beach like that felt unreal because it had happened so fast. One minute our clothes were in a pile, the next we were walking toward the water with nothing on, careful not to make eye contact like we were in a locker room. But no one reacted. No one pointed. No one laughed. People walked past with groceries and beach chairs like it was Tuesday. Kids built sandcastles. A couple argued about where to put the umbrella. A volleyball thumped back and forth behind us. After a few minutes the awkwardness didn't vanish, it just lost its power. We stopped covering ourselves, stopped acting, and kept walking.

The lieutenant, still wrapped in bruises and stitches, stayed up on the dunes with our backpacks, watching us like we were crazy. I couldn't blame him for being utterly confused, but I think even he should laugh at the sight of us running wild and free on that bizarre, beautiful stretch of coast.

Chapter 24

First Come, First Served

Leaving a place like Cap d'Agde wasn't easy. It felt like a secret world you stumbled into by accident. But we couldn't stay even if we wanted to. Overnight accommodations were for residents, and we were tourists. So we walked deeper into the dunes, found a hidden pocket of sand, and laid our sleeping bags down where no one would bother us.

As the sun dropped, we headed back toward the boardwalk. To our surprise, it was even more alive than before—bars and restaurants overflowing with people wearing the loosest definition of clothing. Some women wore nothing but a skirt. Others had a shirt hanging low from their waist like an afterthought. Plenty of people didn't bother with clothes at all. For us, it was a lot to take in.

At one point I stood in the center of a crowded bar watching a completely naked man shove his way through the bodies. No pouch. No pockets. No concern. The whole scene felt surreal, like we'd crossed into a parallel version of the world where the rules had been quietly suspended.

When the night thinned out, we returned to the beach after the lieutenant insisted on watching our gear. We turned our packs into pillows, dug our sleeping bags into the sand, and lay down under the open sky. The waves swallowed every other sound. The Mediterranean breeze cooled the salt on my skin. I slept under the stars with the calm certainty that this memory would stay.

Morning was a different story. The air was peaceful and cool, the waves steady and soothing, but my back complained like it had been insulted. Every muscle felt stiff from sleeping on sand. We didn't linger. It was time to move on.

Next: Interlaken, Switzerland.

We'd heard stories—two lakes, snow-capped Alps, clean streets, green mountain views. Just saying the name out loud made us sit up straighter. We shook the sand out of everything, packed fast, and made our way to the train station in Montpellier.

The ride took a while, with stops that gave us time to stretch, eat, and stare out the windows. As we approached Switzerland, the scenery changed in stages: flat fields to rolling hills, then hills folding into mountains. The world outside looked arranged on purpose.

We arrived in Interlaken at night. The town was quiet, the air cold and sharp. It was nothing like the warm coastal breeze we'd left behind. We called a hostel other travelers had mentioned, hoping for beds. No luck— every spot was taken. They told us the system was simple: show up early and claim it. First come, first served.

I could feel everyone's irritation start to rise. Julio and Alejandro scanned hotel lists near the station. While we walked through a tunnel beneath the tracks, I noticed people sleeping on cardboard, packed close together to stay out of the wind.

I looked at my friends. "I think I'll just crash here," I said, pointing to the tunnel.

They stared at me like I'd lost my mind. Alejandro asked if I was alright.

I shrugged. "Why not? I'm tired. I'm not wasting time or money chasing hotels that are probably full."

Julio gave a nervous laugh. "You're nuts, Botero. What if something happens?"

"Nothing's going to happen," I said, and sat down on a piece of cardboard. "Go look. I'll meet you in the morning."

They argued with me for a few minutes, then left.

I put on my Walkman. The music drowned out the station, the tunnel, the cold. After a while, the man beside me woke up and started talking. His

English wasn't good, but we managed. He'd lost his job and didn't have anywhere else to go. Sitting there next to him, I felt how thin the line was between "traveling" and "stuck." We were both passing through—just in different directions.

I fell asleep.

A few hours later, I woke to familiar voices. My friends were back, tired and irritated.

Julio dropped his jacket on the ground. "Couldn't find anything," he said. "Looks like we're staying here with you."

"This is insane," Alejandro muttered, "but at least we're not alone."

We spent the rest of the night in that tunnel. It wasn't comfortable. By morning we were cold, sore, and laughing the way you laugh when you have no better option. We went straight to the hostel and got there early enough to secure beds this time.

Inside, it was buzzing—travelers swapping tips, languages blending, backpacks everywhere. Outside, a giant chessboard drew a crowd of spectators who watched games like it was a sport.

Once we dropped our bags, we went out to explore. Interlaken delivered exactly what everyone had promised: streets clean and bright, lakes smooth as glass, mountains sharp and white in the distance. The air smelled like pine and cold water. Every view felt composed.

That's where I met Adrienne.

She was from New York—quick humor, calm confidence, the kind that makes you pay attention without trying. She invited us to join her for Swiss National Day that night—fireworks, drinks, crowds.

The celebration filled the park beside the hostel. I smelled grilled sausages in the air, heard music drifting over laughter. People moved in every direction, happy and unhurried.

At some point Adrienne and I drifted away from the noise and ended up at a playground—rusted swings creaking softly in the dark. Two near-strangers sitting on cold metal, talking and laughing like we'd known each other much longer than a few hours.

We kissed under the stars.

By morning, she had to leave. Greece was next for her. Before she went, she wrote her address in New York on a piece of paper, and then—like she was testing whether life could be that cinematic—she told me she'd be in Santorini on a specific day.

"You have to come there," she said.

I wasn't sure I could. I still had Cairo waiting, the base, the return. But I wrote the details down anyway.

We kissed one last time, and I watched her walk away. If I was going to see her again, it would have to happen before Cairo pulled me back into uniform and routine.

The last days in Interlaken were hiking—meadows full of wildflowers, cows scattered across hillsides, the Alps looking too perfect to trust. It reminded me of the Heidi stories I'd heard as a kid, the kind of landscapes that feel invented until you're standing inside them.

When it was time to leave, our group split. Alejandro and Julio wanted Berlin. Ricardo and Rogelio stayed with me. We had a different destination in mind: Elena.

Elena was the girl I'd met on a bus ride back to New York at the end of my exchange year. Before this trip, I'd told her I was coming. She sounded glad and said she'd meet me at the station in Zurich.

Of course we missed the train we were supposed to take. By the time we arrived, it was late. I stepped off and scanned the platform. She wasn't there. I pictured her waiting, checking the time, then leaving.

Ricardo and Rogelio came with me as we tried to find her building. The language barrier slowed everything down, but people were patient— pointing, walking us part of the way, repeating directions until we understood. One man stopped what he was doing and gave us a lift. I wasn't sure I would have done the same for strangers. It made me hopeful in a quiet way.

We reached her building—a basic three-story place with a glass door. I hesitated, then pressed the buzzer. I didn't know which apartment was hers, so we tried all three. No answer.

While we waited, an older couple approached. I asked if they knew Elena. The woman smiled. "Oh yes. She lives upstairs, but she isn't home right now.

You can wait in our apartment," she said. "Come have some bread and cheese. Leave her a note."

They brought us in like we belonged. Bread, cheese, hot chocolate—simple, warm, generous. Waiting didn't feel so heavy anymore.

Hours passed. Then a knock.

Elena walked in.

For a second, it felt like time folded and we were teenagers again. Then I noticed the man beside her—tall, blonde, comfortable near her. She introduced him, just his name. The way he stood close, the way he reached for her hand, told me what I needed to know.

My heart dipped, but I didn't let it spoil the moment. She hugged me. We reminisced about Minneapolis, laughed at old memories, and for stretches of time it felt easy. Still, the truth sat in the room with us.

Later she invited us upstairs. Her boyfriend, sensing what I wanted, disappeared into another room. Ricardo and Rogelio took the couch. Elena and I sat at the table and she pulled out an old photo album.

Flipping through those pictures, I felt happy and sad at the same time. I wanted to tell her how much she'd stayed with me, how long I'd waited for this moment—but the words didn't come. So I stayed present. I let it be what it was.

The night got late. Our conversation faded. Her boyfriend appeared and rested a hand on her shoulder.

I understood. I smiled, thanked her, and moved quickly to my friends' couch.

Elena hadn't changed. I had arrived with an expectation and left with closure. Not what I wanted—what I needed.

In the morning, we parted. She squeezed me tight and said, "Take care of yourself, Federico."

On the train, I watched the scenery blur and felt the loss shrink into something manageable. Not every wound needs to be reopened.

We rode in near silence on the way to Venice. The sun rose over fields and rooftops and no one talked much. My mind kept circling back to Elena—not because I still believed in the old spark, but because closure has its own weight.

Venice greeted us with warm, salty air and canals that felt impossible—like the world had built a city on water just to prove it could. We met up again with Alejandro, Julio, and Lieutenant Montero. Alejandro and Julio were already drunk and only wanted to party. I wasn't in the mood. Venice deserved better.

We agreed to meet later and split up.

Walking through Venice felt like stepping into a different century. We crossed the Rialto Bridge, stood before St. Mark's Basilica, and got lost in narrow streets that kept turning into small squares and quiet canals. When we returned, Alejandro and the others were gone. No note. Nothing. We kept moving without them.

Florence, Pisa, Rome—each one rushed and beautiful, each one leaving a quick imprint. Then Brindisi.

From there we caught a ship toward Greece. We didn't have a cabin—just a spot on the open deck, thanks to our Eurail passes. But that was the best part. Backpackers gathered up top. The roof turned into a party: laughter, music, bottles clinking, salt air pressing in from every side. The Mediterranean at night made you forget responsibility existed.

After a while, I wanted quiet. I carried my sleeping bag and backpack near one of the ship's big chimneys. The metal was warm, so I leaned into it like a heater and zipped myself in.

I woke up early feeling rested—until my back reminded me where I'd slept. I found my friends and they lost it immediately.

"Botero," one of them managed between laughs, "have you seen your face?"

I found a mirror and understood. The chimney had left soot across my skin. I looked like charcoal. I stared for a second, then laughed too. This trip kept turning embarrassment into story.

We arrived in Patras that afternoon and squeezed into an overcrowded train to Athens. Every aisle, every seat, every standing corner was packed. Babies cried. People sweated through their clothes. The air smelled like bodies and impatience.

Still, Athens made it worth it. The city felt alive on top of its own history—ruins scattered through modern streets, markets buzzing, stone and noise layered together.

Everyone else wanted souvenirs—small statues, painted bowls, anything to take home. I couldn't stop thinking about Santorini. Adrienne's note sat in my pocket like a dare. I had come too far to not try.

Rogelio was easy to convince. He liked a good adventure.

We made a plan: I'd tell the police I'd lost my wallet, get a report, and use that as our excuse to stay longer. The moment the words left my mouth, I knew it was wrong. But I was young, stubborn, and convinced that one more day could change everything.

The officer barely spoke English, but he understood enough. He typed a report, stamped it, and handed it to me. I folded it without reading and put it in my pocket.

That was our ticket.

We booked passage again.

Sometime later—after a crossing I refused to sleep through—we finally stepped onto Santorini.

White buildings clung to cliffs. Blue water below looked too bright to be real. The air smelled like sunscreen, olives, and salt. I walked through narrow streets scanning faces, half believing Adrienne might appear like the trip itself had been arranged around her.

By night, Rogelio and I returned to our hostel. Earlier we'd claimed two bunks on the roof, but when we climbed up, every bed was taken.

Bags and shoes marked territory. Two men in one of the bunks played cards and laughed in low voices.

"New here?" one of them asked. His Israeli accent was strong and he looked amused.

"No," I said, keeping my tone flat. "We had beds earlier. Now they're gone."

He laughed, set his cards down. "Rookies. If you want a bed, you leave something on it. Backpack, sleeping bag—anything. Nobody cares about reservations. First come, first served."

Rogelio rubbed his forehead. "So what now? Sleep on the floor?"

The other guy—messy ponytail, relaxed grin—said, "You can sleep under our beds if you want. There's space. Just watch out for scorpions."

"Scorpions?" Rogelio repeated, staring at me like all of this was my fault.

The first guy grinned wider. "Relax. I'm kidding. No scorpions. Maybe a lizard."

"Comforting," I said.

He slid a deck of cards toward us. "You want to play? Or do you need a moment to mourn your lost beds?"

I sat down cross-legged. "Deal me in. Maybe I'll win my bed back."

He laughed. "Dream on."

Rogelio leaned back already half asleep. "Just don't snore."

The ponytail guy winked. "No promises."

They were Avi and Daniel. Eventually they shifted their things and made room. Rogelio and I crawled under their bunks and rolled out our sleeping bags. It was tight. Springs hovered inches above my face. But it was a spot, and travel teaches you to be grateful for spots.

Above us, Avi and Daniel kept playing cards and talking in Hebrew.

After a while I called up, "So what brings you here?"

Avi leaned over the edge. "Backpacking through Greece before heading home. We heard Santorini is mandatory."

Daniel asked, "And you? What's your story?"

Rogelio groaned. "Don't get him started."

I laughed. "We were supposed to leave Greece yesterday. But there was a girl involved."

Avi's grin widened. "This is already good."

"So," I said, "we walked into a police station and I reported a lost wallet—complete lie—just to buy time."

Daniel burst out laughing. "You faked losing a wallet for a girl?"

"Pretty much."

Rogelio added, "The cop probably wrote: 'These idiots want to party.'"

Avi shook his head, still smiling. "You guys are insane. But that's how the best stories happen."

We talked for a long time—places, mistakes, favorite stops, the strange brotherhood of strangers who share food and advice for no reason other than they can. Eventually the rooftop quieted. The breeze off the water cooled everything down. The town below still made noise, but up there it felt like we'd climbed out of the world for a few hours.

Then, at six in the morning, church bells detonated the silence.

I shot upright and hit my head on the bunk above me.

"Ow," I groaned, rubbing my skull.

Rogelio started swearing in Spanish.

Avi and Daniel just laughed, completely used to it.

Daniel called down, "Welcome to Santorini!"

Still half-asleep, we crawled out. Avi and Daniel shared breakfast—bread and coffee from the market. Simple, perfect. The kind of kindness you remember longer than monuments.

For me, travel wasn't only the places. It was sitting with new people in a new location and turning inconvenience into laughter. Messy, inconsistent— sometimes flawless in exactly the wrong ways.

Later that day, Avi and Daniel offered to help us look for Adrienne while showing us parts of the island. With them, the search felt lighter. It wasn't desperation anymore. It was walking with a goal and letting luck decide what it wanted to give.

We left Santorini with the bells still ringing in our heads, the taste of coffee still on our tongues, and the quiet knowledge that not every chase ends the way you want it to—but it still changes you.

Then the pull back began—Cairo, the base, the uniform. I felt it in my chest as the ship cut forward and the islands fell behind us.

Chapter 25

The General's Call

By the time we rattled back into Cairo, Rogelio's passport was gone, vanished somewhere between checkpoints, another small disaster stacked on the trip's chaos. The delay pushed us late, shadows crawling up the walls as we rolled through the North Camp gates.

We had just gotten off the bus, and I could feel it: punishment was in the air, thick and close. We had perhaps gone too far this time. In Colombia, disappearing for more than four days was not "late." It was desertion, and it could land you in a military courtroom.

Morning came too fast, dread simmering in my gut before my eyes even opened. Something waited just outside the door, hungry. Rule-breaking had felt simple out there. Here, at base, every lie and excuse felt thin as paper. When the knock landed, hard and steady, it snapped through me. Not a private playing games. Something official. Serious.

I opened the door. Five MPs stood in the hall, boots planted, faces carved from stone. Their sergeant stepped forward, gaze pinned to mine. "Botero, you're coming with us."

The hallway stretched forever as I followed, boots echoing off the tiles. I didn't bother asking why—every step spelled it out. Rogelio would be somewhere close, probably getting the same treatment. Sure enough, when we reached the commander's office, there he was: standing rigid, shoulders tight, eyes darting, jaw set in a sheepish grin. We exchanged one quick look. No words—just the silent truth between men in trouble.

The colonel swept in, uniform immaculate, rage contained in every movement. He didn't sit, didn't relax. He set himself behind the desk, hands braced, eyes burning holes through us.

"Where were you?" His voice cracked the air, sharp as a rifle shot. "You know what this means?"

"Yes, sir," I answered, pulse thumping in my throat. Rogelio echoed me, quiet, almost defeated.

The colonel's glare could peel paint. "Unacceptable. In Colombia, you'd already be in a cell. But here, this is a multinational force. There are procedures, and I don't have the freedom to handle this the way I would back home. That doesn't save you. It just changes the way you'll pay for it."

I swallowed, felt the sweat on my palms. I knew I couldn't stay silent—not now. "Permission to speak, my colonel?" My voice stayed steady, but every nerve buzzed with fear.

"Speak," the colonel said, arms folded tight, gaze sharp as a blade. "But it better be good."

I drew a breath, heart pounding, and unspooled the story Rogelio and I had practiced, careful and smooth. "Sir, I lost my wallet in Athens. All my documents were gone. The Greek police said we should stay a few extra days, in case someone turned them in. Rogelio stuck with me. I didn't want to be stranded alone." I fished the paper from my pocket, the police report the Greeks had filed after we told them our story, complete with stamps and signatures.

The colonel snatched it, eyes scanning, face a wall. He flicked it back at me, barely glancing. "This is in Greek," he snapped. "I can't read a damn word."

Silence pressed in, thick as desert heat. He leaned in, knuckles white on the desk. "Don't think your cousin, the Minister of Defense, can get you out of this. He's already called. Told me to handle it my way." His mouth twisted. "You're both going back to the desert. Pack up. You'll finish your assignment in isolation, at a remote control center. Dismissed."

There was nothing left. Rogelio and I stood at attention, saluted, and slipped from the room—shoulders stiff, skin prickling with the brush of disaster. In the hallway, I glanced at him and muttered, "Well, at least we had a hell of a time."

He snorted, lips twitching into a crooked smile. "Worth it."

We packed our bags under the blank stare of the MPs. No privacy, no banter—just the clatter of boots and the cold snap of orders. A truck waited outside, dust swirling under the tires. They loaded us in, drove out, and the last familiar lights vanished behind us.

The new control center was lonelier than anything I'd known so far. Bare cots, rattling fans, old paint curling off cement walls. The days blurred into routine: static on the radio, sand in every crease, sun hammering down. At night, the wind kicked up, whistling through cracks, gritty with sand and thoughts I couldn't silence.

Then, suddenly, our orders came. My time in the desert did not end with a bang, but with the tired shuffle of boots on sand and a plane on the cracked runway. As we rose, the empty ground below the grey clouds receding, I felt a mix of relief and grief, pride and angst.

Sinai had been brutal, wild, unforgettable. I'd chased a dream to the edge and back again. Now, it was over.

When we landed in Bogotá, the high-altitude chill went straight into my lungs. Green hills ringed the city beyond the tarmac. Then routine took over: officers waiting, roll calls, duffels stacked, and a long line of tired soldiers queued for debrief.

I could think of nothing but home: a bed, momma cooking, family faces after so many months. I grabbed my duffel and headed to the door ready to board the bus that would take us to the base.

And then I saw two men, not out of the stream, impossibly neat and wearing pressed suits. Their eyes roamed the terminal with sharpness. I just glanced at them till they pushed their way through the crowd and stood directly before me.

"Private Botero?" the taller one asked, voice clipped and precise.

I stiffened. "Yes, that's me," I answered, nerves prickling.

"We're with General Botero's security detail. He's requested your presence immediately."

It caught me by total surprise. "The Minister of Defense?"

"Yes, sir. General Botero."

My father had always spoken about how close he and the General were, but the connection had never mattered, not here. He was a giant in uniform and politics. I was nobody, just a name in a file. I nodded. "That's correct."

"Come with us." He gestured toward a black car waiting at the curb, polished to a mirror's shine. I glanced back. A few of the guys had stopped walking, pretending not to stare. My heart hammered. The colonel had said the General had already called about Greece. *Was he summoning me to dress me down in person? To make sure I understood exactly what I'd risked?*

The drive through Bogotá felt unreal, skyscrapers and ancient trees blurred past the bodyguards as they sat in silence with their eyes on the city outside the glass. The car was a dizzying luxury after months of heat and grit. My brain churned, trying to think of any scenario.

We paused in front of a lofty apartment building in one of the wealthiest sections of the city, and the doorman opened without a word.

The city noise fell away into marble and soft light as we came inside. I had a knot in my stomach. I kept replaying the colonel's words and wondering what waited for me upstairs.

The guards took me through the silent corridors, with their steps ringing on smooth marble. The apartment opened to us; broad windows, indirect light, all selected and arranged with taste. There was power in the air, delicate and unobtrusive, worked into every line and surface.

I sat in the living room alone, staring at the art on the walls, my hands twisting on my knee. When the General walked in, the room filled with him: his uniform crisp, medals hung in neat rows, his lifetime of command in his bearing. As he moved nearer, however, the edge was smoothed. I could read in his eyes the touch of family underneath the authority.

"Federico," he greeted, hand outstretched, voice warm. "It's good to finally meet you."

"General," I managed, rising and gripping his hand. "It's an honor."

He gave a faint smile, waving me toward the couch. "No need for ceremony. We're family."

We sat. He got straight to the point, eyes fixed on mine. "I wanted this meeting because I've heard good things about you in Sinai," he said. "Your

185

colonel speaks highly of you as resourceful, steady, and a credit to Colombia."

Relief washed over me, tension easing from my shoulders. Whatever rumors had reached him, my mistakes hadn't made the list.

"Thank you, sir," I said. "It was an experience I'll never forget. I learned more than I thought possible."

He nodded, studying me, every word measured. "I want you to know—I never interfered in your deployment. You earned that assignment on your own. But once you were in Sinai, I made sure the Colonel knew we were family. Just in case you needed a steady hand."

His honesty cut through the formalities, leaving only the truth between us. It explained a lot—how I'd felt an invisible margin for error, a bit of room to breathe when things went sideways.

We talked for a long while. I kept my stories light—brotherhood, lessons learned, the strange camaraderie only found in the desert. He listened, sometimes nodding, sometimes sharing pieces from his own years in uniform: close calls, tough decisions, pride and regrets. The conversation drifted—part debrief, part family reunion, the weight of military rank fading as the evening stretched on.

"You've done well, Federico," the General said at last, his tone softer than before. "I'm proud of you. Keep going like this and you'll go far."

"Thank you, sir." My voice held steady, but inside, the pride nearly floored me.

Before I could leave, he turned to his bodyguards with a smile. "Show him the city. Take him out to eat somewhere nice. And make sure he gets back to base in one piece."

Chapter 26

On the Razor's Edge

When I got back to the base that night, the contrast landed fast: no privacy, bad food, and cold showers. I was back to the grind I'd left behind.

Within the week, I was cleared to go home. The road home ran through the city, then into the familiar rhythm of small towns and countryside. My heart thudded as we turned down the old street. In the yard, the house looked exactly as I remembered, washed by the late afternoon sun, geraniums blooming on the porch.

We pulled up in front of the garage and killed the engine. The front door was already open. Through the iron gate, I saw movement inside, and then my mother appeared in the doorway and stepped out.

When I stepped out, she crossed the yard quickly and held me tight. "Thank God," she said, and her voice broke. "You're home."

My father came next.

Inside, nothing had changed. The kitchen smelled like fresh arepas and dark coffee. The walls were covered with family photos.

My mother had gone out all the way and set the table with my favorite foods. My brother made fun of my "Sinai" tan. We both told stories and the months of sand and silence were swept away as we talked.

Laughter filled the house, plates scraped clean, music drifting in from the neighbors' window. For the first time in months, I let myself relax.

***

But even as I settled in, my mind kept drifting. I found myself pacing the hallway the next afternoon, thinking about her, my ex. The breakup had felt final, but in the quiet, I realized I still owed her honesty. Her letters had kept me going through some hard nights. She deserved to hear the truth, not just rumors or silence.

That evening, after hours of indecision, I finally picked up the phone. My hands shook as I dialed. When she answered, her voice was soft, cautious— familiar in a way that made my heart ache.

"Hey," I managed, suddenly awkward. "It's me. Federico."

A breath, then: "Federico... I didn't expect to hear from you."

I swallowed. "I know. I just, I'm back. And I was hoping we could talk. Just for a bit."

She hesitated, the line quiet except for her breath. "Okay. Pick me up at my parents' apartment, around seven?"

"Yeah. I'll be there."

I arrived early, my nerves restless. I sat in the car and watched the building's windows glow in the fading light, rehearsing what I would say. When she finally came out, my heart jumped. She looked exactly as I remembered, maybe even more beautiful.

She moved with the same quiet assurance I remembered. Her smile was very warm, and it did not conceal her wariness. Both of us tiptoed through a reunion neither of us had really prepared for.

"Hi," she said, slipping into the passenger seat, her voice low and steady.

"Hi," I said, working to keep my nerves out of my hands as I gripped the wheel.

We chose an old favorite, a small restaurant away from the city. Inside, the other tables faded into the background. Sitting across from her, the old habits came back: the way she ordered for both of us, the way her laugh reached me on my hardest days.

We got a chance to talk and share stories, even laugh about some memories we had in common. Still, there was something between us, something hanging and unspoken.

After dinner, we wandered to a nearby bar for drinks. There, the conversation danced around the real reason we'd come. Only later, parked in the car under the faded glow of the distant city lights, did she finally ask what we both knew had to be asked.

"Why did you really break up with me, Federico?" Her voice was gentle but sure. "Back then, when you ended it, you told me your feelings weren't as strong as mine." She held my eyes. "Was that the whole truth?"

I nodded, hands on the steering wheel. "Yes. That was the truth." I swallowed. "And I'm sorry for how I handled it. I left you with questions you didn't deserve."

She went quiet, eyes bright. "It hurt," she said. "I spent a lot of nights thinking it was my fault."

"It wasn't," I said. "Not even close."

"I wondered if I did something wrong. But hearing you say this now, honestly... it helps. I needed to hear it."

"I never wanted to hurt you," I said, the words thick in my throat. "Your letters kept me going out there. I should have said thank you—really thank you—for that. You reminded me what home felt like."

Her lips curled in a soft, almost sad smile. She looked down, hands twisting in her lap. "I'm glad. Even if we couldn't be together, I wanted you to be okay."

We sat there. Silence settled between us. It was uncomfortable and felt like a sense of closure, the final piece slipping into place.

"You deserve so much more than I could ever give," I said at last, voice low, meaning every word. "I hope you find someone who truly sees you, for the incredible person you are."

She smiled, small and genuine. "Thank you. And I hope you find whatever it is you're searching for, Federico."

We lingered there, talking softly about old times and futures we both knew would go separate ways. When I dropped her back at her parents' apartment, we hugged—a long, gentle embrace that was goodbye, and gratitude, and forgiveness, all at once.

Driving away, I felt lighter. She'd been a light in my life, and even now, that mattered. I hoped she would find happiness—I truly meant it.

***

Back at the base in Armenia, a new chapter began—one that couldn't have felt further from Sinai. My next assignment was with the Commander Company, a role that brought new responsibility and more risk than ever.

I was chosen as a personal bodyguard for the brigade commander's family, his wife and children. No uniforms now, just civilian clothes, blending in, alert to every shadow. Colombia was on edge: guerrillas, paramilitaries, organized crime. The families of senior officers were always at risk.

Every morning, I checked the jeep—mirrors, tires, undercarriage. My partner and I rode shotgun, holding our G3 rifles and 9mm pistols close, eyes scanning the streets for anything out of place. Getting the children to school and back safely became an exercise in vigilance. Every intersection felt like a test. Each stranger's glance, each slow-moving vehicle, each flicker in the rearview brought a spike of adrenaline.

The city around us bustled—street vendors, taxis, mothers with groceries—but beneath it all, tension simmered, never far from the surface. This wasn't peace. This was a fragile balance, one we guarded with our lives, every single day.

When the wife of the commander had to run any errands, be it to the doctor, groceries, a quick dash across town, I was there, following her car so close that her mirrors could not see me.

We merged into the traffic with my companion swiveling his eyes in the rearview mirror and the sidewalk, each stranger a question mark. There was more at stake than before. When I made a mistake, it was not only my life at stake, it was the commander's family that suffered.

It was an honor, but it came with a price. Around the base, I could feel the stares. To most soldiers, I was "Sinaco," the Sinai guy. They said it with a smirk or a sneer, half-joking, half-resentful. To them, Sinai sounded like a break, a vacation compared to the relentless grind in Colombia. "Must've had it easy out there," they'd mutter, not knowing or caring what it had really cost. I got it. Life here was harsh, and their bitterness was real. But Sinai had its own challenges. I kept my head down, focused on my work, refusing to rise to the bait.

Just when I thought I had the rhythm down, it all changed. Orders came sudden, clear. I was promoted again, now assigned as personal bodyguard to the Commander of Intelligence for the Brigade. The air tensed up. This was different. The stakes, the danger, everything dialed up.

The major I now guarded ran operations against drug cartels and guerrillas. He planned raids, mapped seizures, kicked the hornet's nest of organized crime every day. My job: protect him at all costs. I shadowed him into meetings, through alleys, sometimes on raids themselves, never knowing where we'd end up or what we'd face. We never took the same route twice. Civilian cars. Quick turns. Always watching for a tail, for a trap.

They issued me an MP5—a compact submachine gun, weighty and cold in my hands. I wore it like a second skin. Every time I felt its weight under my jacket, I remembered what was at stake. In this line of work, you never forgot—not for a second—how quickly things could go wrong.

There's one mission I can't shake, even now. We were rolling into Pereira, coming from Cartago, the four of us wedged into a battered civilian jeep—major in the passenger seat, my partner and I squeezed in back. Just outside the city, a motorcycle locked onto our tail. Two men, both in black, eyes hidden behind tinted visors. It's a classic move—motorcycles are fast, nimble, perfect for ambushes, the favorite tool of assassins and cartel hitmen.

Their movements set off every alarm. They didn't just follow. They stalked, weaving in and out of traffic, closing the gap every chance they got. My partner and I raised our MP5s, fingers tight on the triggers, nerves singing with adrenaline.

"Major, we've got a tail," I said, my voice low, eyes never leaving the side mirror.

The driver didn't wait for orders; he had mashed the pedal, tore through the snarl of city traffic, attempting to shake them. Horns blared as the jeep bounced down potholes all around us. My heart beat fast, the motorcycle remained on our bumper, no more than a few meters behind.

Everything narrowed; the street, the seconds, the pounding in my head. If they drew a weapon, it would be over in a heartbeat. My muscles burned from the tension, every instinct screaming to stay ready, to survive.

At the last moment, the driver cut sharply toward the San Mateo Battalion gate. The guards saw us coming, recognized the major's face, and yanked the barriers open just in time. We burst through. The motorcycle skidded to a stop, the riders hesitating only a moment before peeling away, lost in the chaos of city traffic.

We sat in the jeep, breathing hard, sweat soaking through our shirts. We'd made it. Barely. Another second, another move, and it could've gone the other way. That's how it was—every day, a razor's edge.

Looking back, those bodyguard days left a mark deeper than any deployment. The risk was constant, but so was the sense of mission. I learned to keep cool when the world caught fire, to trust my training, and my gut. The weight of the MP5 on my shoulder, the hours of nerves, the quick glances with my partner. Those things carved out a new shape inside me.

Sometimes, the isolation stung. The other soldiers saw me as different— envy, suspicion, distance I couldn't close. Still, I wore the job with pride. In plain clothes, weapon hidden but always ready, I wasn't just a soldier. I was a shield. Every morning, I carried that responsibility out the door, knowing someone's life might depend on me coming home with mine.

***

The days blurred into weeks. Each night I would hang my civilian jacket in the same spot, clean the MP5, and lie awake hearing the city outside the barracks. The bodyguard life had made me sharper, more cautious, more proud but so bone-weary it hurt to think about it. Nevertheless, pride remained with me: I served my duty and did my best to guard every life entrusted to me.

By the time my stint in the Commander Company wound down, I felt ready—maybe even hungry—to start life on the other side of the uniform. I thought I'd paid all my dues. But the army had one last test waiting, and nothing in the desert or city could have prepared me for it.

As the calendar crept toward discharge, my orders changed again. Along with the others preparing to get out, I was sent back to the same recruit company where it had all started. Gone were the days of shadowing commanders and scanning for threats. Here, rank didn't matter. Everyone wore the same plain fatigues, and whatever you had done before was treated like it didn't exist. It was supposed to be a holding place, a quiet transition before civilian life. For me, it turned into a crucible.

Trouble started even before we'd moved over. In the Commander Company, López had always watched me with resentment. He never got over missing out on Sinai—a chance I'd earned, and he hadn't. While I'd been away, he got shuffled to communications, and from the moment I returned, he made it his mission to undermine me.

Every minor mess became my fault. "Probably Private Botero," he'd say with a crooked grin, just loud enough for the officers to hear. I took the blame for things I'd never touched: extra push-ups, laps until my lungs burned, punishments stacked on top of each other. I tried to reason with him, but every conversation slipped off his smug, practiced indifference.

It took me back to the day I finally lost it on the school bully. I had promised myself I'd never do that again, but every day he pressed, every time he smiled in the barracks, the strain built.

Then one night, when I had been on duty a long time, and came back to our quarters, I walked toward my bed, and there he sat on the bunk by mine, with an expression of mocking innocence in his eyes. I was there with my toothbrush still wet and in my hand, and a loud pounding in my ears.

"You need to stop this. You need to stop now," I said, voice low but clear.

He looked up, shrugged. "Stop what? I'm not doing anything to you."

It was that smile, that mock innocence, which broke something in me. My hand was instinctively on his collar and I jerked him up and pushed him against the wall. Down went my fist, and fast, all the rage of days in it. He merely gaped, in surprise, with blood on his lip.

I shook him. "You better fight back. Come on. Fight back."

He stood frozen, eyes wide, blood at the corner of his mouth. I let him go, dropping him onto the thin mattress. "Enough," I said, voice tight and shaking. "No more."

The whole room had gone dead quiet, soldiers pressed back in their bunks, eyes darting from me to him. Nobody moved, nobody spoke. They all knew this had been building for weeks. Now that it was over, everyone waited for the fallout.

I slumped back onto my own bed, muscles trembling from the adrenaline. I tried to steady my breath, but it came ragged, mixed with a bitter taste of anger and relief.

The bullying didn't die—it festered. The soldier I'd confronted whispered poison to the newcomers, stoking their resentment. Sinai, my service, the scraps of respect I'd earned, they'd all become a mark. Every day, someone found a way to twist the knife.

One night, deep asleep on the bottom bunk, I woke to a thunderous crash and a sudden, icy shock. A metal trash can—huge, heavy, and full of water and garbage—tumbled down on top of me. The filth seeped through my clothes, cold and choking, thick with the stench of old food and rot. Laughter flickered in the dark, then vanished as the culprits melted into their beds, masks of innocence in place by the time I clawed the muck from my eyes.

It was humiliating, like a cruel joke, except this was my life, night after night.

Retaliation only fueled the fire. Every time I fought back, the officers cracked down harder. They stopped looking for the source, stopped caring about the truth. All they saw was a troublemaker, a stubborn problem they could punish into submission.

One night, they handed down a punishment so absurd it almost felt like a joke. Every hour, I was woken, handed a towel, a bar of soap, a broom. Boots with no laces. At the main gate, I balanced a plate of water on my head and stood rigid for fifteen minutes—just enough time to ache—before stumbling back to my bunk. Each hour, the ritual repeated. No rest. No dignity. Just humiliation, wrapped in routine.

After a few nights, something inside me snapped. When they came to shake me awake, I just stared up and said, "No. I'm not going." I didn't care about the consequences. I was done.

The officers didn't like that. They doubled down with heavier punishments and harsher labor. I hauled sacks of bricks on my shoulders, boots pulling blisters as I circled the square, with my lungs burning. I swung a machete through coffee fields, sweat stinging my eyes, every weed another tick off the calendar. I did it all, teeth gritted, counting the days until my sentence was finally over.

The army was not really a uniform or a line of commands. It was a crucible, hot, unrelenting, smashing all of the old certainties I had and making me do what I never thought I could do. The work every day challenged my boundaries, strained my tolerance, and pounded at whatever ego I had brought in with me when I first stepped through the gate. What I used to be was torn down and reconstructed, bit by agonizing bit. In retrospect, it is as though looking at a mosaic, pieces which at the time of breaking had no meaning, but they do now.

The demands were constant and unforgiving. Marching mile after mile under a sun that felt angry, my pack grinding raw stripes into my shoulders, legs threatening to give out. Some days, exhaustion blurred the edges between mind and body. But it wasn't just my muscles that ached. There was a pressure deeper inside, the constant sense that whatever I did, it would never be enough for the ones who held rank above me.

The abuse was out in the open. Yelled insults, punishments designed to break more than bad habits. It was about power, reminding us where we stood, day after day. I'd lie awake at night, sweat soaking the sheets, staring at the ceiling and wondering: *was this meant to strip me down or was there something new I was supposed to build out of the rubble?*

It wasn't all strength. For years I carried bitterness toward the men who made it harder than it had to be. Time gave me perspective, but it didn't excuse anything.

None of the abuse was justified. Still, I took something real from it: adaptability, control under pressure, and the ability to keep moving.

The army stripped me down. The rest was my choice.

Chapter 27

Forty-Five Minutes

Sunday mornings at home with my mother were always quiet and unhurried, with nothing urgent waiting in the day ahead. The sun slipped through my window, striping the floor and the tall mirror. My room was clean, everything in its order: the desk, the mirror, and downstairs the soft clink of my mother's ceramics as she worked. I was cross-legged on my bed, reading through a set of study notes a friend had lent me for my new insurance job, half-distracted by numbers and scripts, trying to concentrate.

The door creaked open. Eduardo, my youngest brother, slipped in. He wore nothing but swimming trunks—bare-chested, all skinny arms, hair still rumpled from sleep. He paused in front of the big mirror, eyeing his own reflection. A mischievous grin spread across his face. He puffed up, striking exaggerated bodybuilder poses, flexing what little muscle he had, making faces as if he were in a gym ad. He caught my eye in the glass and grinned wider, waiting for a reaction.

"One day, Federico," he said, voice light, almost dreamy, "I'm going to be just like you."

I snorted, shaking my head, barely looking up from the workbook. "Sure you will, champ. You've got the look already." I tried to keep my tone light, teasing, but half my mind was still chasing the numbers on the page.

Eduardo only laughed, bouncing on his heels, his energy crowding the room. "My friend's here! We're going to a friend's farm to play volleyball." He darted out, pausing long enough to lean in to the living room where Mom sat surrounded by ceramic art, pottery and paint brushes. He bent down, kissed her cheek, and she brushed his hair from his forehead, her smile soft and distracted as she told him to have fun.

The house felt filled with nothing but light and simple, ordinary hope.

Not long after, a car horn blared outside. I leaned over the window and saw Eduardo skip down the walk. A battered pickup stood idling by the curb, its wooden bed jammed with children, seven of them, perhaps more, laughing like they owned the street. Eduardo sprang up and smiled towards the house, and off they trundled down the street, their yells dying in the summer air.

The house went quiet.

Only forty-five minutes later, the phone rang. It was a jarring sound that broke the gentle hush. I heard my mother's voice from downstairs, cheerful at first, then confused, her words faltering. Then the panic hit—sharp, raw, a sound I'd never heard from her before.

"Federico!" she screamed. "Come here! I don't understand what they're saying!"

I tore down the stairs, my heart in my throat. My mother stood by the phone, face drained of color, tears streaking her cheeks. Estelita, our housekeeper since we were kids, hovered beside her, wringing her hands, silent with fear.

I took the phone, bracing myself. On the other end, a voice shook and stuttered, searching for words. "There's been an accident. Eduardo... he's in bad shape. They're taking him to the hospital."

For a moment, everything stopped. The words echoed in the stillness. My mind blanked, then snapped into motion.

I turned to my mom, gripping her shoulders. "Let's go. We need to get to the hospital. Now." My voice held steady, but inside I was unraveling.

We ran to my truck, my hands shaking as I crammed the key in the ignition. Heat shimmered off the asphalt. Red lights flashed through the blur of traffic, and the other cars streaked past in smears of color. My mother clutched her rosary and prayed in broken whispers. Estelita stayed behind, promising she would call my father, who lived closer to the hospital.

My dad had already been waiting at the emergency entrance, pacing as he looked at each car as it pulled in. We hurried into the building and met only confusion. The staff shook their heads. No one matching Eduardo's description had arrived. The waiting room was a noisy place, yet to us, the world had been reduced to one question, one desperate question: where was Eduardo?

A nurse caught my father's arm, voice gentle but urgent. "They might have taken him to the other clinic."

I nodded as my throat felt tight. "We'll meet you there." We rushed out, hearts pounding, the world reduced to headlights and the blur of streets flying by.

The second clinic's waiting room was chaos. Eduardo's friends huddled in a corner—some scratched, one limping, all pale and haunted, refusing to meet my eyes. I searched the room, desperate, but Eduardo wasn't there.

"Where is he?" I demanded, nearly shouting. My hands shook as I grabbed one of the boys by the shoulders.

He wouldn't look at me. Another friend, younger-looking, finally said in a trembling voice, "Federico... I know. Come with me."

A cold dread settled into my bones as I followed, my father at my side. My mother stayed behind, rooted to a plastic chair, fists pressed to her lips, her eyes wide with fear.

The boy led us down a corridor lined with harsh lights and doors that all looked the same. He stopped at one, tears streaming. He pushed it open and whispered, "He's gone, Federico. He's dead."

I stepped inside. My legs barely held me. A body lay on the table, covered by a thin white sheet. My dad hovered in the doorway, unable to cross the threshold. I forced myself forward, hands numb and shaking. I reached for the sheet, heart pounding so hard I thought it might burst.

I pulled it back. It was him. Eduardo. His face looked calm, almost peaceful, as if he might wake any second. But he wouldn't. He couldn't. The truth slammed into me—hard, merciless, final.

"No," I whispered, the word catching in my throat. "No, Eduardo... you can't be gone." Tears blinded me as I touched his cold hand, still hoping for warmth, for movement, for some miracle that wouldn't come.

Behind me, my father's shoulders heaved. He gasped, fighting for air, grief wringing every sound from his body. I'd never seen him crumble, not like this, not so helpless.

I made my way back to the waiting room, my body moving without thought. My mother looked up, searching my face. She saw the answer in my eyes before I could speak. She screamed, the sound ripping through the hospital.

"No! Not my Eduardo! Not my baby!" My mother's cry tore through the air, raw and unbearable. Estelita gathered her close, her own face crumpled in anguish. She had always felt like a second mother to me, and in that moment, I could see that she was not just comforting us, she was breaking too, loving Eduardo as if he were her own son and sharing in the weight of our loss. I sat beside my mother, arms around her as we wept. The world shrank to the weight of loss. Just an hour before, Eduardo had filled the house with laughter and hope. Now, all that remained was silence and the shape of what we'd lost.

***

We learned the details after. The truck had flown down a little country road when one of the tires had exploded, causing the driver to lose control. The truck swerved and flipped over. Most of the children hobbled off, bruised and shaken. But Eduardo landed wrong. His neck broke in the fall. He was gone before anyone could help.

I replayed it in my head again and again, searching for logic where there was none. Why him? Why wasn't he saved like the others? The anger ran deep—at fate, at God, at every unfair thing the world could throw. It made no sense. I clung to his hand at the hospital, stroked his hair, begged him to wake up.

"Why, Eduardo? Why?" I whispered, until my voice was raw and useless.

Burying him felt like burying part of our family's heart. At the cemetery, we held each other close—my mom, my older brother who traveled from Bogotá, my dad, Estelita—everyone hollowed out, holding on to what little we had left. Eduardo was the spark that filled our home with life. His laughter carried through every room, turning an ordinary house into a place that felt alive. Everyone loved him—he had no enemies, no bullies, only friends. He lived a beautiful, healthy teenage life, full of energy and joy. Remembering him now, it feels impossible that someone so good, so full of light, could be taken from us.

Strange stories floated in, thin threads of hope and mystery. The mother of one of his friends told us she'd heard Eduardo's acoustic guitar—the one he sometimes left at their house when the boys practiced there—playing by itself the night after he died. She said she could hear the strings, faint and indistinct but unmistakably real. No one had touched it. The guitar was still propped in the corner, gathering dust.

I could not know what to believe. Perhaps sorrow has deceptions. *Is it the mind that creates comfort when the pain is too clear?* Perhaps there was still a chance that Eduardo was somewhere out there, his soul winding in the music, seeking ways to tell us that he had not really gone away.

The guitars were no longer just instruments. They were a part of him, dreams locked in the middle of the song. I even picked up his electric guitar when I was in the house alone and fumbled with a couple of chords, half hoping I could feel him there, half thinking he would come around the door flexing, grinning, still trying to keep up with me.

We were all groping, trying to make sense of the loss, clutching at every story, every weird dream, every suggestion of his presence, anything to fill the gap. Even the young driver, who felt haunted by the guilt himself, told us that he dreamed that Eduardo came to him, calm and smiling. He said to him that it was all right, that he should not reproach himself.

Healing took time, and maybe never came. Mourning took a new form and never disappeared, and even as I write about my brother's death, it still brings tears to my eyes. I came to understand what loss entailed as time passed: that life is delicate, unruly, and unforeseeable. I also learned to carry Eduardo with me not only as a memory, but as a part of me. I take time to remember him, and sometimes I intentionally summon those memories, so his presence does not fade from my thoughts. Losing him taught me to value life, and it deepened my friendship with my oldest brother. We became very close, and we both strive to never let anything, not even material things, come between our bond. I no longer stand before that tall mirror where his smile once met me, and I no longer live in that house. Yet in my heart, that reflection still exists: Eduardo, forever young, forever hopeful, forever dreaming.

Chapter 28

The Silence After the Shot

How much drama can a person endure before something inside gives way? I used to think there was a limit, a breaking point that everyone eventually reached. For me, it felt different. Each wave of chaos seemed to harden me, like leather under the sun. Ordinary setbacks that should have hurt barely left a mark anymore. They faded into the background. However, beneath that calm, a quiet doubt lingered. *Was I building strength, or slowly hollowing myself out?*

When I got to Manizales that January to celebrate my 20th birthday, the city was alive in its own way. It sat high in the coffee region, the air carrying hints of roasted beans mixed with wood smoke from the houses. The streets were full of noise and color. Music poured out from the plazas, drums beating over shouts and cheers, and banners swayed above the crowds. At the heart of it all were the bullfights, a tradition people still held onto.

My grandfather had raised me on them back in Cali. Every year, he bought season passes and shared them with the entire family as we gathered at his house to celebrate the Christmas season. From then on, I tried to attend every bullfight I could. Manizales always had the best ones, and I liked to think the bulls there performed better, maybe because the cooler mountain temperature was closer to the climate where they had been raised. After one of the matches, I followed tradition and joined the *fiestas de remate*, a time to drink, dance, and celebrate until every bar and cantina finally closed. My friends and I, three guys and three girls, pushed through the crowd until the beat of a nightclub pulled us inside. The room was heat and rhythm.

The smell of rum and aguardiente mixed with perfume, and the floor shook with the beat. The DJ played American pop, the kind that made you dance without the effort required by salsa or merengue. The girls lined up in front of us, their hips moving under the lights, mouths close to each other's ears, trading quick comments over the music. For a while, the outside world felt far away.

Then the night split apart.

An arm pressed down on my shoulder, firm and deliberate. I turned and found myself staring at the dark mouth of a revolver.

The first shot cracked, and sound ripped through the room, then two more. Bullets cut between my girlfriend and the girl beside her. The club fell into chaos. My ears rang, my body froze, and then the flood came. People screamed, shoved, and fought to reach the exits. In seconds, joy had collapsed into terror.

I couldn't move.

The man with the gun dropped his arm and backed away, disappearing into the mess around us. I never caught his face, only his back fading into the crowd as people screamed. The music stopped. All I heard were shouts, chairs dragging, and the heavy push of bodies fighting for the exit.

Two figures lay on the dance floor, crumpled and still. My friends pulled at my arm, their voices sharp with fear, urging me to run.

"Come on, let's go!" one of them shouted, eyes wide and wet.

"Leave it, man, just leave it!" another cried.

Something in me refused. Call it stubbornness, call it defiance. My feet carried me back inside.

The club had fallen into an eerie silence. Lights flickered across spilled drinks, broken glass, and chairs knocked on their sides. My jacket still hung on the back of a chair, just a few feet from the fallen couple.

The woman still breathed. Her chest lifted in short breaths, each one weaker than the last. Blood ran from the wound on her throat and spread across the floor. Her hand moved a little, like she was reaching out. I stood there, not moving. I wanted to help, but I had no idea what to do.

Then she stopped.

I took my jacket. Its fabric was damp and cold from the chaos around it, and turned. The man beside her was already gone, his eyes fixed on the ceiling with nothing left behind them.

Outside, the night air slapped me into my senses. My friends huddled on the curb, faces pale, bodies trembling. One of the girls pressed her hands to her face, crying into the hollow of her palms. They looked at me as though I had returned from somewhere they couldn't follow.

"What happened in there?" one of them asked.

I slid my jacket on and walked past without a word.

That night stayed with me, though not in the way I expected. No nightmares. No tears. No restless hours staring at the ceiling. Instead, it burrowed into me, quiet but heavy. It stirred old memories I thought were buried: the man shot by police when I was a boy, the weight of violence I had seen again and again.

And through it all, I hadn't cried. I hadn't screamed. I hadn't even panicked like everyone else.

That silence inside me frightened me most of all.

Was this resilience, or was I simply growing numb?

I wanted to believe it was strength. I wanted to think that staying steady in those moments, pulling myself back together while everything else collapsed, proved I could survive anything. But another thought whispered at the edges. Maybe I was not strong at all. Maybe I was just laying bricks around my feelings, sealing them away so tightly that one day I might not feel anything at all.

When I left the club that night, the jacket felt heavy on my shoulders. It had become a reminder that even in the middle of all that chaos, I had something to hold on to.

I still see the woman's last breaths, the man's empty stare, the flash of the revolver. They carved themselves into me, sharp and permanent. But I also remember how I walked out of that place calm, my steps even, my face steady. I would not let it break me.

In the days that followed, I kept replaying that night, not because I wanted to, but because it had become a part of me. I realized that what I carried out of that club wasn't just my jacket. It was the weight of knowing how fragile the line between life and death really is, how quickly music can turn to silence, how suddenly the air can shift from laughter to screams.

I had faced death before, in the army, in the streets, but this was different. There was no enemy, no mission, no reason. Just chaos. Just someone's finger on a trigger and lives cut short. I thought about the woman's hand, barely moving, as if she was asking the world to stop, just for a second, so she could hold on a little longer. No one could give her that second. Not even me.

And yet, I walked out. I survived.

In that survival, I found a hard truth. Life was never going to give me certainty, and death would always be closer than I wanted it to be. I could choose to fear it, or I could choose to keep walking, to keep building, to keep living like every moment mattered.

That night did not make me fearless, but it made me deliberate. It taught me that strength is not loud; sometimes it is quiet, measured, almost invisible. It is the choice to put one foot in front of the other, even when your soul wants to collapse. It is refusing to let fear own you.

I have often wondered if that silence inside me was numbness. Maybe it was. But maybe it was also the beginning of a decision, a decision to carry what I had seen without letting it crush me. To remember, not to be haunted. To keep my heart alive, even if it meant rebuilding it brick by brick.

Walking away that night was not weakness. It was survival. And survival, I came to learn, is not about escaping death, it is about daring to keep living.

Chapter 29

The Fruit Business

After leaving the army, I was determined to build a civilian life with structure, something that could anchor me as I started over. So when the opportunity came to study at the university in Pereira, I didn't hesitate. My hometown offered a new rhythm and enough work to keep me focused.

Life turned hectic the moment I started studying industrial engineering at the Universidad Tecnológica de Pereira, UTP. My mornings began before sunrise. By four-thirty, I was already out on the road, waiting by the highway for the milkman's jeep. He let me ride to the farm, squeezed between tin cans that clinked with every bump. The cold air woke me up, and the sound of those cans became the first rhythm of my day.

The work at the farm was tiring, but it gave me energy. I oversaw the weighing and sale of the milk, making sure everything was fair and exact. That supervision mattered because I'd discovered that some workers were stealing milk, moving it through the rail-side settlement by the Cauca River and selling it to the community that lived along the tracks, leaving very little for us to sell to the milkman.

At the same time, I had taken on a pineapple plantation. My partner and I planted 150,000 plants, far too many for someone my age, but I was eager. I didn't know much, but she was always encouraging.

"You'll learn," she told me one morning, wiping dirt from her hands as we walked the rows. "You work harder than anyone I've seen. That's enough."

I shook my head. "I don't even trust myself half the time."

"Then borrow mine," she said.

She believed in me more than I believed in myself. That carried me.

Once the milk was loaded, the jeep brought me back to town. By six-thirty I was already in class, the smell of the farm still on me. After lectures, I hurried to my bank job and stayed until nine at night. Homework came late, sleep came short, and then the cycle started again. I told myself it was worth it, each day laying another brick in my future.

Things shifted when a friend offered me a job at a clothing factory. They needed someone with English, and my year in Wisconsin and experience in the MFO gave me the edge. The U.S. deal the factory was chasing never came through, but for me, the job mattered. It pushed me to leave the program and transfer to night school for industrial economics while I worked full-time. It felt risky, but I saw it as a practical investment. By the time I graduated, I wouldn't just have a degree. I would have years of real factory experience, processes, deadlines, and accountability already behind me.

I was hired as warehouse and dispatch manager, and within days we started inventory. That weekend the town hosted a fair, and the factory had a stand to sell overstock and discontinued items.

I assumed we'd pull product the right way, with records and controls. Instead, the owner went to the warehouse behind my back. When he found it locked, he climbed the fence and broke in, grabbing armfuls of clothing to sell at the stand. In one move he undermined the inventory work and showed everyone that "security" was just a suggestion.

The next Monday I confronted him. He didn't appreciate being challenged. He fired me.

I didn't have many choices. My father's old Fiat had been sitting in a shop, broken and forgotten. I pulled together enough money, paid the bill, and got it running again. It wasn't the right car for farm work, so I sold it and bought a pickup. That truck changed everything.

My uncle asked me to transport his papayas to the market, and in return, he'd cover the fuel. At first it seemed small, but I saw the chance to make more. I started buying the papayas myself and selling them in other towns for better prices. Soon I wasn't just hauling papayas. Oranges, limes, tangerines, and watermelons filled the truck as well.

The business grew quickly. Farmers let me buy on credit, trusting I'd pay once the produce sold. They were financing me, whether they realized it or not. Every peso I made went back into buying more, and with each trip, the work grew larger.

As my work grew, I rented a large house and turned it into a warehouse. There, we sorted, stored, and packed fruit for delivery. My days ran together, hauling produce, making deals, and trying to keep up with classes at night. It was exhausting, but it also made me feel alive. I was building something real, one step at a time.

One afternoon the buyer from a grocery store, one of my best clients and a friend, came by unannounced. No call, no warning. The warehouse door was open, and baskets of fruit rose in high towers, filling the space with the sweet, sharp smell of ripeness. He stepped in, nodded to the guys working, and walked straight between the stacks. He didn't ask permission or wait to be guided. Outside of work, he had invited me on a few fishing trips. We weren't just buyer and supplier. We were building a trusting and lasting business relationship.

His eyes moved methodically over the baskets until they stopped. First-grade granadillas, set apart and labeled for Bogotá. He walked closer, tapped one crate with his knuckle, and looked at me.

"And these?"

"For another customer," I said.

Something shifted in his face. Not anger. Not drama. Just a tightening around the mouth, the kind that comes when a decision has already been made. He nodded once, turned, and walked out without buying.

After that, the rhythm of my week changed. His driver didn't show up. The usual call never came. I kept a space in the warehouse for his order anyway, telling myself he'd come back. In my mind, he didn't have many options. I was the only steady granadilla provider in town, and sooner or later he would need me again.

When I finally got him on the phone, he kept it short.

"We're covered," he said. "I already have someone else."

I stood there with the phone in my hand, then looked at the crates stacked around me. From then on, I never played games with grades or pricing. If fruit was grade B, I called it grade B and priced it that way. If my best product was going somewhere else, I said so up front. Trust was harder to build than a warehouse full of fruit, and far easier to lose.

But fixing that didn't fix everything. At the height of it, I made the mistake of growing arrogant. I expanded too quickly, chasing every opportunity without the discipline that had gotten me this far. My uncle introduced me to a granadilla farmers' association, and I tried to control the flow of the market without knowing how it truly worked. I paid farmers in advance, trusting their word, only to watch them sell to competitors. The association fought back with a price war. My finances were a mess. I had no system, only scattered notes and guesses. What I thought was growth was, in truth, decline.

***

The farm carried its own struggles. Theft, sabotage, and dishonesty seemed to follow me everywhere. The worst moment came with my pineapple plantation. I arrived one morning to find the field ruined. The plants were crushed and burned. The leaves lay black and brittle. The field looked beyond saving, and even the engineer advised me it might be too risky to invest another peso into it.

But I wasn't ready to give up. I decided to try a fertilizer designed for coffee trees, one known for excellent results, even though it had never been tested on pineapple plants. It was a leap of faith. Not only did the plants survive, they thrived. They grew taller than any pineapples I had ever seen, so vigorous and heavy with life that we eventually had to brace them to keep them from tipping over.

As if that wasn't enough, whispers of a possible kidnapping reached me at the farm. These weren't rumors I could dismiss. Neighbors repeated them, and even workers hinted that strangers had been asking questions about me. Fear settled into the days, heavy as the heat, and followed me through nights when I barely slept.

The pressure finally broke one morning. I found more deliberate destruction in the pineapple fields. My anger boiled over, and I called the workers together. They gathered around, machetes hanging from their belts, tools of their labor but also quiet reminders of the power they held. I stepped into the middle, grabbed the supervisor's machete straight from his waist, and closed my hand around it.

I stood there with the supervisor's machete heavy in my hand. Their eyes followed me, some hard, some uncertain. My heart pounded, but my voice came out steady.

"If you have a problem with me," I said, lifting the blade just enough to show I meant it, "let's settle it here. Right now. Do not take it out on the farm. Do not destroy what we have built. If you think you can challenge me, step forward. Bring your machete and face me like a man."

No one moved. The silence pressed against us, louder than shouting.

One of the workers muttered, "We don't want trouble, patrón." His voice cracked, and he kept his eyes low.

"Then stop making it," I answered. "This land feeds us all. If you sabotage it, you're not only hurting me. You're hurting your own families."

The men shifted uneasily. Some exchanged glances, testing each other, but no one dared to step out. I felt their fear, but also their guilt.

I lowered the machete slowly. "You want to see if I will break? I will not. You want to see if I will give up this farm? Never. But if anyone here betrays me again, he will not stand among the rest. He will be gone."

The supervisor's eyes met mine, and in them I saw the truth. He had been part of it.

"You are finished," I told him. "Leave your tools. You do not work here anymore."

His jaw tightened, but he said nothing. He turned and walked away, and the others parted to let him go. I dismissed a few more men whose loyalty I no longer trusted. The rest I kept, the ones who could still look me in the eye.

I continued to invest in the field, refusing to give up on it. After two and a half years of hard work, when harvest finally came, the crop was enough to repay the loans. We did not make a profit, but it was still a victory, not just for me, but for the trust others had placed in me. More than anything, I was grateful to save my partner, who had believed in me blindly; disappointing her would have been the greatest loss of all.

That experience taught me that perseverance is never wasted, and that faith can carry you when logic says to stop. What we call instinct is often God's voice—quiet, persistent, and right. Sometimes victory isn't profit. It's honoring the people who believed in you—and walking away with your integrity intact.

Chapter 30

The Machine

I lived inside a machine I built with my own hands—fast, noisy, and hungry.

The fruit business didn't run on inspiration. It ran on timing. On volume. On sleeplessness. When it was working, it felt unstoppable. I was sending trucks to Bogotá at night—five, sometimes six tons—so the load could arrive before dawn and still taste fresh when it hit Corabastos, Bogotá's massive wholesale market." Night shipping wasn't a preference; it was strategy. In that market, arriving early meant you were alive. Arriving late meant you were discounted into irrelevance.

In Pereira, my world revolved around Mercasa, the city's wholesale produce market. I rented two warehouses there, and the place felt like a living organism—competition and camaraderie breathing in the same air. You could see your friends and your rivals loading their trucks side by side, all of us chasing the same thing: speed, quality, and a price that didn't punish you for being honest.

The selection process lasted all day. It was exhaustive and almost sacred—opening samples, checking color, scent, firmness, bruising, ripeness. Then the loading began, and loading had its own laws. Some nights we were still stacking crates at ten. Sometimes eleven. Sometimes midnight. I loved it. The fatigue didn't bother me because it didn't feel like work. It felt like purpose.

I also opened two neighborhood produce stores. The operation grew until money moved through my hands like water. Checks from grocery stores, stacks of cash, small debts, big promises. Each day I deposited what needed to be deposited and withdrew what needed to stay liquid, because cash was king. Cash gave you leverage. Cash got you fruit before anyone else even knew it existed.

I dealt with brokers—fruit seekers—men who moved between farms and markets like hunters. They'd bring samples from growers: a few fruits, a smell, a texture, a color. I'd decide if it was real, ask how much they had, and when it would be ready. Then I'd pull out cash and hand it over as earnest money, and they'd disappear back into the countryside. A few days later a truck would arrive like a promise made physical.

But the machine demanded attention at all hours. That was the problem: I was trying to build an adult life while still living a student life, and the two didn't respect each other.

Most nights my workers were loading the truck while I was in class, with no way of communicating once the night started. I couldn't call. I couldn't correct. I couldn't manage in real time. So my instructions had to be crystal clear—counts, standards, packing order—and then I had to do the hardest thing for a control-minded young man: trust.

One night, during one of the most boring classes I had ever been forced to sit through—history of music, one of those required humanities courses— I felt the machine pulling at me from a distance. The professor had a way of trying to add weight to his subject by being difficult, as if resistance itself proved importance. He played strange sounds and spoke with the confidence of a man certain that everyone else was wrong for not enjoying them.

I sat there listening and thinking about Mercasa—about crates, workers, timing, risk. I could feel the business moving without me. I could feel money on the table and decisions happening in my absence. Something inside me snapped, not loudly, but cleanly.

I stood up and grabbed my things.

The professor stopped me. "Where are you going?"

"I'm leaving," I said.

"You can't leave."

"Yes, I can," I told him. "And I'm never coming back."

I didn't wave goodbye. I didn't justify myself. I walked out, got into my pickup, and drove toward Mercasa like a man running back into his own blood.

The truck was still being loaded. The air was alive with the familiar chaos—voices baskets passing hand to hand, the scent of fruit, sweat and diesel. That disorder didn't feel like disorder to me. It felt like life.

I didn't feel guilty. I wasn't afraid of failing. I was afraid of setting myself up for failure—of staying trapped in something I couldn't respect, something that drained my will. I wasn't afraid of failing. I was afraid of choosing failure. What I couldn't accept was choosing a path that I knew would slowly break me. Staying in something you don't love is like staying in a relationship without love: you can call it commitment, but it's really just delayed collapse.

So I kept moving.

My nights belonged to loading. My mornings belonged to opening the warehouses for local sales—street vendors, small markets, neighborhood stores. Twice a week I came back at three in the morning. The rest of the week I came back at six. Sleep became negotiable. I didn't mind. I liked the pace. I liked the pressure. I liked being needed.

But the fruit business is volatile. It can turn in a day.

Sometimes it felt like the stock market. You'd buy a full load of limes, confident in the price, and then several trucks would roll into the market from another region and the price would collapse before you could even understand what had happened. You could lose everything so fast it felt like you lost your last name.

Still, the worst risk wasn't price fluctuation.

The worst risk was people.

Two of my biggest customers in Bogotá stopped paying. Not because they were broke. Because they were smart enough to turn informality into a weapon. Under one excuse or another, they insisted I send another truckload so they could "recover" money they claimed they had lost. It was a trap disguised as a plan. And because we operated on trust and habit—no signed documents, no real enforcement—my leverage was thin.

I traveled to Bogotá to talk face to face. I wanted a solution. They agreed to partial payments and new terms, but every agreement came with the same demand: "Send one more load."

They didn't honor any of it.

A friend suggested a different approach—show up with someone who could make them take me seriously. I was young, proud, and tired of being played, and I agreed. We traveled by bus and reached Corabastos at three in the morning. The market was already alive—lights harsh and cold, trucks reversing, men shouting, the air thick with produce and ambition. We kept our distance, watching for hours, because I didn't want him to see us and disappear.

He never showed. His mother, who usually worked with him, didn't show either. Someone had warned them.

So we went to their apartment.

I announced myself alone at the entrance. I wasn't looking for violence. I was looking for repayment. But the moment the door opened, things accelerated beyond what I had planned. Fear moves faster than reason. Suspicion moves faster than mercy. In seconds, a situation that should have been a conversation became something else—something sharp and irreversible.

For a brief moment, everyone involved was trapped inside a truth no one wants to admit until it's too late: when weapons enter a room, pride becomes meaningless. One wrong movement and the story ends in blood.

I talked until the air cooled. Until everyone lowered what they were holding. Until we could sit and speak like humans again. We negotiated new terms.

He never paid.

And I never went back.

That was the lesson: you can build a machine, but one cracked gear can destroy the whole system. Two major customers defaulting didn't just cost me profit—it hit my cash flow, my stability, my ability to protect the people depending on me. Bills don't care about your pride. Employees don't eat promises. Stores don't stay open on hope.

The stress started digging into me, and stress has a way of searching your soul for old habits like a thief checks doors for unlocked ones.

Around that time, I was in love. Ana. I loved her, truly. One day I was counting cash at my mother's dining table, running quick messy numbers in my head, and I decided I was ready to start my own family. The next day I proposed. She said yes. Six months later—twenty-one years old—we were married.

I rented a beautiful apartment and filled it with good furniture and top electronics. Life looked great. It looked like I had won early.

But a life can look stable while the structure is already cracking.

The business pressure didn't ease. And when it started bleeding, everything felt louder—debts, demands, the feeling of being cornered by consequences. Ana didn't want to continue law school. I didn't want her drifting, because drifting is how people disappear from themselves. I told her if she wasn't going to study, she needed to help me, at least for a season.

She tried.

I brought her to one of the neighborhood markets. I gave her simple work—sorting produce, learning the rhythm, becoming part of the reality I lived in. On the third day, when I came back to pick her up, I found her still working, tears on her face, tissues on the floor. She looked up and said, quietly, "I want to go back to law school."

"Excellent," I told her, because I meant it. That was always how I saw her. A lawyer. Not trapped in a produce market under fluorescent lights.

She said she needed time away first—she wanted to visit her sister in Bogotá. I agreed. I told myself she would come back renewed, focused, ready.

But the days stretched. Communication thinned. Silence grew legs.

Meanwhile, the stress kept drilling into me, and I started slipping—quietly, the way relapses begin. Not dramatically. Not constantly. Just enough to take the edge off. Just enough to convince myself I was still in control.

Then one night I called her sister, and Ana finally answered. She was with friends. Her voice carried something that wasn't anger and wasn't love—

detachment. In that tone I heard what my mind didn't want to accept: she wasn't coming back the way I needed her to.

My world collapsed in a single moment.

That night I drank alone for the first time. Alone—not in celebration, not with laughter—just me and a bottle and the kind of pain that turns a man into his worst version. I called my mother from the rotary phone, crying like I was too young to be married, too young to be responsible for so much loss. Anger rose with the grief, and I broke what was in reach. Glass. Shelves. The phone itself—until only the frame remained.

My mother came. She cleaned the mess with me. She saved me from myself without making me feel smaller than I already did.

Ana returned after I demanded it. We tried to fix things. For months we lived through small battles—trust, suspicion, exhaustion, resentment. And then the marriage ended the way some endings happen: not with one explosion, but with slow surrender.

When it was over, I realized something that hurt to admit. I had built a life that looked impressive, but it was built on speed, informality, and my refusal to slow down long enough to see what was breaking under me.

The divorce didn't just end a marriage. It ended an era.

That's when I left everything behind.

And with nothing left to prove in Pereira—only scars and lessons—I turned toward Popayán, where another test was waiting.

Chapter 31

Popayán Beginnings

I can still see my mother's office. Light over the table, dust hanging in the air. I rolled a pen in my hand, working up the nerve. My mind wasn't spinning with doubt. It was lit with certainty. I had always been like that. I acted first. I adjusted later if I had to. Standing still was the only thing that scared me.

Finally, I lifted my head. "Mom," I said, steady but charged, "I am going to college."

She looked up from her papers. Her brow lifted and a slow smile pulled at her mouth. "That is great. Where?"

"Popayán," I told her. I could already see the cobblestone streets and the white walls. "I want to study civil engineering."

Her smile widened. "Popayán, huh. Beautiful city."

I nodded, the weight settling in. This wasn't only about a degree. It was about leaving—the farm, the business, the trees I had planted with my own hands. All of it. And I still had to tell Dad. That conversation was already playing in my head. I knew it wouldn't be easy.

***

That evening I sat across from my father on the farm. The smell of soil and the quiet rustle of trees hung between us. I explained my plan. I would hand over the thousand trees I had planted, and in return he would help pay for my tuition. It was fair, I told him. Popayán was not as expensive as other cities, and this way the farm would not lose what I had already built.

He leaned back in his chair and studied me for a long moment. Then he nodded once. "All right," he said. Nothing more, just that. Relief poured through me. One step closer.

But life never let things stay simple. After contacting the university to apply, the woman at the admissions office informed me that the civil engineering program was full. The words struck me with a shock, though this did not last long. Giving up was not an option.

"What about other programs?" I asked.

There was a pause, the sound of papers shuffling. "There is another university," she said. "It is private. They still have openings in mining engineering."

"Mining engineering?" I repeated. The words felt heavy in my mouth. It was not what I had planned, but it was something. "Can I transfer later to civil engineering?"

"Yes," she answered. "Many of the classes overlap."

That was enough for me. "I will contact that school," I said. The determination came back to life in me, sharper than before.

It was like shedding part of my personality to sell my pickup truck and close my fruit business. It was difficult, but it had to be.

***

The road to Popayán climbed through the land as it changed, green hills unfolding beneath a high, clear sky. The air grew thin, alive with the slow breath of the mountains.

Then the city began to show itself. The whitewashed structures shone in the sunlight, their colonial fronts calm and proud. There were narrow cobblestone streets that wove like veins through the center of it. Every stone was askew. Every step carried centuries. Popayán's beauty was quiet but striking. The houses were old. Churches too, with thick doors, wood dark with age. Iron on the balconies. Archways left open.

The square was full. Vendors shouting. Smell of corn roasting. Students walking fast, laughing. The Cathedral stood high. In its shadow, old men sat talking. Pigeons moved around their feet.

We came to the house. I stopped. White walls, thick and rough. Aged tile roof, sloping heavy. The door creaked when it opened.

Inside, the air was cool—shade breathing over stone. Pots of ferns and flowers leaned toward the light, their leaves whispering in the quiet. Outside the doorway, a small rose garden struggled on, half-forgotten, with a few cracked eggshells scattered in the soil for strength. The landlady appeared, moving slowly but with presence—an older woman with kind eyes and a calm that seemed to belong to the house itself. She carried the quiet grace of the city: timeworn, warm, and quietly alive. She lived with five other students. We came from different worlds, but soon we were eating together, studying together, becoming a strange kind of family under her care.

My room was simple: a bed, a small table, and a window with wooden shutters that opened onto the quiet inner corridor and the little rose garden beyond. I set my suitcase down. The sound echoed off the old walls. I waited a moment and drew a breath in the silence. This was it, a new chapter.

The following day I attended the university. It was located outside the city, approximately half an hour away, and the road was winding through the eucalyptus trees and the open fields. The sky felt bigger out there. When the campus finally appeared, I just stopped. Red clay roofs stood out against the dark green of the pines. The verandas stretched wide, looking over the hills. It didn't seem built so much as grown out of the ground itself.

I stayed there for a long moment, staring. The first sight of it had left me without words. Now, standing at the gates, I felt it pulling me in. The city had welcomed me. The house gave me a place to rest. But this—this was the reason I had come.

When I stepped onto the grounds, I felt it right away. Students stood in groups. Some laughed loud, others spoke low and serious. The walkways were lined with trees in bloom. Red, yellow, sudden bursts of color. Birds sang from above. Their calls mixed with the faint sound of a lecture drifting out of an open classroom.

I glanced at my schedule, heart racing just enough to remind me that this was real, and walked toward my first class. Geology. The lecture hall was small, the kind where you could see every face. I slipped into a seat, pulled out my notebook, and felt something anchor inside me. This was where I belonged.

Chapter 32

Thresholds

I moved fast. First semester I was picked to lead the Student Well-being Committee. It let me stand for other students.

By my second semester, I held the highest grades in the university. I'd earned a scholarship, taken a seat on the Academic Council—the lone student in a room full of professors. I spoke only when it mattered.

The first time I raised my hand in that room, the air shifted. A few heads turned like they hadn't expected a student to carry weight. I kept my voice calm and my words simple. When I finished, one professor nodded—not politely, but with the kind of recognition that told me I wasn't pretending anymore. I belonged there.

Leadership kept coming my way.

Soon I was president of the Mining Engineering Student Committee and the University Student Committee. These were not just titles. They were chances to prove to myself that I belonged.

What had started as a quick choice, almost reckless, turned into something extraordinary. I had left the farm and everything tied to it, but in exchange, I had found a new life. The idea of transferring to another university no longer made sense. Civil engineering had been the dream, but here I was thriving. The classes fit me, the people fit me, and the work lit something inside me.

Sometimes success is the signpost. Sometimes it tells you without words that you are already on the right path.

Popayán was not just a city anymore. It was becoming a character in my story. Its quiet beauty enveloped me and reminded me of the sacrifices I had made to come here. Its colonial streets and whitewashed heart were the arena of my metamorphosis as the days went by.

Life settled into a rhythm, one that felt like it had been written with me in mind. The classes inspired me. The professors challenged me. And the friends I made gave me a sense of family I had been missing.

The house where I stayed was alive at every hour. After classes we would spill into the streets together, searching for the same little restaurants. We squeezed around rough wooden tables, bowls of hot soup steaming between us, plates of rice passed from one hand to another. We laughed about professors, about each other, about the strangeness of life. It was more than food. It was family—one that did not need blood to feel real.

Even at the house itself, silence was rare. I would sit down to study, pen in hand, only to hear a knock at the door. A face would appear in the gap, smiling for no reason other than to say hello. It was impossible to stay serious for long. Their energy carried me with it.

At the corner of our street was a small shop run by an elderly couple who seemed to embody the kindness of Popayán. They treated us students like grandchildren, teasing us about being broke and keeping a little notebook of our debts. We would scribble down chips, drinks, loaves of bread, and pay at the end of the month. It was practical, yes, but it also felt like trust. That kind of trust turned the simplest errands into something warm and human.

The university itself became everything I had hoped for. The courses in mining and geology opened my eyes to the earth as something alive. Rocks and minerals were not just objects anymore. They were chapters in a story older than anyone could imagine.

***

One professor in particular, a woman whose voice carried the thrill of discovery, announced a field trip to Puracé Volcano. The moment she spoke, the room lit up.

When the day came, we piled into a battered minivan—every seat taken, bags on our laps, laughter bouncing around the cramped space. As the van pulled out of the city, the road began to climb and twist. The air thinned. Green hills gave way to starker beauty. The landscape turned rugged and cold, the vegetation fading into the silence of stone.

Ahead, the volcano rose—desolate and immense, a mountain of rock and wind, its slopes scarred and lifeless, standing alone under the pale light like the memory of an ancient fire. Thin trails of steam drifted from the crater above, ghostlike against the sky. The sight filled the windows, and for a moment, we all fell silent, breathing it in.

The van climbed. My lungs tightened. At first just a little pressure. I thought I could shake it off. Breathe slower. Wait it out.

The air thinned. The pressure grew. Each breath came short, slipping away before it reached me.

Cold crept in, even with my coat zipped tight. Then the stars—tiny specks at the edge of my sight. Darkness pushing close.

"Stop," I croaked. My own voice startled me. It sounded smaller than I had expected. "Please stop the van."

The driver braked, and the students tumbled out, stretching and laughing as if nothing was wrong. I tried to follow, but when my foot touched the ground, the world disappeared.

Everything went black. I was blind.

I staggered forward on instinct, hands out, legs moving without direction. There was no ground, no sky—only a void pressing in. Panic rose fast and hot, and before I could cry out again my body gave in. I hit the dirt hard, my face pressed into the cold earth. Voices drifted toward me—scattered, muffled, more like echoes from inside a tunnel than sounds from nearby.

When I opened my eyes, the darkness had lifted. Shapes came back first, then color, then the faces of my friends leaning over me. Their voices were close now, sharp with worry, overlapping each other.

"What happened?" "Can you see us?" "Stay still, don't move yet."

I blinked against the light. "I don't know," I whispered, my voice trembling. "I couldn't see. Everything was gone."

They helped me sit up, brushing dirt from my coat. My hands shook as I explained. This was not the first time. It had happened when I was younger. The doctors had run tests, checked everything, and always came back with the same shrug. No answers. No cause. Nothing to hold on to. It haunted me like a ghost that refused to show its face.

That was it for me. The trip ended there. The others went on toward the crater. I stayed in the van, wrapped in a blanket. I watched them walk up the trail. Their voices and laughter faded until the mountain swallowed the sound. Envy burned in me along with frustration. I wanted to climb with them and see what they saw. But I sat there alone, because my body had failed me again.

The hours dragged. Wind rattled the windows, each gust a hollow reminder of what I was missing. I stared at my hands, then at the floor, my mind circling the same thought—that something inside me was not right. Not pain, not sickness, just a silent threat moving beneath the surface, waiting for its moment. I couldn't name it, but I could feel it, like a shadow that might one day decide to take everything without warning.

When the group returned, their faces flushed from the climb, they were buzzing with stories. They laughed, describing the steam rising from the crater and the view that stretched forever. I forced a smile and nodded, asked them questions, pretended to share their excitement. Inside, I felt something different. I felt the weight of what I had lost, a chance I might never get again.

It humbled me. It reminded me that no matter how strong I believed myself to be, there were limits I could not argue with. Plans could be made, but the body has its own laws.

***

Back in the van, their voices filled the cramped space, bright and unstoppable. I sat quietly, a knot forming in my stomach. Why had I been the only one left behind? What was happening inside me that no doctor could explain?

A few days later I was at a friend's house for dinner when someone brought up another trail. This one was harder. It cut across several volcanoes, stretched over days, and demanded everything from you—endurance, navigation, the strength to carry packs filled with food, tents, and stoves. The starting point was the very same mountain that had defeated me.

Their eyes shifted in my direction. They didn't say it, but I heard their doubt. I forced a smile. "I can handle it," I told them. Maybe I was trying to convince myself as much as them. I could not let that moment of weakness be the story that followed me. If I gave in, fear would hang over me every time I thought about altitude. This trip became a test I had to take.

We spent the next month planning. Buying gear, mapping routes, arguing about food, arguing about weight. In the end, five of us committed.

When the day came, we rode a bus to a small town at the base. The idea was simple. Start low, climb slow, give our bodies time to adjust.

We stepped off the bus with packs strapped to our backs. They felt heavy enough to crush us before we had even taken the first step. Doubt whispered in my mind, asking if my body would betray me again. I pushed it aside. I lit a cigarette. My friends scolded me, reminding me of the thin air we were about to walk into. I laughed it off and took the first steps onto the trail.

The path wound through cattle fields at first, grass bending under the cold wind. Higher up the land changed. The green fell away and left bare ground, tundra-like, where every step crunched.

Hours passed. My legs grew heavy, my shoulders ached from the straps digging in. Still, I stayed with them. The music in my ears kept a rhythm, and I refused to fall behind.

By late afternoon we chose a spot to camp. Halfway up, the air was sharp and cold enough to bite through our layers. We pitched the tents with stiff fingers. The smell of canned stew drifted from the small stove, mixing with the thin mountain air.

It was only then that someone noticed Orlando was missing.

Orlando was the strongest of us, the one always chasing the next challenge. He biked up mountain roads for fun. If anyone should have been fine, it was him. I volunteered to look.

I found him not far off, sitting on a rock ledge without his shirt. His eyes were closed. His skin already pale in the fading light.

"Orlando, what are you doing?" I shouted. The wind cut through me even with all my layers on.

He opened his eyes slowly, smiling like he knew a secret. "Acclimatizing, man. You should try it."

"It's freezing. Come on. Dinner's ready."

He chuckled, but he followed.

That night his body shook so hard the tent rustled. No blanket warmed him, no coat stopped the tremors. Hypothermia had found him, and his calm bravado was gone.

In the morning his face was gray, his lips cracked. He could barely stand.

We argued quietly among ourselves. Go on, or stop. Stay together, or turn back. Orlando ended the debate himself. "I'll go down," he said, his voice thin. "It's lower. It's warmer. I'll be fine once I'm moving."

None of us liked it, but we let him. We watched him strap his pack with trembling hands. Then he started down the trail, his figure growing smaller against the stone and the grass. The four of us stood there, watching him vanish, our numbers cut by one.

We kept climbing. The slope grew steeper until hands were as necessary as feet. My lungs ached, every breath harder than the last. For a moment I wondered if the mountain would beat me again.

Then I realized we had passed the altitude where I had failed before. Nothing happened. No darkness. No stars closing in at the edges of my vision. Just the sound of my breath and the crunch of rock under my boots. A spark of hope lit inside me.

At the summit we stood on the crater's rim, bent and sweating, caught between exhaustion and joy. I had done it. I had beaten the mountain, beaten myself. The fog was so thick we could barely see a few steps ahead, and the sulfur stung our throats, but none of it mattered. I had made it.

The fog made it impossible to push on to the next peak. My friends suggested we head down, look for safer ground.

I shook my head. "I'm too tired to move," I said. "Let's stay here."

They did not like it, but they agreed. We set the tents close to the crater, fighting the wind and choking on the bitter smell of sulfur.

That night the fumes slipped inside our shelters. We coughed until our throats burned, our eyes watering, lungs on fire. Sleep never came. Nausea rolled through me, dizziness spun the tent around in my head.

When morning broke we knew. We were too weak to go on. The dream of crossing several volcanoes ended there. We started down, each step heavy, each breath tasting of sulfur.

The mountain had given me a victory and a warning at the same time— a reminder that conquering something outside of you means nothing if you lose sight of what's within.

Up there, in the thin air where pride can't breathe, I understood something simple: not every summit is meant to be reached. Some exist to reveal the limits of your will, and to teach that restraint can be as powerful as endurance. Survival itself is a sacred kind of victory.

***

Back in Popayán, the nights carried a different kind of challenge. The streets twisted like a maze. By day the white buildings stood proud. The same buildings leaned in at night, shadows stretching across the stones. Lamps flickered but their light did not help; it only made the dark thicker. The silence pressed close, broken sometimes by a dog barking far away or the buzz of an old bulb.

I walked home alone often after classes or meetings. I kept my stride steady. I would not let fear tell me when to move. Still, some nights the sound of my own steps grew too loud.

That night was one of those. My shadow stretched long under a lamp, sliding across the wall like it was alive. For a second it felt like the city itself was watching me.

Then they came. Boys stepping out of an alley. First shadows, then faces. The light caught them and I saw they were young, close to my age, maybe younger. But their eyes were already hard. We met eyes for a single moment.

Then one of them lunged. His hand clamped around my neck and shoved me against a metal pole. Before I could breathe, a fist drove into my stomach—hard, deep, knocking the air out of me in a single, brutal rush.

They closed in. Fingers yanked at my jacket, my pockets, my belt. Instinct took over. I swung at them, twisted, tried to tear myself free. For a second I broke loose.

Then something crashed into the back of my skull. A bottle. The crack echoed louder than my own breath. The street tilted and I hit the ground, my cheek scraping across rough asphalt.

Hands pinned me down. One pressing my back, another gripping my wrists. My head throbbed and blood crept warm down my neck, pooling beneath me. They took everything. My shoes, my wallet, even my pants. I lay there stripped, humiliated, too dizzy to move.

"Chúzalo! Chúzalo!" one of them shouted. He held a jagged piece of metal like a knife, his arm trembling but his eyes wild. The point hovered at my throat. Another voice rose from the group. "Kill him. Do it."

Everything narrowed. The cold of the metal against my skin. The hammering in my ears. The smell of sweat and fear choking the air. I could not breathe, could not speak, could not plead. In that second, I believed it was over.

Then headlights cut through the dark. A taxi turned into the street, its beams slicing the shadows. The boys froze. The spell broke. They bolted into the night, their footsteps scattering against the walls.

I stayed where I had fallen, curled on the pavement, shaking.

The taxi screeched to a halt. The driver jumped out, his eyes wide, scanning me where I lay. "¿Estás bien? Are you okay?" His voice snapped me back to the world.

I tried to nod, but it felt weak, half a lie. My head throbbed. The taste of blood sat heavy on my tongue.

"You're bleeding," he said, pointing at my neck. His voice was steady, but I could see the alarm in his face.

"They broke a bottle on my head," I whispered. My words shook as they left me. "I... I don't have any money. They took everything."

"Don't worry about that," he answered. He didn't hesitate. "Get in. I'll take you home."

The taxi was warm. I sank into the seat and watched the city slide by in streaks of light and dark. In the window my face looked pale, almost not mine.

The driver said nothing. He only looked back sometimes to see if I was still sitting up, still breathing.

Later, in bed, the pain set in. My body ached everywhere. My pride was in pieces. But the side of me that counted—the side that could not bend—stood erect. I would not tell myself I should have been at home, I should have taken another road. That was not me. Freedom was the point: to walk as I pleased, even at night, even at peril.

Still, as I lay staring at the ceiling, the corners of the room felt heavier. The shadows clung tighter than they used to.

***

It carried me back to another night. Pereira. I was sixteen. Just a boy, really, though I thought I was older.

I had left my girlfriend's house not long before. We had sat with her family, talking, eating, laughing. They lived simply, a small place on the backstreets of downtown. Her mother worked hard, did her best, but everyone knew those streets were not safe after dark.

I stepped outside into the thin light. The lamps flickered, throwing long shadows across cracked sidewalks. It was only two blocks to the main street. Two blocks to flag down a cab, two blocks to home. My feet tapped softly against the pavement. My head was still full of the warmth of her smile, the sound of her family's voices.

At the first corner I saw them. Five boys. They seemed to grow out of the shadows, walking across the street toward me. Their laughter was low, jagged, like it could draw blood. I told myself not to think much of it. Groups like that were common. Boys with nowhere to go, nothing to do, letting the night swallow their boredom. Still, something in their tone made me slow my step.

230

When we crossed paths, I felt it. Something changed in the air. Two of them slid in front of me, their steps slowing just enough to cut me off. The other three drifted behind, close, too close. My chest tightened. It was not loud, not obvious, but I knew—I was boxed in.

Their footsteps echoed harder now, matching mine, louder than before. I tried walking a little farther, hoping it was nothing, hoping I was imagining it. But the tension thickened until I could almost taste it.

One of the boys in front snapped around fast. His fist caught my shirt, yanking me forward so hard I stumbled. Before I could react, the rest pressed in, their faces hidden in the poor light, but I caught it—the shine of teeth, the curl of ugly smiles.

Something shot through me. A surge went through me. I did not think. There was no time for thought. My body moved before I knew it. I jerked back, tore free, and threw a punch with everything I had. My fist cracked against his jaw. His head snapped back. He stumbled, cursing, spitting.

But there were still four. Hands shoved at me, pulled at me. My shirt ripped open across the front. Someone grabbed my arm, and I wrenched it free with a strength I did not know I had.

I did not run. I should have. Any sane person would have. But I planted my feet. I clenched my fists. I stepped toward them.

"Come on then!" I shouted. Adrenaline thundered through me, but my voice came out steady, like someone else had spoken for me. My eyes jumped between them, daring them, telling them without words that I was ready.

Then the street went quiet. Their eyes flickered. I saw it—the hesitation. They shuffled, glanced at each other, not so sure anymore. Maybe they had not expected a fight. Maybe the sight of their friend holding his jaw was enough.

"Let's go," one of them muttered, spitting to the side. Their voices trailed off with the threats. Then came the laughter again, like nothing had happened.

I stayed where I was, gasping, shirt torn, my breath jagged in the night air. Slowly, I began to walk again, each step steadier than the last, until I reached the main street. The headlights and noise of the city washed over me like a tide. I was shaken, but I was standing—and that felt like enough.

That night in Pereira left a mark I didn't see at first. It gave me a kind of confidence that looked like courage but was built on defiance—the belief that if I had faced danger once and walked away, I could do it again. In Popayán, that belief followed me through every dark street.

But life has its own ways of humbling the proud. Popayán reminded me that survival isn't about fearlessness—it's about awareness. It's knowing when to move, when to pause, when to listen. Being cautious isn't weakness; it's wisdom paid for in scars.

Of course I felt fear. Anyone would. But what stayed wasn't the fear—it was faith. I began to believe that some battles were allowed only because I was meant to face them, and that anything beyond human reach could only be faced through God's protection. More than once, I felt that invisible shield—not because I was fearless, but because I was never truly alone.

I didn't think much about healing. Life did not stop coming. It kept testing me. I decided early that I would not hide from it. Avoidance felt like surrender, and surrender spreads.

So I faced things as they came. Sometimes it hurt. Sometimes it cost me more than I expected. But I would rather take the hit than live in fear of it.

Over time, I realized something even quieter: understanding isn't what brings peace—acceptance does. Understanding begs for "why." Acceptance learns to breathe without it. Some things aren't meant to be solved; they're meant to be surrendered to.

In time, I saw that this wasn't only a way to cope. It was who I had become. I no longer lingered on what was behind me. I had learned to face the storm instead of running from it, to stand there until it passed, and to keep standing after.

Chapter 33

North Bound

The university sat on a hill above the town, quiet and apart from everything else. Cobblestone paths ran through tall eucalyptus trees, and the air felt new after rain. My days were busy, but not like other students'. They went to class. I went to meetings or worked in the archives. The smell of old paper stayed on me as I turned page after page, trying to piece together stories of floods, landslides, and earthquakes for a geology book I was hired to help with.

Classes still mattered, but they came second. I studied at night, my desk lit by a flickering lamp, the quiet of my room my classroom. By Friday, the halls were almost empty. Most students slipped away early, chasing the weekend.

***

Something had started happening in Popayán, something I kept to myself at first.

For several nights in a row, sleep turned hostile. I woke up drained, as if I'd been fighting through the dark and only my body remembered it. I didn't know what it meant, only that it wasn't stopping.

One day, as we waited for the bus that picked us up at the city-center square, right by the cathedral, I told my friend. He was an Ecology student from Cali, and I respected him for how spiritual he was. I thought he could understand and guide me.

"I'm not sleeping," I said.

He looked at me. "Because of studying?"

"No," I said. "Because of my dreams."

His brow tightened slightly. "What kind of dreams?"

"I'm being killed," I said. "Every night. Different ways."

He didn't laugh. He waited.

"Pulled out of a car in the middle of town," I continued. "A black cover over my head. They try to kill me, but I don't die." I swallowed. "Another night I'm chased down an apartment building and stabbed. Another time I'm shot from far away. I can't remember all of them. I just remember I never die."

"And when you wake up?" he asked.

"Exhausted," I said. "Like I've been running all night."

He nodded slowly, as if he were listening past my words. "That's not normal."

"I know," I said. "And it's not stopping."

The bus still hadn't arrived. People shifted their bags. The cathedral bells rang in the distance, dull and heavy.

After a moment he said, "I might know someone."

"Who?"

"An older man who lives past the university," he said. "Some people call him a botanist. Others say he's a French doctor. He runs a greenhouse— plants, herbs." He hesitated. "I've heard stories about him helping people."

"With what?" I asked.

"With things that don't always have names," he said. "Look—maybe it's stress. But if it's not... he might be able to calm it."

I stared down the street, half waiting for the bus, half hoping it wouldn't come.

"Let's go," I said.

"After class," he replied. "When we're both done."

We went. My friend waited outside.

The man listened without interrupting. When I finished describing the dreams, he looked at me and asked, almost casually, "Do you believe in the Virgin Mary?"

The question caught me off guard, but I said yes—I do.

He reached into a drawer and pulled out a prayer written on a piece of paper. Then he pulled out a second paper and wrote down herbs he wanted me to get at the market. He gave me instructions, simple and specific.

"Once you have the herbs, go home. Soak them in water and bring it to a boil. Let it boil for ten minutes. Let it cool some. Take a shower, then rinse with the water from the pot. After that, go to bed, say the prayer to the Virgin Mary, and sleep."

I walked out feeling strange. The whole thing felt unreal, half faith and half ritual, but I followed the instructions.

I had my own private bathroom in the house, so I could do it without anyone rushing me. My room was painted ocean blue. A wooden shelf ran wall to wall, filled with rocks and minerals collected from field trips. An aquarium with goldfish sat in the middle of the shelves, the water quiet, the fish gliding like they had nowhere to be.

I had no curtains. I had replaced the windows with two pieces of stained glass a good friend had made for me. They gave me privacy and turned light into color. Outside was the corridor, then the rose garden. Sometimes the corridor light was left on, and it would spill through the stained glass and paint my room in dim blues and reds.

The window and the door had small air gaps near the top. Behind my bed on the wall there were candle holders, and more candles sat on the shelf.

That night I closed the door and the window. I showered. Then, with whatever light I had from the candles and the faint corridor glow filtering through the stained glass, I read the prayer softly.

I started to feel sleepy.

Then a current of air invaded the room—stronger than anything I had ever felt indoors. It hit like a sudden presence, pushing through the air gaps and moving with purpose. The candle flames flickered hard, bending and trembling, until they went out.

I sat up fast.

And then, above my bed, where the wall should have been, I saw her.

The image of the Virgin Mary appeared as if the wall behind me had been replaced. She wore a blue tunic and white cloth over her head. Her face was slightly tilted, and she didn't take her eyes off me. She raised both hands and placed her palms on my forehead.

Hundreds of images started passing through my mind—too fast to recognize, like flashes of a life I couldn't name. Then I saw a number. I always believed it was a date, but I couldn't hold on to it long enough to remember exactly what it was.

And then she vanished.

Popayán was a city where people spoke freely about faith and apparitions, as if the veil between worlds was thinner there. I didn't know what to do with what I had seen. I only knew it left me shaken—and strangely calm.

After that, the dreams stopped.

***

One Friday I walked into my mining lecture and found no one there. The professor stood at the door, arms crossed. He looked at me and said, "If you're the only one here, there's no point in holding class." His words felt strange—half dismissal, half freedom.

With the afternoon open, I decided not to wait for the four o'clock bus. I didn't feel like sitting in the cafeteria over a cold coffee. I walked down the hill toward the main road. It was long and covered in eucalyptus leaves—the kind of road that gave you time to think. Students used to hitch rides there. Drivers were used to seeing us waiting. I stopped at the curve. The faint crunch of dry leaves under my boots began to fade, and with it, the sharp scent that once lingered in the air.

Nearly an hour passed with no ride. Then a beat-up pickup came down the road. A few Indigenous men were standing about half a block away, as if waiting for the public bus. The truck slowed and stopped halfway between us.

The boards on the back were split and rough. I lifted my hand anyway. The driver's face sat in shadow under his cap. I climbed in first, and the men walked up from where they'd been standing and climbed into the back with me. The air smelled like cacao beans, as if that had been the last thing carried in the back.

The truck jerked forward. After a bit, something started to feel off. My pulse jumped hard and fast. I tried to ignore it and held the rail, staring at the road behind us. It didn't help. My heart started pounding. My breath came short. Something told me I needed to get off.

I leaned forward, pounding the roof. "Stop! Stop, I need to get off!"

The driver turned his head, shouting over the wind. "What's wrong with you? We just started!"

"I don't know," I said, louder this time. "Just stop the truck!"

One of the men beside me frowned. "You're fine, *hermano*. Sit still. It's a long road."

"I can't," I said, shaking my head. "Please, tell him to stop."

Another man muttered, "What's his problem?"

The driver swore under his breath but slowed anyway, pulling to the side of the road. "This better be worth it," he said.

The men looked at me, some curious, others annoyed. One of them leaned forward. "You sick or something?"

"I don't know," I said, trying to catch my breath. "I just need to get off."

The driver waved me out. "Then get off, *hombre*. We don't have all day."

I climbed down. A strange feeling settled over me—something between dread and revelation. I stepped back as the truck went on, the wood creaking, the men still staring until they turned the corner.

I stood there, stunned, waiting for the feeling to return. Confusion hung over me, thick and still. Nothing moved except my breath. The feeling was gone. I felt stupid. Maybe I made it all up.

I began walking back up the hill. The road shimmered ahead. With each step, the air grew cooler, and the faint scent of eucalyptus returned as I got closer to the point where I would start hitchhiking again. A small car pulled up beside me, its tires hissing softly against the asphalt.

"Federico!" a voice called.

I turned and saw four students from the university, faces I knew well. "What are you doing out here?" one of them asked, leaning out the window.

"I was waiting for a ride," I said, still catching my breath. "Got one, but something felt wrong. I got off."

They looked at each other, half amused. "You jumped off a ride on a Friday afternoon, hermano? You're crazy," another said.

"Maybe," I answered. "But I don't know. Something told me to."

"Man, you're lucky we came this way—we're going to town. Get in."

I climbed into the back seat, squeezed between the door and my friend in the middle. The car was tiny, its seats torn and engine coughing as it started to move—probably older and more beat-up than the pickup I'd just escaped. They kept talking, teasing me.

"You and your gut feelings, man," one said. "Next time just take the ride."

"Maybe I'll listen to my gut again," I replied, looking out the window.

The laughter didn't last long. We had to halt.

The pickup I'd left behind had flipped and was lying on its side, the bed ripped open, wood splintered across the road. The men who had been riding with me were flung out, their bodies scattered across the asphalt. One of them lay completely still.

The driver whispered, "*Dios mío.*"

Nobody else spoke. I froze, and for a second I couldn't move. I just stared. "That's the same truck, isn't it?" one of them said quietly.

"Yes," I said. My voice was barely there.

The man on the road did not move. His poncho was torn. The others knelt beside him, shouting for help that would come too late.

Before we left, we tried to help. One of the guys checked for a pulse, another waved down traffic. I remember kneeling beside the man, my hands trembling as we lifted him carefully toward the edge of the road. His body felt weightless and heavy at the same time, like the air itself was holding him. We didn't speak, but our eyes met—a quick, wordless exchange that said everything: the shock, the disbelief, and the quiet understanding of what I had just been spared from. The noise of the highway filled the space our words couldn't reach.

I couldn't look away. The image carved itself into me: the pickup on its side, the torn bed, the still body—too close to the kind of crash that had taken my brother. The memory came rushing back so fast it stole my breath.

We stayed until help arrived. When we heard the ambulance and saw it pull in, we stepped back and let them take over.

***

As we drove away, nobody spoke. Some whispered what they had seen. I said nothing. I stared out the window, the blur of the road passing like a reel of unfinished thoughts. It didn't feel like coincidence—more like grace disguised as fear, the kind that speaks through the body before the mind can understand.

Finally, one of them whispered, "You'd be dead if you hadn't gotten off." I nodded slowly. "I know."

And I did know. I knew it down to my bones. The godly voice that pushed me to get off that truck had saved my life.

After that, I made a promise to myself. I would never doubt that voice again. I didn't care what name I gave it—instinct, faith, something divine—it didn't matter. What mattered was that it was there, waiting for me to hear it.

Staying alive was only the outcome. The lesson was trust. I started to see the voice inside wasn't only warning me; it was leading me. To listen, I had to let go. I had to stop thinking I knew everything and step into what I didn't understand.

Then I looked back and saw all the times I had turned away from it—the moments I ignored it, the choices that hurt more than they had to. A pattern emerged: that voice wasn't just keeping me from harm; it had been trying to move me forward. The voice hadn't changed. It had always been God, the same Man in the stars, guiding me from the beginning.

That moment on the road stayed with me. It taught me to slow down. To notice things. To trust what I couldn't see. Some lessons aren't taught.

They're revealed They come in quiet. In the pause long enough to hear what's been there all along.

That day, I didn't just survive—I woke up to something greater. It wasn't coincidence. It was grace—quiet, patient, relentless.

***

Strikes were common in public universities: heated debates, locked gates, chants echoing through hallways, and sometimes violent protests. It was part of student life. But my university was private, and strikes didn't happen there. That was why the chaos that morning caught me off guard.

By the time I arrived on campus, the gates were chained shut. The chains sat tight across the metal, unmistakable. Students gathered in groups, their faces set and grim. The air was dense. I didn't have to be told what was happening. I knew a strike when I saw one. But this time it felt different. It had been planned without anyone coming to me first.

As I paced through the university square, trying to comprehend the situation and locate the leaders, a professor approached me, his face tense with urgency. Without hesitation, he motioned for me to follow him toward the principal's office.

The office, usually a sanctuary of authority and calm, carried a different weight that day. The polished desk, the rows of legal books, the flag in the corner—those symbols of control now seemed meaningless. The air was still, and I could sense the anxiety in it.

"Federico!" The voice came from the doorway. It was the principal, the father of the academic director. His face was pale, his confidence gone. "My daughter's inside," he said quickly, words tumbling over one another. "She's locked in with them. She's pregnant—very advanced. She can't stay there in that noise, in that chaos. Please, you have to help."

As president of the student council, it was my job to mediate conflicts, but this was more than a conflict. It was a rebellion.

I moved from group to group, scanning faces and listening, trying to understand what had triggered it and to find who had organized it. The main gate was still chained shut, thick links wrapped through the bars and locked tight. Students shouted over one another, anger spilling into the air. The barricade did not just divide the campus from the outside world. It divided us as students. Ironically, many had come to private universities precisely to escape this kind of unrest, only to find themselves pulled into the same cycle of rebellion they once tried to avoid.

When I finally reached the gate, I saw them. The leaders stood together, hard and sure of themselves. I knew some of them, faces I had trusted, people I had worked beside.

Seeing them there brought a deep sense of betrayal and disappointment.

"What do you want?" I asked.

They shouted over each other. "Better facilities! Better transportation! New bathrooms!" The noise tangled into chaos.

I raised my hand. "Quiet," I said. "You've locked the gates and trapped a pregnant woman inside. You call this leadership?"

One of them stepped forward, a wiry student who always wanted to be at the center of things. "We had no choice," he said. "No one listens unless we do something drastic."

"Drastic?" I said. "You think this helps you? You think this makes anyone listen? If you want to be heard, make sense. Pick what matters most and drop the rest."

They looked at one another. The shouting stopped. Slowly, they began to sort through their demands. We cut the list down to what truly mattered: transportation, classroom repairs, bathrooms that worked. The rest was noise, and we left it behind.

"Now," I said, looking at the one who had spoken, "you're going to open the gates. No one here is staying locked in—not her, not anyone."

There was hesitation, but finally the chains came off. The gates creaked open. The academic director stepped out, one hand on her stomach, the other gripping the metal for balance. Her father rushed to her, his face a mix of relief and weariness.

When things finally settled and the list of demands was ready, I carried it to the principal's office. The meeting took place in the boardroom—a quiet, formal space with a round wooden table that reflected the afternoon light from tall windows. Around it sat the principal, a few academic advisors, and representatives from the student body. Papers were neatly arranged; pens clicked softly against notepads. Despite the tension that had filled the day, this meeting felt different—structured, almost ceremonial, as if everyone knew the importance of ending things with dignity.

As I listened, my father's words returned to me: "A true leader is neutral—someone who can feel for both sides. Pull too hard toward your own, and peace slips away." I understood then that leadership wasn't about authority but about empathy, the willingness to understand both sides and carry the tension without turning it into war.

By evening, the strike was over. The students got what they came for. The principal got his school back.

A few days later, one of my teachers from the School of Mines caught me in the hall. There was a look in his eyes that made me pause. "The director wants to see you," he said.

The office was quiet. The principal handed me an envelope without saying anything at first. His face gave nothing away. Then he said, "This came for you."

I opened it and read fast. My heart started to race. The Liberal Party was asking me to lead its youth wing for the department of Cauca.

They wanted me at the national youth presidential convention in Barranquilla, with eight delegates under my responsibility.

When I looked up, still processing, the principal smiled. "You've earned this, Federico," he said. "You've shown leadership and wisdom beyond your years. I'm proud of you."

Barranquilla was hot and humid. The air never stopped moving. Students from everywhere filled the halls of the convention center. We talked, argued, and made quick plans that felt big at the time. At one point I sat with one of the presidential candidates and his wife, asking questions specific to education and youth initiatives. Then we moved through the crowds, gathering allies for what was coming.

The party leaders had decided to exclude a neighboring department— mostly Black—from representation in the next main national convention in Medellin. It was wrong, plain and simple. When my turn to speak came, I walked to the microphone and said what needed saying.

"They deserve a seat," I told them. "We can't claim to represent everyone and then shut our own people out."

They tried to brush me off. A few told me to step away. I didn't. I took the microphone and started walking as I spoke, moving through the crowd so they couldn't corner me. By the time security began pushing in, the room was already with me. The hall erupted with students shouting and clapping, backing me up. The pressure built until the leaders gave in. The department would be represented.

It felt like victory, but not the kind I expected. It wasn't about winning an argument. It was about standing for something larger than myself.

When I returned to Popayán, I stepped down from the youth wing and handed the position to someone I trusted. I had seen what power could do to people, and I did not want it to do the same to me. What mattered was the work, not the title. Still, I did not disappear from politics overnight. A friend had started a new political group, and he asked me to back him up and introduce him at the universities. I agreed.

Politics looked bright at first. It was energy, speeches, and plans to make things better. But it changed fast. I began to see the darker side: the envy, the threats, the way one voice can stir admiration and hatred at the same time. In Popayán, every meeting I attended and every introduction I made won me some friends and earned me enemies—serious ones.

It started small. A few whispers in the hallways, a note slipped under my door, a warning I ignored. I told myself it was nothing, part of the game. But then the calls started. Voices in the night. Words meant to shake me. By the end of the semester, they knew too much—where I went, who I cared for, how to reach me.

The semester break was supposed to be a break from it all: a peaceful Christmas back home, time with family, room to breathe. But the calls didn't stop. The phone continued to ring in my birthplace. My stomach tightened each time it did. The tones on the other end were colder.

One evening after dinner, I sat my parents down. My mother looked at me, already sensing what I was about to say.

"I have to leave," I told them. My voice felt heavier than I expected. "It's not safe anymore. I need to go far away. As far as I can."

My mother's hands trembled as she held her rosary. "Where will you go?" she asked quietly.

"Alaska," I said without thinking.

The word came out like an instinct, but it wasn't random. I had seen magazines about the mines and oil platforms there—issues I used to read with my cousin Santi in my uncle's home office during a family visit to Columbus, Ohio. We'd sit there, flipping through the pages, dreaming out loud about working in a place like that someday. It was Santi who first said he'd love to go there, and I suppose the idea stayed with me. Alaska felt far enough to be safe from everything that hunted me, and remote enough to keep life interesting—a place where survival itself could become a kind of redemption.

"Yes," she said slowly. "But Alaska?"

"Yes," I repeated. "Alaska."

That night, we started making arrangements.

I stayed three days at my grandparents' house in Cali, waiting for the ticket that would take me away. Those days felt heavy, suspended between the life I had built and the one waiting beyond the horizon. My career—split in half by circumstance—had once promised a bright future, and my friends from Popayán, more like brothers than classmates, now lived only in the corners of my memory.

The house itself was alive with its own rhythm. Wind chimes sang softly every time the afternoon breeze slipped through the open front door, passing through the metallic screen and out toward the backyard. The parrots argued loudly from their perch, filling the air with familiar chaos, while the sweet smell of ripe mangoes drifted in from the old tree that had never failed to give fruit. It was a house that breathed, that carried the spirit of family in every sound and scent.

My grandfather, the most honorable man I have ever known, had passed not long before, and now only my grandmother filled the home. She moved gently through it, her voice softer now, as if reaching across time to the ones who could no longer answer. That night, I walked from room to room, touching the tables, the framed photos, the doorknobs—small relics of a life that had shaped me. I didn't know if I would ever return.

Both my parents came to say goodbye. My mother's tears fell silently, though she tried to hide them with small smiles and gentle touches, as if her love alone could shield me from what was coming. There was pride in her eyes, but it was buried under fear—the kind of fear only a mother knows, when love has to let go.

My father stood beside her, not grieving but almost hopeful. He saw it as a new beginning, a chance for me to rebuild, to reclaim what life had tried to take from me. For him, this departure was proof that I was strong enough to start again.

When morning came, I stepped outside and listened one last time—the wind chimes, the parrots, the rustle of the mango leaves. Then I picked up my bag, looked back once more, and walked away from the world that had made me who I was, into the unknown that would make me who I would become.

After a string of airports and layovers, I finally boarded the last flight north. As the plane began its descent toward Anchorage, the world below looked remote and untouched. The window filled with white. Snow blanketed the mountains, vast and endless, as if I was being delivered into another realm—one stripped of comfort, one that would demand something new. The warmth I had known was behind me now, and ahead lay the cold honesty of beginnings.

There were only a few passengers on the plane, four, maybe five at most. Each sat alone, wrapped in silence, their faces turned toward the small oval windows. No one spoke. The cabin held that practiced, travel silence, broken only by the engine's steady drone and the occasional rustle of a jacket sleeve.

I breathed on the glass and watched it fog, then clear. Below us stretched white and distance, mountains and frozen flats with almost no sign of life. It hit me then how far I was going, and how alone it might feel when I landed.

When I stepped out, the cold hit hard. It wasn't just the air—it was everything I had left behind. My friends. My family. My work. The person I used to be. All of it stayed somewhere behind that long stretch of sky.

This didn't feel like starting over. It felt like stepping into a silence that could swallow me whole. The fire that had once kept me moving had burned down, leaving only the faint glow of something I couldn't yet name. In Alaska,

I was no one—just a man with a small suitcase, standing in the wind, watching his old life disappear behind him.

But even then, something flickered inside, a quiet spark that refused to die. I told myself this wasn't the end. I had left everything behind, yes, but not myself. And that had to be enough.

As the cold pressed against me and the weight of all I had walked away from settled in, I made a promise—not spoken, not written, just felt.

I would rebuild. Slowly. Faithfully. However long it took, however far I had to go.

Not back to what once was, but forward—toward something true.

This wasn't defeat. This was grace in disguise—the beginning hidden inside the end.

About the Author

Federico Botero was born in Pereira, Colombia. A natural entrepreneur from a young age, he built his first ventures before making a life-changing decision to leave everything behind in pursuit of higher education—a defining chapter that led him to earn a degree in Mining Engineering and, ultimately, to discover his deeper calling as a storyteller and seeker of purpose.

Over the next two decades, Federico worked in the oil and gas industry, advancing from field operations to high-level management and executive roles. His career took him across countries and cultures, teaching him both the rewards and the costs of ambition.

But life, as it often does, had other plans. After years of professional success and personal upheaval, he felt called to walk away from the corporate world and begin anew, this time on the open road. Today, Federico lives and works as a professional truck driver, embracing the freedom and solitude that come with a life lived between horizons.

From entrepreneurship to corporate leadership to life on the road, Federico's story is one of transformation, a continuous journey toward simplicity, faith, and purpose. Beyond his career and travels, he is a loving father of three and a lifelong seeker of spiritual truth.

Through that search, he has discovered one enduring truth: that no achievement or destination compares to the peace found in building a deep, personal relationship with God.

The Walk Away is his first memoir and the beginning of a trilogy exploring survival, faith, and the redemptive power of walking away to begin again.